The Cooking of Provincial France

The Cooking of Provincial France

by

M. F. K. Fisher

and the Editors of

TIME-LIFE BOOKS

photographed by Mark Kauffman

TIME-LIFE BOOKS, ALEXANDRIA, VIRGINIA

Time-Life Books Inc.
is a wholly owned subsidiary of
TIME INCORPORATED

FOUNDER: Henry R. Luce 1898-1967

Editor-in-Chief: Henry Anatole Grunwald
President: J. Richard Munro
Chairman of the Board: Ralph P. Davidson
Executive Vice President: Clifford J. Grum
Chairman, Executive Committee: James R. Shepley
Editorial Director: Ralph Graves
Group Vice President, Books: Joan D. Manley
Vice Chairman: Arthur Temple

TIME-LIFE BOOKS INC.
MANAGING EDITOR: Jerry Korn
Executive Editor: David Maness
Assistant Managing Editors: Dale M. Brown (planning),
George Constable, Thomas H. Flaherty Jr. (acting), Martin Mann,
John Paul Porter
Art Director: Tom Suzuki
Chief of Research: David L. Harrison
Director of Photography: Robert G. Mason
Assistant Art Director: Arnold C. Holeywell
Assistant Chief of Research: Carolyn L. Sackett
Assistant Director of Photography: Dolores A. Littles

CHAIRMAN: John D. McSweeney
President: Carl G. Jaeger
Executive Vice Presidents: John Steven Maxwell, David J. Walsh
Vice Presidents: George Artandi (comptroller); Stephen L. Bair
(legal counsel); Peter G. Barnes; Nicholas Benton (public
relations); John L. Canova; Beatrice T. Dobie (personnel);
Carol Flaumenhaft (consumer affairs); James L. Mercer
(Europe/South Pacific); Herbert Sorkin (production);
Paul R. Stewart (marketing)

FOODS OF THE WORLD
EDITORIAL STAFF FOR THE COOKING OF PROVINCIAL FRANCE:
EDITOR: Richard L. Williams
Chief Researcher: Helen Fennell
Associate Editor: Irene Saint
Designer: Albert Sherman
Assistant Designer: Robert Pellegrini
Staff Writers: John Stanton, Jeffrey Tarter
Chief Researcher: Sarah B. Brash
Researchers: David Arnold, Joan Chambers, Helen Isaacs,
Julia Johnson, Eva Smidth
Test Kitchen Chef: John W. Clancy
Test Kitchen Staff: Fifi Bergman, Joel Levy, Leola Spencer

EDITORIAL PRODUCTION
Production Editor: Douglas B. Graham
Operations Manager: Gennaro C. Esposito,
Gordon E. Buck (assistant)
Assistant Production Editor: Feliciano Madrid
Quality Control: Robert L. Young (director), James J. Cox
(assistant), Daniel J. McSweeney, Michael G. Wight (associates)
Art Coordinator: Anne B. Landry
Copy Staff: Susan B. Galloway (chief), Celia Beattie
Traffic: Kimberly K. Lewis

CORRESPONDENTS: Elisabeth Kraemer (Bonn); Margot Hapgood,
Dorothy Bacon, Lesley Coleman (London); Susan Jonas,
Lucy T. Voulgaris (New York); Maria Vincenza Aloisi, Josephine
du Brusle (Paris); Ann Natanson (Rome). Valuable assistance was
also provided by: Judy Aspinall, Karin B. Pearce (London);
Carolyn T. Chubet, Miriam Hsia, Christina Lieberman (New
York); Mimi Murphy (Rome).

THE AUTHOR: M. F. K. Fisher is one of the wittiest, most fluent and sensible of the great modern gastronomes. She acquired much of her kitchen knowledge while living in southern France and has shared it with appreciative readers in nearly a dozen books, including *The Art of Eating,* and in several magazines, including *The New Yorker.* She now lives on a ranch in Glen Ellen, California.

THE CONSULTING EDITOR: The late Michael Field relinquished a career as a concert pianist to become one of America's first-rank food experts and teachers of cooking. He conducted a school in Manhattan and wrote many articles on the culinary arts for various magazines. His books include *Michael Field's Cooking School* and *Michael Field's Culinary Classics and Improvisations.*

THE CONSULTANT: Julia Child has been a welcome guest in millions of homes on her television program, *The French Chef.* Mrs. Child studied at the famous Cordon Bleu cooking school and, with two other women, founded the cooking school, L'École des Trois Gourmandes, in Paris. She is the co-author of *Mastering the Art of French Cooking* and the author of *The French Chef Cookbook* and *From Julia Child's Kitchen.* She and her husband, Paul Child, a painter and photographer, divide their time between Cambridge, Massachusetts and southern France.

THE PHOTOGRAPHER: Mark Kauffman, a graduate of the photographic staff of LIFE, is one of the world's foremost journalistic—and food—photographers. He joined LIFE in 1941, and covered major news assignments on every continent; he has been a freelance photographer since 1960. For *The Cooking of Provincial France* he drove through every part of that country, then spent six weeks creating pictures of processes and finished dishes in the "Foods of the World" test kitchen.

THE COVER: A dessert soufflé, delicately puffed and golden brown on the peak, is a perfectly achievable dish—if properly prepared. A recipe is on page 189.

For information about any Time-Life book, please write:
Reader Information
Time-Life Books
541 North Fairbanks Court
Chicago, Illinois 60611

Contents

The Recipe Booklet that accompanies this volume has been designed for convenient use in the kitchen. It contains 61 recipes printed here plus 40 more. It also has a wipe-clean cover and a spiral binding so that it can either stand up or lie flat when open.

Introduction: Welcome to the Country Kitchens of France

The title of this book about the food and cooking of the French provinces has words in it with many connotations. Plainly it is about French cooking. But to nine out of ten of us "French cooking" means an elaborate and expensive way of complicating or at least masking foods with sauces, which rightly but sometimes impatiently are referred to as *French* sauces. (When I stopped in Scotland with my young children after a long stay in Provence, elderly and rather insular friends exclaimed in wonder at how well we seemed to be, "in spite of those dreadful thick rich concoctions covering everything and making one bilious, not to mention gouty.") Unfortunately "French cooking" can also mean mediocre or poor or dishonest cooking, served with pomp in pretentious restaurants everywhere, including the city of Paris itself.

There is, of course, another side to the cooking of France. What is called *haute,* or *grande, cuisine* may be one of modern man's nearest approaches to pure bliss. Every dish must be prepared with skill and artistry by cooks trained for years in the great tradition of blending, balancing and transforming such plain ingredients as butter and eggs and fresh herbs into masterpieces of subtlety. Final proof of this control is that the dish must always be as good as it was the time before, exactly as a fine actor will always come on stage in Scene Two with the same heart-rending sob.

Where the master chefs began

French provincial cooking means something quite different from *grande cuisine.* First it must be made clear that the word provincial, in this context, does not mean countrified, rude, narrow, limited, oafish, intolerant or bumpkinish—connotations fastened in our minds by only one facet of the term. It means simply the cooking that springs from the regional areas called provinces for many hundreds of years in the highly diversified country known as France. *Grande cuisine* owes a great deal to true provincial cooking, but has very little in common with it. It is true that most of the great chefs have come from villages in the provinces. They have learned how to be deft and knowing with the trout from their native streams, the cream from their pastured cows. Then they have gone on to the kitchens of famous and fabulous and above all very rich people, where infinite variety must provide the spice of life, and where truffles and caviar grow on bushes. Such people must be ready at all times to feed their guests in myriad courses and with unlimited supplies of the rare, the ostentatious.

Escoffier, still called the great modern chef although he is long since gone, said that the whole of French cooking, which to him of course meant the *grande cuisine,* stood or fell upon its essential stocks, and on the five basic warm sauces: *espagnole, velouté, béchamel,* tomato and hollandaise. A little earlier, Queen Victoria's French-trained and Italian-born Francatelli, giving his own list (of course) of Grand Sauces—*espagnole* or brown, *velouté* or white, cream *béchamel, béchamel* and *allemande*—stipulated the following supplies to make the basic stocks: two legs or 40 pounds of white veal, the same of gravy beef, the same each of leg of beef and of veal knuckles; carrots, turnips, celery and leeks; lean ham for both brown and white sauces, with wild rabbits for the first and hens for the second; and so on. (And after intricate directions for the construction of the basic stock, and recipes for the Grand Sauces, he gives recipes for 83 hot and 11 cold sauces.)

In true provincial cooking there is no need for such complexity, simply because most dishes that come from country kitchens make their own juices, right in the casseroles in which they are cooked, and often without any need of the strainings, the additions, the final touches intrinsic to a great chef's unfaltering performance.

The food that grows nearby

This matter of natural as opposed to fabricated sauces is probably the main difference between real provincial cooking and *grande cuisine.* Another important one is that provincial kitchens use what grows nearby, even in today's period of rapid and expert transportation.

Today in many countries, as in much of France too, the basic ingredients, whether deep-frozen or fresh from the garden, are available almost everywhere. Mass-canning techniques have been perfected. The marketing of both fresh and preserved foods is a highly specialized profession. In other words, good food is available at decent prices to all of us who can seek it out, pay for it and then prepare it with both sense and pleasure.

French cooking as it has evolved in the provinces is, to a reasonable degree, anyone's to command. True, leeks from the supermarket in their cellophane packaging may not have the same flavor (nor the same gritty sand) as those pulled from the kitchen garden on a French farm. Overlarge strawberries in colored plastic boxes are not like *fraises des bois,* the tiny wild berries of France. But given the intrinsic wish to continue as long as possible, in this chancy world, the rituals of eating in order to live, we can all follow with rare enjoyment the patterns of people who for centuries have managed to subsist on what their nearest hills and brooks and meadows provide for them. They have survived because they use their wits as well as their teeth, and so can we.

It is good to remember, in the kitchen or out of it, the firm advice of Escoffier, one of the greatest chefs of the last or possibly any century in the Western world. From his little village near Nice, in southern France, he rose to be master chef of all the Ritz hotels, to teach and practice haute cuisine in its purest form, to invent over 7,000 dishes beyond the provincial recipes he had first learned at home, and still to say to all his disciples, *"Faites simple"*—Make it simple!   —*M.F.K. Fisher*

I

Provinces and Palates

The provinces of France, which actually have not existed as classified legal departments of the government since the Revolution of 1789, cover more than 30 regions, each one an ethnic pocket of its own culture and history and way of speech, as dictated by its special geography.

So firmly have the centuries proved that as a man eats and works, so is he formed, that in bone structure as well as in accent a Burgundian can generally be told from a Provençal, a vineyardist from a fisherman, a mountaineer from a farmer. The sparse rocky pasturage of Auvergne, west of Lyonnais, has bred a different fellow from the man who lives in the gentle meadows of the Jura, even though one tends sheep and the other cows, and in the same way the food these Frenchmen have fed on for hundreds of years has irrevocably shaped the ways they look, feel and think. (A fine-nosed Swede who has lived for a long time in Paris once said to me, "I can tell immediately and with my eyes closed, when I am next to a man in the Métro, what province he is from. Garlic? Provence! Apple Brandy? Normandy! Sauerkraut? Alsace! It does not matter how long ago he left home: he is *made* of it!" My friend then shuddered a little, being Swedish and therefore fastidious about odors other than his own, inborn and unsuspected, of herring and aquavit! Some Westerners say that Orientals smell of tea. Some vegetarians among the Seventh Day Adventists even say that other Christians smell of meat. . . .)

In America we have short memories, in the sense at least of atavistic gastronomy and compared with older nations. Within a comparatively few generations we have been wrenched from set patterns of eating as our fore-

A brooding mansion stands guard over an inlet of the Atlantic in Brittany, a province rich in gifts from the sea. In the foreground are rocklike oysters, delicately patterned clams, feathery shrimp and tiny black winkles.

fathers did, in this high tiny valley or on that broad salty plain. We may remember with nostalgia, and even manage to re-create now and again, the Sachertorte or the borsch or the steak-and-kidney pie our grandmothers made for special occasions, family gatherings when a few memories of the Old Country and the Old Days were brought out with the last delicious crumbs and the heeltaps in the party glasses. But mainly we live in a new gastronomical world, and not always for the better.

The patiently awaited seasonal feasts

The same is true of the modern French housewives, of course, in even the little fishing towns and rocky villages of the provinces. They too have bottled, canned and processed foods which a decade or two ago were unknown. But most of them still live near where their ancestors lived, even in the same houses. They still understand and grow and use unquestioningly the old herbs for the old dishes, and they still cook and eat in a seasonal pattern. When lamb is at its best, thyme on the hillsides will have sent out new supple shoots to tie around it for roasting, and the peas and lettuces are at their tenderest, all to make a feast provincial families wait for as patiently and instinctively as birds do the coming spring. When cherries are ripe, everyone eats them, fast, fast, and bakes them into warm tender *clafoutis*, and preserves them, with the most beautiful ones kept on their stems and covered with good brandy, or *eau de vie*, for a special treat. They are picked at their prime, ready for local uses or fast shipping to the nearest big markets—easier in France than in America, where distances are so great and produce must often travel hundreds of miles, near-ripe and oftener near-green.

In the main towns of the French provinces, markets run by the municipalities still supply every local fruit, vegetable, cheese and sausage as it is ready for the eating, and in an odd way these places triumph over the new supermarkets, at least in their ever-changing variety and fresh delights.

In villages of anything more than 50 souls, there is at least one general store where farmers will leave whatever is ready to sell that day: a basket of green beans or tomatoes, a sack of potatoes, some strings of garlic, a keg of freshly brined olives. The supply may be less varied and less dependable than in the marketplaces, but it is always fresh.

There are bakeries wherever there is a community of people. Myself, I know of only one village in all of France without its own bread, and that is Le Truel in the Aveyron, on the wild banks of the Tarn. By now this strange situation may have changed, but—when last I heard—all the bread had come from neighboring places for many years, since the startling suicide of a baker who was felt to have betrayed his trade and his village by leaving so unexpectedly, with nothing edible in his ovens.

There is sure to be a special kind of loaf, or at least one shape of loaf, peculiar to each region, sometimes even to each small locality: flat to fit into a hunter's bag, long and thin to stand alongside the bottle of wine in a shepherd's deep cape-pocket. Some regions will like a salty flavor in their loaves, or the crust will be brushed with olive oil or egg yolk or garlic, or the flour will be a different color from Parisian custom. In Aix-en-Provence there is a bread called simply *pain d'Aix*, but few people seem to know about it, and it is impossible to get in most restaurants, because the famous curative water used in the dough makes it come out rather gray and heavy and less conventionally attractive. In other words, the bread is completely local, as well as provincial.

Then, of course, in any good bakery, anywhere in France, there will be the regular loaves, made fresh before dawn six days a week: round, long, flat, fat, of crusty white; small solid dark ones, called somewhat disdainfully "health bread"; perhaps some short loaves for the schoolchildren, who almost always eat a small piece of chocolate with their afternoon snack. In at least one town I have known, the local bakeries made the school-rolls with a nugget of chocolate baked in the middle, a refinement which may well be common everywhere, but which I am unable to check on because of my currently limited acquaintance with that age level of consumers. (I do know about one elderly music teacher in France who fascinates her pupils by coming into the classroom every morning carrying a short split loaf of fresh bread and a small bar of bitter chocolate, which she solemnly puts together in a sandwich and then wraps again and sits upon at her piano until the midmorning recess, when she proceeds to eat the gently warmed and melted snack.)

Spices and herbs differ with the climate and geography of each place, too, so that the cooking in the high mountains of the Savoy tastes and smells of meadow plants, while much the same dishes (a stew, a soup, an omelet) will have another savor, another aspect, in Brittany or the Île-de-France.

Ancient ways remain

In spite of constant political turmoil and periodic war and invasion, the French nation since 1789 has kept an administrative uniformity which has protected its educational system and its whole cultural life, but the striking diversity of its natural regions, which we still call its provinces, has never changed. Formerly each of these regions, with its own reasons for independence, was a separate historical unit: a duchy, even a kingdom. Now, split into about 100 political departments which make up the country, but referred to by the old names like Burgundy, Provence, Alsace and Lorraine, they are the true divisions of the France we recognize, economically, geographically and above all gastronomically.

There is a great deal of ethnic dissimilarity in such an ancient country, somewhat as in the United States but of much longer and firmer standing. Just as many people speak with a hint of German accent in Milwaukee, for instance, or Spanish in El Paso, so in Alsace and parts of Lorraine, stepchild German is easier than pure French for people still living partly in the days of the Franco-Prussian War (a hundred years last longer in an ancient country than in a new one), and in the same way the dialects of northern Spain shape the vowels and voices from Bayonne to Perpignan. In Picardy and Champagne, near the Belgian border, Flemish is heard and understood, and in Béarn, Basque. In three of the French provinces, Brittany in the far north and Provence and Languedoc in the south, there are distinct languages, spoken and sung for centuries and still in daily use. More than a million Bretons use their own Celtic tongue, and along the Mediterranean the melodious sounds of *langue d'oc* are as vivid as when the troubadours used them in the 13th Century.

11

Provincial France: Ancient Names Signifying Great Food

The historic provinces of France no longer exist as political entities, but the names of many of them are as expressive as ever in characterizing traditional ways of life—especially ways of preparing food. On this map the provinces are grouped into 11 regions (designated A through K). Some of their notable contributions to good eating are described opposite and discussed more fully in the text of this chapter.

Belgique

La Manche

Allemagne

Boulogne-sur-Mer

ARTOIS

FLANDRE

Amiens

PICARDIE

Cherbourg

Le Havre

Rouen

ÎLE-DE-FRANCE

C

Reims

LORRAINE

Strasbourg

Caen

LA MARNE

Nancy

NORMANDIE

B

Argenteuil

Paris

CHAMPAGNE

LA SEINE

LES VOSGES

LE RHIN

F

Brest

A

MAINE

Chartres

ALSACE

BRETAGNE

ORLÉANAIS

Mulhouse

Orleans

BOURGOGNE

Dijon

D

E

FRANCHE-COMTÉ

Angers

NIVERNAIS

Nantes

Tours

Beaune

LA LOIRE

ANJOU

TOURAINE

BERRY

Suisse

SAUMUROIS

BOURBONNAIS

G

POITOU

Poitiers

Bourg-en-Bresse

LE JURA

AUNIS

MARCHE

Clermont-Ferrand

LYONNAIS

SAVOIE

Océan Atlantique

SAINTONGE

Cognac

LIMOUSIN

Lyon

I

Grenoble

ANGOUMOIS

LA GIRONDE

AUVERGNE

Italie

Périgueux

H

LA DORDOGNE

LE MASSIF CENTRAL

DAUPHINÉ

Bordeaux

LANGUEDOC

LES ALPES

GUYENNE

J

LE RHÔNE

GASCOGNE

LA GARONNE

Toulouse

Nîmes

PROVENCE

Nice

Bayonne

Aix-en-Provence

BÉARN

Castelnaudary

K

Marseille

LES PYRÉNÉES

Carcassonne

Espagne

FOIX

Perpignan

ROUSSILLON

La Méditerranée

12

A BRETAGNE (Brittany) takes its food and cooking simply. The sea supplies an abundance of fish, and excellent Belon oysters are taken from carefully tended beds along the Breton coast. Bretagne can be credited with inventing the French version of the pancake, the delicate crêpe.

B NORMANDIE can boast the richest milk, cream and butter in all of France. Norman cream is an important ingredient in some of the best French dishes, and much of the milk goes into the world-famous Camembert cheese. The region's meat is excellent, especially from the sheep and lambs pastured in the salt marshes along the coast. Apples grow abundantly, most of them going into cider, the favorite accompaniment to Norman meals, or into the fiery brandy called Calvados.

C CHAMPAGNE makes one supreme contribution to the table—the famous sparkling wine named after the province. Although its repertoire of food is limited, the region produces excellent sausages, and neighboring Flandre has invented many different ways to serve the lowly herring.

D TOURAINE is often called "the garden of France." Its recipes can be as delicate as Loire River trout in aspic or as robust as roast pork with prunes, a survival from medieval times. The Loire Valley that cuts through the province is "châteaux country," where French kings relaxed in the splendor of their country estates while their chefs made the most of the region's fine fruits and vegetables. France's greatest table grapes grow in Touraine.

E ÎLE DE FRANCE, the fertile land surrounding Paris, is the birthplace of the classic cooking style known as *la grande cuisine*. It was here, in the cavernous kitchens of kings and lords, that French cooking became a high art. Cooks competed with one another to invent ever more elaborate dishes, and their employers developed ever more sensitive palates to appreciate what was served. The cooking of the Île de France lacks a strong regional personality, but it draws on the culinary genius of all the provinces.

F ALSACE and LORRAINE have often come under German domination, and this is reflected in their cooking. Alsatian food, with its sausages and sauerkraut, has a Germanic heartiness. The food of Lorraine is slightly more French in character. Its most famous dish is the *quiche lorraine*, an egg, cream and bacon tart; the province also is known for its excellent *potée*, a cabbage soup with pork and vegetables. The fruity Rhine wines of Alsace rival those of Germany.

G BOURGOGNE (Burgundy) is justly well known throughout the world for its wines, and these wines—aristocratic whites and mellow reds—play a dominant role in Burgundian cooking. Red burgundy is a key ingredient in *boeuf bourguignon*, the king of beef stews, and in most regional dishes. The annual gastronomic fair held in Dijon, the principal city of Bourgogne and the "mustard capital" of France, draws gourmets from all over the world.

H BORDEAUX and the country around it are best known for their wines, which rank with the Burgundies as the greatest in the world. Bordeaux cooks have developed a highly refined cuisine to accompany these wines, and the gourmets of the region are among the most demanding in France. Bordeaux has given *grande cuisine* one of its basic meat sauces, the *sauce bordelaise*, whose 13 ingredients are bound together by the aristocratic taste of the red Bordeaux wine that is added as the sauce simmers. Also in this region are Cognac, the brandy capital, and Perigueux, whose truffles go into the making of *pâté de foie gras*, perhaps the most extravagant delicacy of the French table.

I FRANCHE-COMTÉ, like its neighboring provinces of Savoie and Dauphiné, is mostly mountain country, and the food is as robust as the climate. Perhaps the greatest contribution of this region to the national cuisine is the Bresse chicken, a small bird whose flesh is so delicate that even the inventive French prefer it simply roasted, without any sauce or spices to obscure its flavor. The cows of the Franche-Comté region produce more milk than the inhabitants can drink, and much of the surplus is made into cheeses, the most distinguished of which is Comté, a French version of the Swiss Gruyère.

J LANGUEDOC, FOIX, ROUSSILLON: Languedoc was once an outpost of the Roman Empire and it has retained traces of Roman influence in its cuisine. The people of Languedoc are especially devoted to the old Roman *cassoulets*, rich concoctions of goose or duck, pork or mutton, plus sausage and white beans. To the west, along the Pyrénées, in Foix and Roussillon, the Spanish culinary influence prevails, particularly in omelets prepared with green peppers, tomatoes and ham.

K PROVENCE has been a favored vacation center since Roman times. Like some other lands of the northern Mediterranean, it bases its cooking on garlic, olive oil and tomatoes. A dish combining all of these ingredients is Marseille's *bouillabaisse*, the famed fish stew which often contains a dozen kinds of Mediterranean fish and shellfish. In general, Provence has a cuisine that is more highly flavored than that of northern France.

In a larger way, not limited by provincial boundaries, the north of France can be called basically Germanic, as the south can be called Latin. Since World War II, additional ethnic challenge has crept in, thanks to the countless prisoners who chose to stay on when the peace was made, and to political wanderers: Italians working on all the buildings, Poles digging in the mines . . . and Algerians . . . and Spaniards . . . and yet the unique character of each province of this extraordinary country remains impregnable, apparently, perhaps even to time itself. Cheese still comes from highland meadows. Oysters still breed along the northern and the western coasts. Olives and tomatoes and almonds still grow like weeds in the south. Vineyards thrive. Grains flourish. And with the ageless adaptability of people determined to survive with grace, no matter what the odds, the French do so in every region of their myriad-faceted land.

Normandy and Brittany

For simplicity, especially when we talk of the gastronomical side of French life, this book will group the 30-some provinces into the regions shown on the map on page 12.

Normandy and Brittany are alike in forming most of the north coast of France, and in supplying fish and apples and succulent lambs fed on salty marsh grasses to its markets, but they differ subtly as well as openly in many other ways. Normandy's coastline is more docile, with the waters of the English Channel slapping gently at it oftener than they lash it. Long, shallow beaches stretch out for sandy miles from the shore at low tide. Small, busy ports harbor fishing fleets to catch the delicate soles we call Dover or Channel, or to head into the North Sea for long weeks of cod and herring catches. And almost at once, behind the flat beaches and the ports, there are the rich meadows and orchards, so green, so lovely in the spring, that people who have not seen them incline to smile at any earnest description. The first time I ever saw France, I went slowly through this magical countryside from Cherbourg, at its northmost tip, toward Paris, and although it is not *quite* the fact, I saw the small fat cows then as I still see them in my mind, colored many delicate shades of creamy rose, like pink butter. They stood calmly in the thick grass, and apple trees hung with garnets and rubies bent over them.

The people of Normandy are strong and brave, as befits a race which contributed William the Conqueror to history, and which has been a force in the French nation for more than a thousand years. They eat well, work hard and are courageous. They live in one of the few provinces without vineyards, but their cider and its distillation, Calvados, are fine substitutes, and the cuisine which has evolved during the centuries, based on jewel-like apples and cream from the little pink cows, is one of the best in the world. Combine such elements with the delicate Channel fish, the fine marsh lambs and meadow calves, the cheese, the honey from the apple blossoms, and "miracles will be seen," as Brillat-Savarin loved to say.

Brittany has meadows too, but they are far inland from the wild rocky coast which juts into the Atlantic and goes down the Bay of Biscay toward Bordeaux. The Bretons too grow apples, but smaller and more tart. There are delicious sheep roaming the marshes, but their meat is saltier and must

be cooked differently from that of most sheep. Even the vegetables taste of the ocean in Brittany, for seaweeds gathered along the beaches at low tide are used for fertilizer there in the farm gardens. The fish caught off the coast are mostly tinned or salted: sardines, herring, mackerel, tuna. But creatures like lobsters, which can hide in their own shells in bad weather, and the equally protected oysters, abound along the edge of the Atlantic, and are shipped alive all over the country and across to England. And there are clams. And scallops. And there are soles too, best skinned, stuffed with salty butter, and quickly fried, *à la Bretonne*.

And there is the one notable wine of the province, the dry, light and lively Muscadet, to drink with all these delicate flavors and textures, or the less elegant cider which flows like heavenly water everywhere in Brittany and is taken as seriously by its partisans as any wine in Burgundy or Bordeaux: its age is known, its place of origin, even its bottler, if it is not served simply from a pitcher.

The people of this craggy country, who make some of the best sailors and

In the open-air market at Villeneuve-de-Marsan, in Gascony, shoppers mingle with vendors whose tomatoes, spinach, garlic, carrots, artichokes and other vegetables have been picked in their own gardens.

fishermen in the world, seem more remote to outsiders than do the Normans. They are pure Celt rather than their neighbors' mixture of many bloods, and many of them still speak, or at least understand, the language called Breton, which came with them when they fled England almost 1,500 years ago. In one way or another they are intimately bound up with the sea, wedded to its mysterious power, and their deep religious feeling goes far back beyond the Christianity they soon learned, joining them in another mystical marriage, with the prehistoric sun worshipers who left their cryptic stone monuments, called menhirs and dolmens, scattered everywhere.

Visitors who come to paint or photograph these strange stones, or to watch the devout religious pilgrimages and celebrations called *pardons,* are inclined to feel neglected, gastronomically, by the Bretons. It is true that much of the produce from both land and sea is sent to Paris and other big markets, and that there are few noted provincial dishes, but there are delicious sausages always, and a spicy fish soup called *cotriade* is usually ready for the asking, and the pancakes are, too: not thick like most American versions of this near-primitive dish, but big and thin, rolled into triangular or rectangular packets to hold the butter or cheese or jam or honey or whatever may be in them, served hot off the black griddle with a dash of sugar or salt on market days, and along the quais, and in countless Breton restaurants.

Boats lie beached at sundown in northern Brittany, along a wide stretch of sandy shore that a low tide has left exposed. The houses lining the waterfront are part of the village of Cancale, a small fishing port that is famous in France for its nearby beds of clams and oysters.

Best of all, there are the lobsters, and the fresh soles and skates and mackerel. They are cooked simply: butter, a dash of cider or Muscadet or the scarcer lemon. And who wants a cooked clam or oyster when he can eat it fresh and cringing right from the sea? Outsiders may turn pancakes into the probably Parisian *crêpes Suzette,* or turn lobster into the suspiciously Provençal *homard à l'américaine.* In Brittany they can still be eaten as they have been for centuries, and the good cider can still be drunk, if visitors know how to push gently through the crowds of other visitors and find a fishermen's pub or a welcoming small inn behind the postcard shops and even the dolmens and menhirs.

The Champagne country

The northern part of this region is like Normandy in its coastline, with the currents of the Channel racing through the Pas de Calais, and Boulogne the greatest fishing town in France. Inland, though, the country is not shaped into curving pastures and orchards, but is flat and with a feeling of great space in it. Fields of wheat and rye seem endless there, and vast, neat plantings of beets and potatoes provide food for much of France, as well as for the hearty northerners who must nourish themselves on plenty of starch and sugar. Everything is strong: the cheeses, for instance, smell of ammonia even when they are not overripe. Beer, and strong beer, is the common drink, and is used in regional dishes like the beef stew called *carbonades à la flamande.* Wild boar's meat is prized, flushed dangerously from the many forests, and unless very young it is perhaps the "strongest" meat in Europe, needing long, slow rest in equally strong marinades to make it fit to serve.

Farther south, into Champagne proper, the country remains flat or gently rolling, and the great vineyards begin. Noble rivers like the Marne and the Seine flow through this famous but little-visited province. Centuries of canny planning have made the land proper for its best human usage. The fine forests have not been razed as in other parts of France during the past 1,500 years, but have been protected for their amazing populations of wild game, almost as essential to Frenchmen as bread and wine. The deep layers of chalk under the topsoil have been respected. They cleanse and drain the vineyards, and make an ideal place for miles of cool deep tunnels where the full bottles are stored.

The making of sparkling champagne—which if it comes from any province but the one it is named for, must legally be called simply *mousseux* ("sparkling") wine—is as complex as its consumption is simple. Unfortunately this makes it costly, and it is impossible to imagine using it in cooking. Recipes which call for "champagne" should never be made with the sparkling wine if they are to be heated in any way; instead they should be made with its still or natural version, bottled without being transformed into the wonderful bubbly stuff that old Dom Pérignon first captured toward the end of the 17th Century. Still champagne is delicious to drink, too, but for cooking as for drinking, if a still champagne cannot be found, any good dry white wine made from Pinot Blanc or Chardonnay grapes will serve nobly. Naturally, in a recipe for a chilled dessert like a *coupe Jacques,* or for punches, the bubbly wine is essential (although wasted on a real champagne lover).

A Breton fisherman transfers live lobsters from a storage basket into a pail to carry them to market. The baskets, immersed in the salt water, protect the lobsters after they are caught. In the background are dike-surrounded reservoirs, filled by the sea at high tide and used to keep oysters while they mature.

The people of northern Champagne are often tall, blue-eyed, blond. They are influenced by the ethnic habits of Belgium and Lorraine along the northeast borders, with their Germanic tastes shaped to combat a harsh climate: plenty of pork, potatoes, cabbage, beer—all things which grow best on the flatlands. Farther south, where the hunting is good and the wine flows, bones are shorter, hair is darker, more Gallic, and the cooking becomes more complex. Because most of the land is either in vineyards or forests, there is not much domestic meat (with the exception of very fine hams), and chickens and the bountiful river fish are important in the kitchens.

Alsace and Lorraine

Lorraine slopes up gently from the flat country, into the high farmlands and meadows of Alsace. Its rich fields grow fine grains, and from its fruits come some of the best distillations in the world, from kirsch and mirabelle and quetsch to the rarest of all, *eau de vie de framboise*. Even so, the same liqueurs of Alsace are more famous possibly because they are scarcer. There the soil, perhaps the finest in all France, is used for a dozen other important crops, first of which is grapes, to make the province, along with Bordeaux and Burgundy, a leading producer of French wines. Next, at least in the eyes of food lovers, comes the cultivation of geese, whose main purpose is to provide oversized livers for the world-famous *pâté de foie gras*, but who also perform in dozens of Alsatian kitchen miracles, as thoroughly taken advantage of as the pig who has nothing left but his squeal. Alsatians are very thrifty, shrewd people, which is probably why they place the pig second only to the profitable goose in their economy, and the sausages and hams of their country are justly famous. So are their fruit tarts, in which every plum, every apple and every cherry not destined for the distillery finds a symmetrical sweet place.

Alsace, so rich in wine and food, has always been a top prize in European conquests for power, but the basic strain in its people is Germanic, as are many of the customs, the dishes, the architectural patterns. Wars or not, salmon still leap from the Rhine and the Ill, a few storks still clatter their long beaks arrogantly and amorously on chimney tops, and the Sunday-noon sauerkraut still simmers until church is out.

To the south looms the beautiful Jura, and between Lorraine and Alsace is the long range of the Vosges, with vineyards on its eastern slopes, and the high meadows filled with fat cows, and rushing trout-filled streams, and small farms where eggs and milk and butter make the industrious owners among the richest in the world.

Fresh white cheeses are much liked in Alsatian homes, used almost like sweet-smelling butter, but the most famous ripened one, Munster, creamy

A street-side stand in the Breton town of Saint-Malo displays mussels, gathered the same day from a reservoir at nearby Le Vivier-sur-Mer.

and crusted, is apt to be very whiffy when at its prime—rather like American Liederkranz, except more so. In Strasbourg in the winter I used to go after a long Sunday walk to a big, noisy, fine beerhall and order a "Munsterplate": a large piece of very strong runny cheese, a bowl of finely minced raw onion, a smaller bowl of caraway seeds, plenty of good crusty bread. This called for the heady blond beer of the town, for no wine ever grew that could stand up to such an assault. Somehow it all vanished, except perhaps for a few stray seeds. And in that cold land, after walking fast through the bare woodlands along the Rhine, and the ice-hard city streets, it

Sheep graze on a seaside meadow near Mont Saint-Michel, in Normandy. Flocks like this yield lamb and mutton called *pré-salé*, prized for the salty flavor the meat gains from the aromatic grasses.

seemed without cavil a proper late-afternoon snack. In Bordeaux or Provence, probably, even a hefty young farmer would be laid out by it . . . as certainly would I, these years later and in a different world.

The good life of Touraine

Several regions have been called the true gardens of the nation, its market baskets, but the sweet Touraine country of fields and vineyards and rivers, fertile and welcoming, is probably the truest one. It has an elegance about it, because of centuries of noblemen who have built beautiful castles there and brought their sophistication to the abundance of the farms and streams. But everywhere the hospitality is noble, whether in a château or in one of the innumerable chalky caves which often serve as pleasant simple homes as well as natural wine cellars. Good manners and good language are intrinsic to the life of this earthly paradise. Its white wines, too casually lumped under one name, Vouvray, can be sweet or dry, and they marry perfectly with the subtle plainness of the regional ways of preparing everything from a delicate pike to a sturdy plum tart. But there are also robust reds like Chinon and Bourgueil, as essential at table as they are in the stews of eel or wild rabbit they accompany.

Shallots are as characteristic of the regional cooking of Touraine as garlic is in Provence, and tarragon, nutmeg, fresh grape-vinegar, all help to add a peculiar freshness to the cuisine. There is ample cream. Butter is plentiful, to make the delicious hot delicate sauce called *beurre blanc,* and to brown eels and meats for the infinite varieties of *matelotes* or stews. And the inexhaustible supply of fish, from the many streams and rivers to the great, gracious Loire herself, seems made for pleasure in the kitchen: salmon, trout, pike, dainty gudgeons, crayfish of course, and up from the sea at Nantes, in Brittany, the rare shad, more salmon, and easy shipments of clams and all the shellfish of the coast.

In Touraine, walled gardens are part of living, whether in the châteaux or the simplest village homes. Vegetables thrive almost the year around in them, and fruit trees are trained against their walls and on trellises. The finest garden produce can reach Paris two weeks before it would ripen in the Île-de-France, and all winter bunches of beautiful table grapes, which drink from vials of water in dark cool rooms until they are shipped away, gladden the hearts of French gourmets rich enough to buy them. The magnificent summer fruits are dried, or preserved, or made into jams and jellies. Dishes and jars and even tubs of them, and of honey, and of the pâtés and *confits,* or preserves, of pork and rabbit, and of the famous *rillettes* and *rillons* of potted goose or pork, line shelves in every respectable kitchen in Touraine, ready to hand, and often to be shipped to great restaurants everywhere or to be used for Aunt Josephine's christening for her new boy, or the Duvals' golden wedding party. In this temperate and gentle province, blessed with rich chalky soil and many fields and riverbanks, people have been able to live graciously for centuries, and it is probably right that they call themselves the realest Frenchmen, and their culture, as their cooking, the most typically "French" in its forthright intelligence.

The Île-de-France—it has Paris!

The province of the Île-de-France is rightly jealous of such claims. But it has Paris! In strictly provincial terms this may seem a menace: the metropolis can appear to be all, everything, a giant absorbing and overwhelming the countryside around it. To anyone flying into *la ville lumière,* though, this is not true, for so lovely is the landscape below, so rich are the fields and forests that press against the edges of the great city, that in itself the city is merely a part of the whole.

It is true that the good things that grow in the woods and meadows and

rivers flow toward Paris, the gastronomical heart of our Western world. Hunting is a fine art in the Île-de-France, as it has been for centuries in the vast disciplined forests of Fontainebleau, Compiègne, and a dozen more, and in the more distant woodlands near Orléans. Recipes for preparing everything from pheasants and thrushes to stags and wild pigs start in the country kitchens, and then grow grander as they reach the restaurants of the capital. Streams flow from every direction into the great rivers named Seine and Marne, alive with fish. Like the excellent beef and pork of the region, they are usually cooked simply, depending for their drama upon the artful sauces which often accompany them.

The finest fruits and vegetables are grown in a great garden circle around Paris, yielding to vast wheat fields toward Chartres to the southwest, and eastward toward Champagne to the fine pasturelands that produce the near-celestial cheese known everywhere as Brie. Mushrooms and wild strawberries grow in the shady woods of this idyllic region, but are also cultivated to

Dairy cattle browse in an Alsatian pasture, in the fertile foothills of the Vosges Mountains. Their milk is used in the pastries of the region, and goes into such creamy white Alsatian cheeses as Munster.

perfection in vast cellars, hothouses, orderly fields, according to their natures. Bees make a honey like no other, called Gâtinais (after the region where the bees live), gathered from all the wild and planted blossoms: pine and gorse, herbs along the riverbanks, apple and peach trees in bloom, meadow flowers. Peas grow best and fastest in one part of this enormous garden, and asparagus or green beans in another. Table grapes almost as famous as those of Touraine, peaches and pears and almonds, all have a flavor that make them undeniable in origin.

Some people think it is the rich soil of the riverbanks of the Île-de-France that gives this special savor, but generations of artists, and the sensitive inhabitants themselves, believe that it is the sky, rather: tender and luminously gray, or a clear, kind blue, never cruel.

The riches of Burgundy

To the southeast, Burgundy makes the small wine-areas of the Île-de-France seem poor indeed. It starts out with the famous Chablis district, before its rolling land gives way to the range of hills known everywhere as the Côte-d'Or, where most (but not all the best) of the wine is red and not white, and where a town like Beaune literally sits on a fantastic maze of cellars holding some of the greatest vintages of the world.

Fortunately the food of this region is plentiful and hearty, to stand up to its bins and bottles. The chickens of Bresse, the fine Charolais beef, the snails that feed on grape leaves, the mustard grown in great honey-sweet fields, all contribute to the robust cuisine which has been typically "Burgundian" for some 2,000 years.

The people who live there eat hugely, and their feasts are historical, whether held in Caesar's day or last week. They drink their own wines and their neighbors', and their dishes depend on the same wines for their special nature, recognizable everywhere: *coq au vin, boeuf bourguignon,* even fillets of sole and pears and prunes, are prepared with red or white wine by the bottleful, not the quarter-cup. The sauces that evolve naturally from the marinating and slow cooking are rich and fruity. . . and call for more wine in the glass alongside. Fish and game are treated handsomely and in the same winy manner. There is good honey for the mountains of gingerbread that come from the ovens of Dijon, and fine jams are made from the firm provincial fruits. Fields of black currants yield their pungent berries for the famous liqueur *cassis,* and mustard is ground with wine vinegar to make the unique condiment known everywhere as Dijon mustard. Dominant, though, in this life and culture, is the magic ridge of hilly land called the Côte-d'Or. It is the heart of Burgundy, as Burgundy itself likes to feel it is the heart of gastronomy (to the scornful amusement of another true capital of the pleasures of the table, its southern neighbor, Lyon).

Franche-Comté: Beautiful and wild

Franche-Comté includes for our own simplification the regions of Savoy and the Dauphiné. To the north is Lorraine. To the east lie Switzerland and then Italy, and southward is Provence. It is a beautiful and often wild region, with the Jura Mountains running down it toward the Lake of

Geneva, and then the great Alps rising. There are serene lakes, and gentle fields and pastures on the lower slopes of the mountains. Excellent wines grow far below the peaks, and are a part of the daily fare of everyone. Many kinds of fish abound in the cold rushing waters, and crayfish too, so that almost any village inn can offer dishes like the freshly killed and quickly cooked trout called *truite au bleu* or a *gratin de queues d'écrivisses*, the tiny crayfish tails, which would make a Parisian restaurateur pale with envy. Mushrooms and truffles thrive in the meadows and in the shade of the forests, and so does game, of course, so that the provincial recipes for jugging wild hares, as well as for venison and boar, are standard wherever there is good cooking.

In the same way, mountain herbs figure largely in this strong but subtle cuisine, and many-flavored honeys, wild berries, chicken and eggs share honors in the kitchen. Some of the fricassees and omelets of the region are copied all over the world, perhaps with never quite the same freshness and simplicity. Pigs flourish there too, for hearty stews to warm people through the long rigorous winters, and for delectable sausages. Best of all, perhaps, the goats and cows flourish. In summer they go up into the mountain meadows; in winter they are stabled close to their owners and fed pungent hay, and pampered like princesses, to supply cream and butter for the cooking, and above all milk for the famous cheeses of this region: Comté

In the village of Ittenheim in Alsace, a farmer's wife helps load cabbages hand-to-hand into a wagon. The outer leaves have been trimmed from the freshly uprooted heads.

(or French Gruyère), and farther south Reblochon, with of course countless local variations that are never marketed.

The people are tough and durable, whether they be farmers or mountaineers. Their cooking reflects their real respect for what the forests and waters
and meadows can offer them, and when they cannot go out into the snow
they sit in their snug simple homes, carving wood, making clocks, and living well on the good food they have put aside during the rich summer days.
The cows and pigs and chickens on the other side of the wall are healthy
and generous. The cheeses are ripening. The wine is bottled. . . .

The exotic and the plain thrive in Provence

Southward, life in Provence is astonishingly different, and the people are
a breed apart, shaped by invasions of every race around the Mediterranean:
short, dark, fiery, with their own language and religious traditions. The
sky can be a fierce blue, or howling with cold dust during the north wind
called mistral. The light that is cast over the landscape is the antithesis of the
gentle luminous light in the Île-de-France, the half-foggy, half-clear blue-
gray one in Brittany. Along the coastline of Provence the fishermen, often

26

The cargo on the sidecar is a basketful of parsley; the vehicle is a Velosolex motorbike. The farmer is bound for the marketplace in Cavaillon, Provence.

Outside the town of Lourmarin, a field of carrots soaks up the heat of a Provençal afternoon. The foods of Provence benefit from France's longest growing season.

working at night by lantern light, bring strange fish from the rocks and inlets for the famous stews and soups like *bouillabaisse, bourride* and plain *soupe aux poissons.*

Good wines grow along the Rhône and on the rolling land, and olive trees first brought by the Greeks flourish wherever they can put down roots in the dry rocky soil of the hills, providing their own fruit and then the oil on which the regional cuisine is based. Tomatoes and garlic, justly synonymous with most dishes *à la provençale*, flourish like weeds. And everywhere, even in the ditches, herbs grow. They make the air heady. They are used by the handful when they are fresh, and dried in myriad bunches to be kept until the next season in jars and bottles, or blended with powdered lavender, dried orange peel and other exotic things to make each household's own mixture for the flavors intrinsic to its cooking.

In the flat plains around Avignon, protected from the bruising mistral by great slanting windbreaks of live cypress and bamboo fences, fine early vegetables are grown, and melons and tree fruits prosper so abundantly that even after the northern demands have been satisfied, Provence has its full share of them in all the open-air markets, which can function the year around in that southern climate.

Ripening in a vineyard on the Gironde River estuary, these grapes will yield a fine red Médoc wine called St. Estèphe. The village for which the wine is named lies north of Bordeaux, in the region that is also the home of the famous Haut-Médoc wines: Château Lafite, Château Margaux and Château Latour.

Truffles grow in Provence, and snails, and tiny thrushes that are made into rich sensuous pâtés. In the desolate salt marshes of the Camargue grow lamb and beef and rice that have their own flavor, to delight lovers of good food—and this includes, foremost, the people of Provence themselves. They eat and drink everything that grows in their seaside province with unflagging interest and enjoyment, but never with the occasional heaviness and excess of Frenchmen who must survive harder temperatures.

To the east there is the Italian influence on dishes like *ratatouille* (tomatoes, eggplant and squash) and *salade Niçoise*. To the west toward Spain, in Languedoc, there is *cassoulet*, the fabled stew of beans and meats, which arouses endless arguments about whether Toulouse, Carcassonne or Castel-

28

naudary makes it "correctly." (All make it very well.) The controversy over which of the three historical versions of the French recipe is the "real" one has been raging, or at least simmering as a proper cassoulet should, for a long time, and inevitably a club has been formed of its *compagnons,* some 200 at the last counting but open to new members at five francs a head. The president and founder, who was about to open a restaurant in Paris when the club began, neatly got around the three-way split by naming his specialty in all simplicity *cassoulet de Languedoc.* "That way, nobody can be vexed," he said.

The fact remains that an addict from Toulouse would be somewhat more than vexed if he were presented with a dish that he firmly believed sprang from *his* town and that did not have *his* preserved goosemeat in it. (What else can thrifty Frenchmen do with all the meat left from the geese who die to make the *pâté de foie gras* of the region, as famous as that of Alsace, and even richer with truffles?) A man from Carcassonne, on the other hand, might well be affronted by the blanket-recipe offered to his aficionados of the Compagnons du Cassoulet by their president-restaurateur, if it proved innocent of lamb, and any decently chauvinistic citizen of Castelnaudary would willingly forego both goose and lamb as long as there was plenty of tender pork in the dish. The Maison du Cassoulet, it was diplomatically agreed, could serve all the components of this gastronomical trinity in one superb concoction, guaranteed to nourish the spirit as well as the body of any true trencherman. And that one must be, to savor and encompass this basically hefty Languedoc dish!

Always in the south there is the beautiful Mediterranean, and the air and the soil that breed good olive oil, bursting, pungent tomatoes, pearly garlic. The staple drink called *pastis* sends its clean licorice tang into the vibrant air whenever work risks becoming a bore and a chat at the corner cafe is indicated. Herbs and salt leave their taste upon the lips with every breath. Life in this region is not always easy, but it is simple and good.

The Bordeaux region

This is true, too, in most of the southwest. The Bordeaux region includes the provinces of Béarn and Gascony along the Spanish border, with their hearty cabbage soups called *garbures,* flavored according to the area with salt pork, preserved goose or whatever other fattish meat is available.

Another dish from the Basque country in southwest Béarn is the popular *pipérade* of eggs and vegetables, a pleasant summer omelet, as a *garbure* is good anywhere for winter. Geese and ducks flourish, to make pâtés and *confits,* with truffles to perfume them, and on the high, bleak tablelands of Rouergue, in southeast Guyenne, roam the sheep that make the world-famous Roquefort cheese.

Along the Atlantic shoreline, especially in the round bay of Arcachon, grow some of the finest oysters in the world, and up the great inlets and in all the rivers and streams there are boundless fish. Forests, sternly kept wild and rich, provide the hunting that is as essential to the people of Bordeaux and the southwest as is winegrowing, and the mushrooms called *cèpes* grow there too, to add flavor to countless dishes evolved by the household cooks to complement their supplies of game and fish.

Needless to say, Bordeaux means wine throughout the world, and to the people who live in the fabulous country at the mouth of the Gironde, and around its capital, wine is life. They cultivate the grapes for it, carefully see them from vine to bottle to table, discuss them, drink them—and of course shape their eating according to what they have thus produced. Wine becomes, perforce, a mystique, and the Bordelais people who practice it stay sound and keen, and the rest of the world is the better for their dedication. And after a meal designed knowingly to complement and compliment the bottles chosen to be savored that day, there is always a taste of one of the two great brandies of the world, Cognac and Armagnac, which come from this grape-wealthy region. The first is better known, but both are noble indeed when they have been properly aged in oaken casks, and as blatantly ignoble, legally at least, if they assume those names and come from any other part of the globe.

More to the east, in the Périgord area of Guyenne, which suggests truffles much as black suggests white, the attitude toward wine as such is more relaxed. The country has everything required to produce a cuisine fitted to good drinking, but the people of Périgord keep the two interdependent, rather than letting the bottle dictate to the palate as in the true wine country. There is the customary game from forest and stream. There are of course the truffles. Geese, ducks, chickens thrive. There is even fresh caviar from the sturgeons wandering up the long estuary of the Gironde. Vegetables grow well, to make the rich dishes more bracing (usually cooked within them instead of apart), and there are crisp salads tossed with walnut oil. Table grapes and fruits thrive on the lower mountain slopes, and plums especially are used in countless ways, both fresh and preserved, or baked into the *clafoutis*, or fruit tarts, which in other provinces would be made with pears or above all cherries.

The gastronomic region whose metropolis is Bordeaux is a kind of summing up of everything that makes regional cooking the source of all other cooking anywhere: that is, it relies on the use of natural products, nurtured by man. In other parts of the unbelievably varied country of France, human beings continue to struggle with rigorous ocean and Channel storms, with deadly cold, and still they have evolved a way of surviving, at table, which has great dignity and pattern. In Brittany, for instance, the cuisine is part of the mystery of the sea, and of the unknown races that have occupied that land in the lost past. In Provence, as in Alsace, life is shaped by centuries of occupation by other ethnic groups, other cultures. But in the country tributary to Bordeaux, which has many of these influences working within it too, there is a synthesis of climate, sea and land waters, mountains and plains, to make it possible for the people there to choose, rather than to have their patterns thrust upon them. They can be wine makers, farmers, hunters. They can raise geese. They can hunt truffles. They can fish, or cultivate oysters, or make cheese. They can raise greengage plums. Life in the Bordeaux region, centuries seem to have proved, can be a well-fed one.

A Burgundian grape picker washes down his sandwich with wine from a bottle he has brought into the vineyard. The grapes will make Vosne-Romanée, a leading wine of the Côte de Nuits, south of Dijon.

II

A Family Affair

In almost any region of France the more intricate cooking, the special dish, is saved for the special day: Sunday, of course, but usually a *special* Sunday, like Easter; or a baptism, a wedding, a betrothal (not necessarily in that order!); above all for birthdays and private family anniversaries like the First Warm Day, The First Frost, The Day in Honor of the Biggest Trout (caught in 1903 by Uncle René), The Last Strawberry Tart until Next Year. These almost childlike excuses to gather together around a dining table are a part of country living that city people try to cling to, with some desperation, amid the increasing pressures of urbanization everywhere, but the French are especially stubborn and even in Paris such festivities are still taken seriously. A few Alsatians from north of Mulhouse can always be collected to drink the last bottle of a prized plum brandy, or some Savoyards to share a couple of Reblochon cheeses fresh and fruity from a newcomer's suitcase.

In America people are basically restless in the kitchen, teased by their subconscious memories of other ways, perhaps, and all the more eager to assemble a Balinese meal, or to try a Hawaiian luau in the back yard, or to gather rose petals for an Armenian sweetmeat. In France, although "foreign" dishes are on the increase in good restaurants, most people are perfectly content to reproduce the same edibles their far-back ancestors liked, yet to enjoy, if correctly prepared by a wife or equally reputable visitor from some other province, specialties of that region: *tripes à la mode de Caen* from Normandy, *carbonades de boeuf à la flamande* as it is made in a village south of Dunkerque, a *cassoulet de Carcassonne*. . . .

In Paris' Rue Mouffetard, Mme. Annie Boulat *(left)* shops for a dinner party. Next to her an old woman shops for melons, testing for a fresh smell, hefting for proper weight and feeling for the softness that means ripeness.

In this same vein, a girl who goes northwest from her native Provence to marry a man from the Bordeaux country, and raise their children there, will usually learn fast and well how to cook the food he considers the only proper food, which is to say Bordelais. For special days, or when her family comes to visit, there will be Provençal dishes. If, on the other hand, a *man* moves from one province to another very different from his gastronomically, his wife will cook as much as possible as he wants it to be, adapting the food at hand in their new home. This is a natural part of the European attitude toward lasting marriages.

The physical as well as moral respect for the pleasures of the table in France has at times seemed laughable to Anglo-Saxons raised by the post-Victorian precepts that one should eat what is set before one, be properly thankful for it, and remain silent, especially on the subject of its edibility. The respect does not, however, seem to have had any adverse effect upon the historical integrity of provincial French kitchens, and perhaps the meals which we non-French can evolve from their time-tested recipes will add to our own stability, in the family if not the world.

The pattern of the meal

If there could be such a thing as a typical French meal, the kind eaten nearly every day by a family able to provide for its natural needs, it would of course vary with the region and even more so with the seasons of the year. It would, however, follow a general pattern, whether in the country or in small or big towns and cities, in somewhat the way that superimposed outlines of many different men will make a recognizable Man.

This meal, usually called dinner, would be served in the middle of the day. With the increasing speed of life there are snack bars and such for hasty eating in the cities, but most Frenchmen make time at noon for a leisurely and solid meal, and eat very simply and more frugally at night. At midday the children have two hours off from classes. The offices are closed. It is the indicated time to devote to one's healthy digestion—and at home if possible.

There is much talk in France about "Americanization," which really means the general speeding-up of the old ways, and of course one of the most vital spots to be hit is the table. Thousands of government workers in Paris now take a 45-minute break for lunch, instead of the old one lasting from 12 until 2. They are reported to have agreed to this after a trial period which most of them found acceptable because their workweek was cut by a half day to five days, and they got home earlier as well. Sly employers like to believe that their people will come back to work after a bite in a snack bar (a correct term now in Franco-Yank) bright-eyed, alert and full of enthusiasm for their IBM machines. This may possibly be true in the metropolis, where there is no place to spend two hours but in a favorite bistro, talking and tossing down one more glass of Beaujolais or Sancerre. In the provinces, it is another thing entirely. Quite probably it will take as long to eliminate the noonday eating-at-home freedom of small-town and country people as it will take to convince them that sliced packaged bread distributed by trucks from enormous centralized bakeries is as good as bread made fresh every morning before dawn at the neighborhood bakery, and carried home warm and crackling, naked of waxed paper or cellophane.

Annie carries her roomy shopping basket through the open-air market, filling it with onions, heads of lettuce and a bag of fresh table grapes.

In Paris, many schoolchildren still come home at noon to eat and relax, whether with one or both parents, with a part-time maid, or with a kindly neighbor. In smaller, quieter places they do not need to be escorted through the streets when they are little, and as they grow older they save half an hour or so for themselves after the noon meal, to ramble on Main Street, wherever it may be, to look at each other and exchange the cabalistic salutations of their peers. Older men who are not at home because they are traveling or because, perhaps, they have become bored with their own dining rooms, find themselves sitting in whatever café is to their taste, sipping a brandy or a glass of mineral water, according also to their taste. But the idea of going back to the schoolyard or office in less than two hours is unthinkable to most Frenchmen.

The typical midday meal, although it will follow a pattern common in almost every social level, need not be elaborate or bounteous. This is true, in great part, because conversation is almost as essential to the act of eating

After arguing over price and quality, Annie buys the fresh chives, tarragon and chervil for her salad. A few yards away are stalls that sell cheese, fruit, sausages and roasted chickens.

as is the food itself, in every reasonably normal French household, and it makes everything taste better and last longer. Worrisome subjects like school examinations, money problems or politics are delicately avoided until digestion has set in, and even such trite subjects as the weather are considered acceptable if they are discussed with intelligence over the sliced tomatoes with chopped basil and olive oil, the boiled beef and potatoes, the green salad and the cheese.

When a news story about a shorter lunch schedule to be tried on Paris civil employees described a "lunch break" as usually spent consuming six-course meals, with wine, coffee and Cognac, in friendly bistros or at home, it was a gross and perhaps malicious exaggeration: few wage earners could afford such a feast every day, or would enjoy it, and six-course meals are almost unknown, except in the grand restaurants or at state luncheons for kings and presidents.

In Paris, with about three million people, in Arles with about 40,000, in Plascassier with fewer than 300, any Frenchman with more than half an hour for his noon meal will first eat an hors d'oeuvre, not tidbits served with a cocktail, but a proper course that is literally "aside from the main work" (which is what *hors d'oeuvre* means), and that is always served at the table. It may be very plain or elaborate, hot but usually cold, and above all it will be tasty and light, to tease the palate and ready it for what is to follow. It may consist of a simple dish of cold sliced potatoes in a vinaigrette sauce and a tin of anchovies or sardines, or a slice of exquisite truffled goose pâté in jelly, but it will be eaten with the correct implements as the first course of the meal. Often in a middle-class family the nearest available child runs around the corner to the bakery or pastry shop to bring back a small hot cheese tart for every diner. But *something*, fresh and tantalizing, is served before the main course, which will usually be fish or meat or fowl, in even the plainest French homes.

An infinity of salad greens

Sometimes vegetables accompany this main course (the entrée in American usage), although never when it is any kind of stew or moist concoction that already contains vegetables. Often, a delicate soufflé of potatoes, or a bowl of fresh green peas or beans, or baked tomatoes, will be served *after* this course. If artichokes or asparagus has been served as the hors d'oeuvre, or some freshly mixed vegetables, there will be no vegetable course at all. Instead there will be, after the entrée, a plain salad of garden lettuces—what is almost always described in America as "tossed green."

Actually this is the only dish Frenchmen really recognize as a salad, culturally and technically, and the kinds of greens grown for it would have to be checked with the largest available seed catalogue, for they are apparently infinite, and grow in everything from window boxes and the steep cultivated banks of railroad tracks to hothouses and neat kitchen gardens, the year around. The bowl of fresh green leaves, lightly dressed at the last possible minute with the simplest mixture of seasoned vinegar and oil, is meant quite bluntly, as Rabelais said, "to scour the maw"—a refresher, a kind of tonic to the palate. It never comes before the main course. Occasionally, at home, it is served on the same plate as was the meat, to catch the last deli-

In her kitchen overlooking the Boulevard Montparnasse, Annie beats egg whites for her dessert, a *mousse au chocolat*. On the counter are other ingredients—including butter, sugar and Cognac. Her kitchen is small, cheerful and well arranged.

At dinner, Pierre Boulat refills his guests' glasses with a red Burgundy, to go with the lamb, roasted potatoes and a salad.

cate flavors, but usually it is put upon clean plates after the entrée, a crisp, cool antidote to the probable heartiness of whatever went before, and a refresher for what will follow.

Except on Sundays or other feast days, cooked desserts are seldom served at the noonday meal in provincial homes. Instead, either with or after one or two cheeses (whatever seemed to promise the most in the market or the dairy shop that morning), there will be whatever fruit is in season, in a bowl, or on a tray or platter. There will be just enough bread left beside one's plate to carry the good taste of Gruyère, or sugared Petit-Suisse, or creamy Bleu de Bresse—the same bread, or course, that has been on the table throughout the meal, crusty, unbuttered and unique in the Western world. And then will come the ripe cherries-plums-pears-apples in their seasonal turns, and the sudden basket of green almonds, and the tantalizing ripe gooseberries, the tart-sweet currants, the handful of wild raspberries, the tiny bananas from Tunisia perhaps, or the pungent dates and figs and the nuts of winter in their shells.

If this typical French meal is indeed celebrating anything, however, anything at all, then there probably will be a dessert at noon. In a simple home it will take the place of the fruit and possibly of the cheese, but never of the salad if a plain green one seems indicated after the entrée. It will be perhaps a baked caramel custard, or Grandmother's Apple Tart, or fresh *fraises des bois* with thick cream, or even a frozen *diplomate au kirsch* from the town's best pastry shop.

And then, as at every noon dinner, coffee will be served—then, and never before, I add firmly and insistently. Coffee mixed with any other flavors, such as meat or fish, is repellent even to think about, for a Frenchman. It is of course drunk (most often with hot milk) at breakfast with some kind of bread. In simple homes it sometimes is drunk from bowls, instead of soup, for supper. But at noon with a good entrée or an hors d'oeuvre? During a real *meal?* Horror!

Old kitchens made new

This basic pattern of the main fare in a French household is carried out in kitchens which to many foreigners seem inconveniently small, or too simple, until they have worked in them and have come to understand their complete functionalism. They are often in houses, even in the big towns, which were built centuries ago, and perforce their plumbing and wiring must be outside the thick stone walls, and their windows may be small, built before central heating was invented to keep out the cold winter air.

But in the decades since the last big European war, many changes have been made in the conveniences of daily life in France, and some of the best have taken place in the kitchen, where so much of life springs from. There are few houses today, in the remotest mountain villages of the Jura, in the most primitive *mas* of Provence, that do not have liquid or natural gas or electricity for cooking, and many have piped water (even though the old well may still give its purest for the table). Often, in very old kitchens, there will be streamlined white enamel stoves and even dishwashers, installed neatly under the broad, deep mantels of the ancient hearths. And it becomes rare indeed not to find some kind of mechanical icebox in any household, poor or well-to-do, referred to always as "the frigidaire," no matter what its make.

Most French kitchens, even the rather dark ones of the older houses, are attractive, partly because of what is universally called The Servant Problem. Young Frenchwomen I know who were raised when a maid-of-all-work was part of any average household now do most of their own cooking, and their innate sense for pleasing the eye helps them make the kitchen as nice as any other part of their homes. They do not start from the beginning, in new houses or new apartments, but they adapt the old ones to the better modern lighting, and to the well-designed cabinets that are available now to almost every pocket. They keep the ancient oak cupboard, too big to go through any modern door, and line it with bright wallpaper or gummed cloth. They put new curtains at the windows, to bring in the light.

(One kitchen I know in France looks out through a tall, deep window across Provençal wheat fields, to the piny hills of Chateaunoir, and another wider one opens onto the treetops and the excitement of the Boulevard Montparnasse in Paris. In the handsome attic where I once lived in Aix, two small windows, in curved alcoves, lit the kitchen dimly, with a northern light better for painting still lifes than for flipping omelets, but there was air always, and the sound of fountains came across the rosy tiled rooftops very early in the morning.)

Kitchens in France (I started to say *all* kitchens there, since I do not know it any other way) have a wooden-topped table in them, sometimes against one wall if space demands it, but most often in the middle of the room. There are benches or stools to fit under it, out of the paths of busy cooks. Sometimes the tabletops are beautiful, waxed dark wood, but more often they are scoured and scrubbed white, somewhat scarred from generations of chopping and cutting and carving, somewhat stained by spilled oils, fruit juices and the like. If they are covered, it is with a length of the gay and often beautiful new patterns of what used to be called oilcloth and is now a plastic-coated material, bought by the yard in any good small-town supply store. With the ancient hearth itself now converted to electricity or gas, this kitchen table may be the hub of a whole family; more and more as young Frenchwomen do their own cooking and share the family wage earning, and perforce simplify their lives, they encourage their husbands and children to eat there, at least at supper, in the room filled with warmth and good smells, where even a few years ago they would have felt it proper to use the more formal dining room for all the family meals.

The importance of eating out

And for a change from this comparatively intensive home life, there is the inimitable position held for centuries by the restaurants of France, whether they be the great establishments in Paris or the inns outside the hamlets of Alsace or Béarn. The public eating place, from a sidewalk barrow of oysters to a small dining room in the best available hotel, has always attracted Gallic lovers of gastronomical variety as long as it is worthy of attention, and there is no family so mean that it has not managed to celebrate in a restaurant some wedding or betrothal or christening, within the memory of even its youngest members.

In provincial towns, as in the *métropole,* there are the elegant quiet places, the stylish new noisy ones, the costly and the very plain. In much smaller towns and villages there is bound to be one good innkeeper, or at least one baker-caterer, to provide for his own price a good long trestle-table, green garlands for the walls, and a rousing and usually lengthy feast.

Not long ago I looked at the bill for a dinner given for some 40 near-relatives, in a village in the Aveyron not far from Roquefort, for a friend of mine who was being feted on his 100th birthday with a noon banquet at the city hall, which was also the grange-hall, the justice-hall and the jail. There was a long list of supplies and their prices, drawn up by the hired cook-baker: 10 large tins of *rillettes de Tours,* 80 fresh trout, 8 quarters of lamb, 40 loaves of bread, and so on. Then there was a bill listing the cost of several of the proposed ways of preparing the foodstuffs: roasting the meats at the cook's bakery, completing the hors d'oeuvre, preparing and sautéing the trout and arranging the salad bowls at the inn (run by the baker's wife but too cramped for such a festival), ordering cheeses and fancy ices from the nearest town. There was a sensibly staggering wine list, and another bill for the service, which was to be handled by a retired schoolteacher-cousin of my old friend, and several of her former pupils from the nearby farms. There was also a modest bill from a photographer, essential to such an important gathering.

Any day can be a feast day

Altogether it added up to a fine celebration, worth every hard-earned penny saved and gladly spent by proud relatives. I could not be there, but I hear that it lasted from noon, with a welcome from the mayor and the departmental chiefs, until the last toasts and re-toasts at dusk. And although there were few men 100 years old in France that day, I am fairly sure, many other worthy festivals were undoubtedly in progress in every province, for they are a part of life there, a part of each private history.

And so are the occasional Sunday Dinners Out, which when the weather is good may be eaten in a garden restaurant as far as 30 miles away, if there is a family car, or at a small, odorous bistro across the square in a little town. Religious obligations are out of the way, everyone is in his best clothes, and most probably the whole family, with visiting relatives serving as the excuse for this festivity, has stopped at a popular café to have some kind of apéritif, from raspberry syrup in milk for little Jeanne to a daring vermouth-gin for Mother.

Once at the restaurant, which may be noted for some specialty brought from another province by marriage or accident, or simply for its way of boiling a hen, the family makes itself serenely comfortable and tucks in. The meal will be long, generous and well laced with somewhat better wines than the ones drunk every day. Friends will exchange greetings, and perhaps an after-dinner brandy. The children will finally grow fidgety or sleepy. If the day is fine, a slow digestive amble for the babies and older folks comes next, and the young ones slope off to meet their friends and perhaps dance. It is Sunday, the best day of the week to restore one's strengths, gather one's forces—at home or, for a treat, "out."

A City Family's Respect for Country Tradition

Even for Parisians, the authentic France is still to be found in the countryside. There the days are calmer, the pleasures simpler, the food straightforward, colorful and full of flavors of the garden.

Parisians Pierre and Annie Boulat own an old stone farm cottage *(below)*, which they rebuilt and decorated themselves, about 40 miles south of the French capital. Annie's days in the country are often built around the meals she will serve her family. In the morning she goes with her children to buy vegetables at a neighboring farm. The rest of the day she spends preparing the food—carefully but without hurry, for the preparation is a joy in itself. The taste of country dishes derives as much from the freshness of the ingredients as from the preparation. In provincial cooking especially, the French technique is to let the ingredients speak for themselves.

On an excursion in the woods, Pierre offers his daughter Sandra a *girolle*, one of the many species of mushroom growing near their house. For many French families, mushroom hunting is one of the delights of country trips. And the subtle flavors are a mainstay of French cuisine, from the simplest dishes to the most elaborate.

Annie, Sandra and Antoinette leave the cottage early in the morning to buy fresh produce for dinner at the farm of their neighbor, M. Marchiset.

41

Two-year-old Antoinette Boulat samples the raspberries *(left)* while her mother picks string beans with the help of M. Marchiset. Before making her choices, Annie Boulat has discussed them with him to find out which will be the greenest or ripest vegetables of the day. As she works, she often pauses to show Antoinette (and Sandra) how to tell the best farm-fresh vegetables, fruits and herbs from merely adequate ones; these are lessons the girls will never forget. Good raspberries, for instance, should be firm, fat, very bright in color and dry on the outside.

In her country kitchen Annie Boulat adds the vegetables to some pickled pork for a *potée* to be cooked in an earthenware pot.

Pierre pours a trickle of wine into Sandra's water glass. He loves good wine and will teach his children to share his appreciation of it. On Sandra's plate is a portion of *potée;* the salad is made with quartered tomatoes, onions, lettuce, chervil, tarragon and chives, all gathered on Annie's morning excursion to M. Marchiset's thriving garden.

The Boulats sit down to a hearty outdoor family dinner at a table of sanded pearwood that Pierre built with his own hands.

III

A Way
of Their Own

The kitchens of provincial France, the more or less typical family meals cooked in them, the Sunday afternoons at home or out, all suggest an especially French set of feelings about cooking and eating. French ways with food and drink are not exactly the same as other people's ways, and some of the differences are worth learning about. At the least, they help explain what makes the French so French.

For example, as already noted, their main meal is at noon, when few American families are together. For another, there are more courses in this meal than some American or English women would encourage or even condone. The French change plates much oftener. They abhor mixing distinctly different flavors, and since they do like variety, with one dish enhancing another, of necessity the plates must be changed meticulously between them. Even in very simple households, neither silver nor plates used for fish, for instance, are used again for meat, vegetable, salad. (A disappearing part of most provincial table settings of even a few years ago is the little oblong bridge, made of anything from wood to sterling silver or crystal, that used to stand to the right of one's plate, to rest the used tips of the knife and fork upon between courses. In the days of traditional white tablecloths at noon, these gadgets were a godsend to housewives, especially those with many children.) Forks and spoons usually are placed face down.

French people want and expect, if they can manage it financially, one meal a day that will interest and amuse them past the acceptance of plain nutrition. They do not consider a one- or two-course meal to be a real *meal*. Once a day they want to sit down to a correctly served repast, and they

Four-year-old Jean-Baptiste Goethals, on a Sunday picnic *(page 47)*, bites into a snack with a snap to it: buttered bread topped with radishes. The open-faced radish sandwich is an acquired taste—best acquired at an early age.

believe, for reasons unfathomable and perhaps even ridiculous to many other cultures, that a good main dish should be preceded by that small something called an hors d'oeuvre. Even if a man is very poor he will still expect, for the noon meal his wife manages to scrape together for him, a nicely hard-boiled egg, perhaps to be shared with her, peeled and cut in two, and decorated with a dusting of fresh pepper and slices of cucumber. *Then* he will put down his goblet or tumbler, his knife and fork, and wait with pleasure for the important part of the meal, the hot dish savory with herbs no matter what they are rescuing, artfully contrived no matter how inexpensively. He would be offended, shocked, to come directly from his work to that delicious dish, or to sit down to a steak and baked potato after a couple of scotches and a bowl of salted cashew nuts.

Bread, well wrapped in ritual

Still another difference is that bread is always on the table in France, from the first course until dessert is served or the meal is over. The bread is never the squeezy-fresh soft slices many Americans accept or permit, but comes crusty and fragrantly fresh at least once a day from the nearest bakery, six days a week, and is sometimes lightly toasted if it must be eaten stale by more than a few hours. In most households it is sliced about an inch thick, quite often diagonally, and placed in an oblong shallow basket. Sometimes a long, thick loaf will be placed on the table and broken or sliced by the person at the head of the table. It is then broken with the fingers by each diner, into proper bite-sized pieces, as he eats it with the hors d'oeuvre, perhaps uses it discreetly to catch some of the sauce of the entrée, and then enjoys it as a foil for the cheese.

When rolls or individual loaves are served, they are put to the left of or above each place setting, or in a basket, since butter plates are not seen in ordinary French homes. (When butter is served, it is always as part of the hors d'oeuvre and is put upon one's plate, although many restaurants now serve it throughout the meal, until dessert, with the small plates and knives their touristic clientele seems to expect.) For supper at home, there is occasionally a loaf of dark bread, round, fat and solid, to be sliced right at the table, instead of the long and relatively thin white loaves that are served at the noon meal and eaten for breakfast with butter and jam, according to one's tastes.

There are really only three other times when Frenchmen eat butter with bread (or anything else at the table), as far as I know: when there are sharp new radishes, peppery slices of sausage, perhaps little shrimp in their shells; or when there is a very strong cheese like a crumbly Roquefort at the end of the meal before or with the fruit; or when there is an American guest at the table. Otherwise the unsalted delicious stuff (once at its best in the northern provinces and the Jura but now available everywhere, so that it is almost as fresh in a village without a milch cow to its name as it is in Normandy or Savoy) is considered part of the cooking, and thus is to be used only in the kitchen, where it belongs.

There are certain other rules of eating as well. Potatoes are considered a vegetable in France, not an automatic and often ignominious accompaniment to meat and fish, and the constant supply of bread acts as the main

   Continued on page 50

The Goethals and the Duponts settle down to savor the view of the river, and the feast in their baskets.

A Family Picnic
High above the Seine

As much as any people, the French love the open-air pleasures of a meal in the countryside—and nothing is quite so hearty as a French *pique-nique*.

For the outing shown on these pages, Philippe and Caille Goethals, an active suburban couple who often go on picnics, took along three of their children and two friends, Georges and Jeanne Dupont, to a hillside overlooking the Seine 50 miles from Paris. Caille brought a tomato-cheese pie baked from her mother's recipe, and lamb, kidneys and livers to barbecue over her husband's fire. She also brought bread, fruit and cheese, and plenty of cider and good local red wine. Jeanne Dupont contributed a spicy Provençal tuna salad, and Philippe topped off the meal with music played on his guitar.

Eight-year-old Jean-Nicholas Goethals, bearing three crusty loaves, watches his father build the fire.

Georges Dupont *(left)* and Philippe Goethals help keep the lines straight as their children try the fishing in a small tributary of the Seine.

The fishermen *(above)* had no luck; these trout, sizzling as Christophe Goethals blows on the fire, were brought as insurance by his mother.

Juicy lamb, well seasoned with salt, pepper and aromatic rosemary sprigs, is neatly skewered on a steel brochette, to be slowly cooked over the wood fire.

Jean-Baptiste Goethals digs into one of his favorite picnic dishes, a hearty plateful of Provençal tunafish salad served with bread and radishes on the side.

Smoldering birchwood adds aroma to the lamb brochettes, set on forked twigs and turned until brown. Lamb kidneys and liver are on the skewer at right.

The tomato-cheese pie, which has been rewarmed over the fire, is set down as the main meal begins. The recipe for this pie is given on the following page.

Tarte à la Tomate

TOMATO-CHEESE PIE

(See preceding page)

To make an 8- to-9-inch pie

1 *pâte brisée* pastry shell *(see recipe, page 67)*
1 pound Gruyère cheese, cut in thin slices
2 or 3 large tomatoes, cut in ½-inch slices
Salt
Freshly ground black pepper
1 teaspoon dried basil or 1 tablespoon finely cut fresh basil
2 tablespoons grated Parmesan cheese
2 tablespoons melted butter

Following the instructions on page 67, bake the pastry shell and let it cool. Sprinkle the tomato slices generously with salt, and place them on a cake rack to drain for about ½ hour.

Preheat the oven to 375°. Arrange the cheese slices, slightly overlapping, in the bottom of the pastry shell, and place the drained tomato slices side by side on top. Sprinkle with a few grindings of black pepper, the basil and the grated Parmesan cheese. Dribble the melted butter over the tomatoes and bake in the upper third of the oven for 25 minutes, or until the cheese has melted and the top of the pie is lightly browned. Serve hot or warm.

NOTE: An 8-inch-square baking dish may be used. If you wish to make a larger pie, double all ingredients and use an 11-inch-square baking dish or a 12-inch false-bottomed *quiche* or cake pan.

source of starch in most meals. Also, as has been said already, salads are always served after the entrée. Another fairly arbitrary rule is that soups are rarely served at the noon meal, unless some famous regional dish like a *bouillabaisse* is to be its feature, and so is considered the entrée or main course. Soup is mainly for supper, for both young and old, in provincial France: in fact, soup *is* supper. Country people simply eat a big bowl of it, often made with potatoes or bread, and go to bed. Townspeople eat heartily of it, with perhaps an omelet or light pudding or fruit compote to follow. The exception to this unwritten rule is at a great noon banquet—state, municipal, wedding—when some such soup as a double consommé with sherry, or turtle with Madeira, may appear on the tables between the fresh caviar and the *soles financière*.

Coffee later, not "with"

Coffee, as has been noted, never accompanies what is properly called a meal, but is served afterward, usually black and in a small cup. With sugar and hot milk it appears for breakfast, and sometimes for the very simple home suppers that may follow a big Sunday dinner. One reason for this firm shunning of coffee with food is that coffee does not ally itself with the wine that is a natural part of dining in France. Another is that Frenchmen drink it very strong; they would soon become poisoned if they tried to drink numberless cups of it during and between meals.

As for wines, they are thought of (or rather, they are not even thought of) as being as necessary to a meal as bread itself, or fish, or meat, as cool, white and dry for most hors d'oeuvre and for fish, as red and room-temperature for most meats and cheeses, and as slightly sweeter or sparkling for feast days with their traditional tarts and pastries and puddings.

Relatively few Frenchmen have their own cellars, in spite of romantic fiction: they buy from the nearest reputable wine merchant, conveniently around the corner if possible, and only as much as they can afford or can store at one time. Tradition-loving winemen, whether producers or consumers, lament the fact that modern living conditions make it increasingly difficult for most families to store wines correctly, and even to know what to store. But a good bottle or two can usually be produced for an occasion and given time to "rest," after which the rules first formally laid down in Bordeaux, one of the great wine centers of the world, are followed almost instinctively: dry white wines are always served before red wines, which in turn are always served before sweet, heavy white ones—those rare good ones called dessert wines. If two whites or two reds are to be served, the light and dry will always precede the heavier one, the less important one will come before the nobler, and almost always the younger one will come before the older, unless their vintage years have had some phenomenal upset.

At the noon and evening meals, every day except for celebrations, wine or cider is left in the bottle or pitcher in which it was fetched from the dealer, or decanted in the kitchen from liter-content bottles into serviceable carafes, one for red and one for white, or in some regions into locally made jugs and pitchers of glazed pottery, which are shaped exactly as they were centuries ago by the invading Greeks, Romans, Saracens, Celts. There is usually a carafe or pitcher of water, too. Water is judged as severely as any wine for its freshness and flavor, and if the locality is not blessed with its own good fountains or other sources, there will be, in even modest houses, a bottle of "bought" water on the table, still rather than sparkling, and most probably geared to the latest dietary demands of the family hypochondriac for its alkalinity, or nonalkalinity, and so on.

Ordinary table wine is often mixed with water for children or old people or an occasional eccentric who actually likes it. Water was believed to be made more antiseptic that way, and my first landlady in Dijon, a wonderfully stingy woman who was plainly uneasy about my obvious enjoyment of her daily allotment of barreled Algerian rejects, tried unsuccessfully to convince me that my appreciation as well as my chances of survival would be tripled by allowing the subtleties of any wine, not just her own mysterious blend, to be brought out by generous dilution.

Most middle-class Frenchmen prefer to think that only the workers—farmers, miners, day laborers—drink wine between meals. It is true that people who sit in offices all day seldom sit down again in a café, in their leisure time, to a little carafe or glass of white or red. Instead they will order a beer, or one of the innumerable syrups of fabricated liquids called apéritifs, which seem more characteristic of their country than of any other, even Italy. These are most often based on a fortified wine, with herbs and spices added to whet the appetite, and they are drunk plain or with water or, increasingly in the larger cities, with gin for an additional whip.

Mother's cocktail hour plot

These so-called tonics and teasers once belonged to the French cafés, and housewives seldom managed to join their husbands there to indulge in them. Lately, in the unending plot of all good Frenchwomen to keep men comfortable and at home, it has become noticeable to anyone who has middle-class friends that a few minutes are spent before either noon dinner or supper, usually in the formerly neglected parlor, while Father tries to forget his favorite café, Mother takes off her apron and looks approvingly at the fresh flowers on the piano, and the children from three to 18 relax around a tray of bottles and glasses never seen there before World War II. There may be a little bucket of ice from the refrigerator, American style. There is a siphon of soda water. There are two or three bottles, from *pastis* in the south to Scotch almost everywhere, and some sweetish, herby wine to be drunk straight, or watered down for the young ones if they do not prefer fruit juices. It is a plot, yes, but it seems to be a successful one, for it is spreading fast. Families like it: they see more of one another, they feel modern and up with the times, and it costs a lot less than two or three noon rounds in a café, or a couple of quick cokes in a student snack bar.

For a time it was considered stylish, even in small provincial towns, to serve cocktails, at least for special occasions, but now they are seldom seen except among internationals. The French, who take wine seriously as the essential partner of all good food, found that mixtures of strong alcohols and fruit juices and such, even in small quantities, did not contribute to their enjoyment, at least past the first moments of false exhilaration. Why, they asked in their eminently logical way, spend money and time on something that spoils the basic reason for spending money and time on a worthy meal?

After an early-morning trip to the inn's garden, Marcel returns with fresh sorrel leaves for cooking and flowers for a bouquet.

At a simple inn in Essarts-le-Roi, just off the highway between Paris and Chartres, Marcel, the gardener and handyman, waters the flowers above the door. For more than 40 years patrons have come to the Auberge des Essarts-le-Roi for strawberry tarts, *steak au poivre* and other specialties.

Many purists condemn the common and popular apéritifs with the same rationality, and will serve only a chilled dry white wine, still or sparkling, before dinner, but the average family enjoys a modest and more varied drink together, of fairly inexpensive concoctions when served sparingly, sometimes with a dry salty wafer or a few salted nuts, before a hearty noon meal and the simpler supper.

Giving old ways a new trial

We who do not live in France might try adapting the good things in French provincial eating to our own potentialities, and our own conditioned hungers. We too can meet together *en famille* for a pleasant, quiet drink before a meal, instead of putting the kids in the rumpus room with soft drinks and TV while we adults brace ourselves with a few vodka Gibsons in the den. We too can eat slowly and well and in good company if

we really want to, and French families seem to believe that it is worth it. And if we cannot do it at noon, thanks to greater distances between jobs, and shorter hours, and so on, there is suppertime—at least now and then!

We can find good salad greens and good bread, and good cheeses and meats and vegetables if we want to. We can try to reach the slower pace of older habits than our own new nervous ones, by serving a small, tasty course at the beginning of a meal, before the main dish, and then skipping the gelatin pudding or ice cream. Novelty will add to the first pleasure, and then plain enjoyment will strengthen the custom (and cut down on the calories) in almost any family. We can learn how to make a dainty fresh tart for a birthday surprise, and how to sniff out good cheeses now and then, and how to buy fresh fruit meant to be eaten on proper plates instead of merely forming a decoration on the dining room sideboard or an after-school snack in the kitchen.

We can relearn a lot of things our forefathers knew, which we have had

In the garden dining area of the *auberge,* Mlle. Renée Bracquemond serves two regular guests chicken stewed in wine. Throughout the provinces of France, a favorite inn and its treasured local recipes play an important role in the patrons' well-ordered, well-fed lives.

to shed in our flight toward other freedoms. Our ancestors might not have found what we have, if they stayed put in the homelands instead of heading elsewhere, but mostly they did remain strong and with their own private independence, because they clung passionately to the resources and traditions of their native provinces. If they were mountaineers and raised goats, they ate goat cheese. They survived. We can eat goat cheese, at least enough of it to compare it judiciously with packaged, pasteurized, predigested, vitaminized, presliced Kentucky Blue-de-Blue. Why not? And we can serve a meal slowly now and then, and substitute a new rhythm for the familiar eat-and-run technique. Why not, indeed? It is not a far-out nor an "in" idea: it is frankly a deliberate imitation of a very old way of life which has served people well for centuries.

Mountain people have always stayed lean: how else could they climb? Plains people have grown longer legged and plumper, the better to follow the plow. Americans must be every type of man, having no long local heritage of behavior, but there is great good, both esthetically and scientifically, in reviving in one's own life some of the table customs that have survived so many centuries in other, older lands.

The supermarket compromise

Today there are countless French homes where it is taken for granted that both father and mother must work, she at least half-time. Often she does not have a maid or neighbor who can market for her, and she must hurry on from her job, at night, to one of the many new supermarkets in France. Oldtimers correctly deplore these as ruinous to the small shops that have so long been intrinsic to family buying. (The same is sadly true in small-town America.) But they are a godsend to the new working parents, since in them everything essential to eating can be bought quickly and thus efficiently under one roof.

The novelty of the self-service, as they are called, has worn off, and in some small towns and neighborhoods where most housewives do not have outside jobs, they have already disappeared: women raised to the pattern of going to one place for good cheeses, to another for the best fresh eggs, to a third for a profitable chat with their butcher, are bored by the sterile efficiency of the new style. In general, though, the somewhat altered French version of the supermarket is plainly a fixture in present-day living, and young housewives blandly ignore their parents' scoldings about the possible lack of flavor and interest in foodstuffs that are distributed wholesale rather than bought laboriously in the open-air markets and myriad small shops. They know that they are making the best possible compromise between the old ways and the new, to be able after their offices close to stop at a convenient, clean, well-lighted store where everything is available to them for a good supper later with their husbands and their children.

Many French housewives, of every station in life, know some basic culinary rules: how to make a soup stock, bone a fish, fricassee or braise a chicken, make elementary sauces like "white" or "brown," roast a piece of meat, make a green salad, do two or three desserts like a custard and a tart, with the correct flourish. Add to this the fact that they have learned these rules more or less instinctively, as a requisite part of their roles as females, single or married, and that they can base all of this knowledge on recipes which are an intrinsic part of their heritage, and you have women who cook, whether or not they really want to, as naturally as they breathe. Fortunately, many do want to, for they are exposed throughout their lives to other people, and especially to males of every age and position, who believe that pleasurable meals are essential to their well-being and dignity.

Frenchwomen go one step further than their mothers ever did, and use concentrated broths and soups, packaged products, canned vegetables, but always with their trained sense of adding and subtracting to achieve the best results. They invent and perfect shortcuts, and have at hand a few good tricks for preparing impressive last-minute dishes "out of the blue" for unexpected guests. They do all these new things partly because they must hold down their jobs, but first and foremost because they must act as good French wives have acted for centuries, in the interest of pleasing their husbands and their families.

In this new way of living, the traditional leisurely noon meetings of parents and children over a good solid meal have had to be shifted this way and that. In such cases, and I know many of them, it is considered as important as health itself that time be spent together in the evening, and that Sunday and if possible the whole weekend be saved for family walks, for special meals which every member of the family knows about and in some way helps to produce, for family picnics, for family visits to other houses. The word "family" is very elastic, of course, and sometimes it may mean two persons instead of 10, but it is rare that a Frenchman will leave his wife alone on Sunday and go to a football game or a café while she watches television. Even if they are mutually bored, they will walk together, go to a concert or movie, sit on a café terrace—and usually after a good meal, which she has prepared especially to please him.

A cuisine with survival value

French girls and housewives take the pre-eminence of the kitchen much more easily and naturally than many of the busy young Anglo-Saxons who are their social and economic counterparts. We Americans are the children of wanderers, of refugees from one kind or another of personal or political or national trouble. More often than not, we do not live where our mothers and fathers were born. We may not even know what our grandparents' homes looked like, much less how they ate, at what table, under what ticking clock. It is of little or no importance to us to bake a certain kind of cookie on a certain day for our children simply because 903 years ago a saint came through our mountain valley and made some like them, to feed, miraculously, a great band of pilgrims. What saint? What valley? We simply do not have the *reasons* for many of the foods that go into everyday regional cooking all through France, any more than we have the inborn habits that go into their continuance.

But we can look, and ponder. We can, above all, be reassured by the basic simplicity of what has survived so many centuries of peace, and war, and invasion, in such a diverse land as France. Its provincial cooking, from which probably the greatest haute cuisine in the world developed, has survived all this, and is ours for the trying, to reassure us.

IV

Hors d'Oeuvre: Overture to the Meal

The first course is as essential to the noon meal in French provincial homes as is the light to eat it by. This course is designed to refresh and amuse the eye, to titillate the palate, and to prepare the gastric juices for the more solid food to follow.

It is the overture to the opera. As such, its variety is infinite, dictated, of course, by the seasons as well as the regions where the food is eaten—in the mountains, by rivers or at the seashore.

An hors d'oeuvre is always correlated to the entrée in home cooking and, of course, should be equally tidily planned when ordered in restaurants. Just as Madame Durosier would not serve stuffed eggs before an omelet, so neither she nor anyone else in his right mind would compose a Sunday dinner to begin with an egg-based *pipérade* and end with an egg-based *soufflé au rhum*.

On the same subject of intrinsic balances, anything as forceful as an *anchoyade* with its tongue-clinging taste of anchovies would probably not be served before a delicate *blanquette de veau*, nor would the rather filling *quiche* be offered before a hearty *boeuf bourguignon*.

Probably the actual presentation of honest hors d'oeuvre, whether in a home or in a restaurant, is more like classical Japanese food design than any other part of Western gastronomy. The dish must be as artful in its colors and patterns as in its textures and flavors. When the hors d'oeuvre consists of a variety of tidbits, it is commonly and rightly said to demand something fresh and crisp (vegetables), something salty (sardines or anchovies or herrings), a dry and meaty taste (like ham or sausages) complemented by a

This fat balloon whisk flashing in a copper bowl is beating egg whites for the soufflé described on pages 64-65. Of all the techniques used round the world for beating eggs, French cooks prefer this one for the airiest and fastest results.

flavor bland and smooth (a mayonnaise, for instance, masking some fresh fish, or eggs). When a single dish is served, either hot or cold, it is just as carefully presented as an esthetic offering; to woo the eye as well as the taste buds.

The hors d'oeuvre is such a natural part of French eating habits that it has no social levels. Affluent diners, or people celebrating a wedding, a birthday, or anything at all, may eat sumptuous, heady pâtés, or expensive lobsters, or omelets bulging with black truffles. On the other hand, in the poorest family I myself ever knew in France, the street sweeper's wife would prepare for each noontime a precisely arranged first course; perhaps one tomato from the market, thinly sliced, with half an olive on each slice, hints of salt and olive oil and a sprinkling of finely chopped parsley. In winter there might be three or four anchovy fillets from the smallest-sized tin, laid in neat strips over a slice of bread cut from the single loaf that was the couple's daily ration. This course was served as correctly as it would have been in a good restaurant, as if the street sweeper and his wife were not eating it in the one room, with its bed, an open hearth to cook on, and a table with two chairs, that served for their whole existence. And the food was eaten calmly, as all hors d'oeuvre are meant to be, with pleasure and anticipation for what might follow. On good days the main course might be half a chicken; on thinner ones, perhaps a small sausage and one potato to divide equally.

Often in good provincial restaurants an alluring array of local specialties is presented for this opening course: seasonal vegetables like tiny radishes in the spring, or thumb-sized artichokes, or beans to eat raw and crisp with salt; olives and mushrooms stewed to the cook's taste or whim in herbs and oil; thin slices of the region's sausages and hams, and a pâté or two or three—all very appetite-arousing.

The art of tasting teasers

If these little teasers are honest and fresh (this morning's tomatoes), or correctly ancient according to their rules of preparation (such as a pâté meant to age six months in its crust), they are almost irresistible. Learning what and how much to eat of them is an art hard to practice, for they can easily defeat their real purpose and ruin what comes next: the main course, the *raison d'être* of the meal.

Sometimes this danger is courted deliberately, as every hungry traveler knows, to disguise the poor quality or stinginess of the entrée, and, indeed, of the establishment itself. Often the hors d'oeuvre are tired or mediocre, but if their appearance is kept appetizing enough, and the diners are hungry and thirsty enough, the innkeeper will succeed in his unscrupulous trick of masking a dishonest kitchen.

In the home, of course, the diner faces no such danger. Often when a housewife plans to serve a light entrée, for reasons economic, religious or simply commonsensical, there will be several kinds of "appetizer" on platters or in bowls before it appears: something fresh and crisp from the garden or the morning's marketing, sardines, stuffed eggs (unless an omelet comes next), a bowl of the new crop of black olives warmed a little in oil and herbs, two or three kinds of sausage, thinly sliced. Or freshly opened shellfish, still alive in their shells, served with lemon and brown bread; mussels in a marinade; a pile of little shrimp or prawns with lemon juice and perhaps some sweet butter for the bread. Sea creatures have always been a welcome introduction to a good meal, served in their own seasons and in almost every region of a country whose borders, like France's, abut water more often than land.

A first course on the run

As soon as cool weather comes, inland, as in every seaport town or village, shellfish stands are set up on the sidewalks, usually outside eating places of high and low position, financially if not gastronomically. Housewives hurry to the stands at the last possible minute before dinner to have three dozen oysters opened and put onto the platters they carry. Little apprentices run to and from the nearby cafés and restaurants with plates designed to hold one or two orders of everything from fresh clams to prickly sea urchins, alone or mixed into what is imaginatively called a *bouquet de mer*—flowers of the sea! And all kinds of people, from schoolboys to bankers, stand unabashedly in the gutter, sucking and gulping a quick snack innocent of any trimming except the half shell the mollusk is still living in, or a dash of vinegar from the common shaker, or juice squeezed from a wedge of fresh lemon.

In one southern seaport I know well there is a whole marketplace with nothing much but shellfish in it, displayed at dozens of stands which spill out onto the streets running down to the Old Port, where the fishermen's wives sell the morning catch from the bows or sterns of the family boats. Thanks to such modern developments as inexpensive ice and enforced sanitation laws—as well, perhaps, as to the fact that most Mediterranean sea creatures are used to warm weather, even when living in the water— the stands in Marseilles seem to operate all year round. Many times I have eaten a half dozen of this or that mysterious shellfish, lying on its thick couch of fresh seaweed and chopped ice, from the open-air counters that stand like tiny oases in the hot, bright July sun.

An hors d'oeuvre, depending upon the season as well as upon what will follow it, often consists of one "made" dish, either hot or cold depending upon whether a hot or cold entrée is to be served. For instance, a light but satisfying *quiche* or tart (of onions, fish, cheese, or, as in Lorraine, of cream and bacon), hot from the oven, could precede an entrée of cold roasted game or poultry, with the traditional green salad to follow, and then, of course, some cheeses and fruits, or a dessert, depending upon the importance of the meal.

Many such made dishes are equally as good for the main dish of a light lunch or supper as they are for a tempting tidbit in the first course of a larger meal. In the same way, some of them can be served cold. A freshly made onion tart, for instance, is fine to take on a picnic, as in the Provençal version of a pizza, the *pissaladière!* There are two common denominators to most of the made dishes: almost all of them can be put into individual dishes or crusts, and many of them are based on eggs, baked in a soufflé, scrambled or poached, and then combined ad infinitum according to custom, the weather and the preferences of the cook.

Mastering the art of making a good soufflé is only a matter of learning a few essential techniques *(page 64)*. Another easily accomplished and useful dish is the *crêpe*. Generally thought of in America as a rather grand dessert dish, it actually relies on a basic recipe that can instead lend itself to dozens of variations *(page 70)* as the opening dish of a meal.

Often vegetables such as eggplant, celery, endives, tomatoes and small squash (*courgettes* in France, marrows in England, zucchini in Italy and the United States) are served either hot or cold in numberless ways, depending on the next courses. One nice thing about this appetizing trick is that such a dish can be made to serve three or four different functions: hot or cold as the hors d'oeuvre, hot as the main supper dish after the prerequisite soup, and hot or cold as the main dish at noon if one lunches in the American and English style instead of serving the heavier midday meal customary in provincial France.

Zucchini or little eggplants or round squashes can be stuffed, and so (to the surprise of some Americans) can cucumbers. The way tomatoes are fixed for the oven in Provence—stuffed with crusty white bread crumbs, garlic and herbs to add zest to the blandness of the vegetable-container—makes the basic and delicious rule for all the rest of the vegetables which by nature and trickery can be shaped to hold a little stuffing. All of them are good as a first course, good as an accompaniment to many entrées, good as a vegetable course served separately after the main dish, good for supper with a light pudding or compote to follow; good hot, perhaps even better cold.

Almost any vegetable can be made *à la grecque* (cooked in a marinade and served cold), as long as it will hold its shape and retain its own characteristics of flavor and color. Many vegetables, especially when at their prime, are served raw in the French provinces, either to be dipped into a strong mayonnaise or tossed in an equally forceful variation of vinaigrette.

The basic dressings and what they dress

Three of the great dressings, mayonnaise, hollandaise and vinaigrette, are basic to preparing many hors d'oeuvre. The first is a smooth emulsion of egg yolks in either olive or vegetable oil, to which either vinegar or lemon juice is added. The second, a richer cousin of mayonnaise, is also egg-based, but served warm and with pure butter incorporated into the egg yolks to make a thick, yellow, creamy sauce. The third dressing, vinaigrette, is made with oil and vinegar (without eggs) and remains thin and clear, but pungent with herbs.

These three basic sauces can be varied endlessly, and are. When vegetables are prepared *à la grecque*, the boiled marinade in which everything is lightly cooked is obviously a kind of vinaigrette, just as the béarnaise sauce that can be served with the steak dish in Chapter 9 is recognizable as a kind of tangy hollandaise.

One of the most elegant of the offspring is *sauce aux fines herbes*, a mayonnaise colored by fresh green herbs, to serve with cold poached bass, or salmon or any other fish with rather dry flesh. It is as useful (and colorfully impressive) with many hors d'oeuvre as it is with cold fish, from delicate pink shrimps to plain hard-boiled eggs cut in half.

A delicious variation on the mayonnaise theme is something I used to

To make a pint of your own fresh mayonnaise, start with three egg yolks at room temperature, a warmed mixing bowl and a whisk or other beater. Carefully whip in lemon juice or wine vinegar, mustard, salt, pepper, oil and boiling water, following the recipe on page 74.

wait for in springtime in the house of a good friend in France, when the asparagus was ready to eat, tepid and drained, at the beginning of a long noon meal. It was called, there anyway, *sauce à la neige,* and it was half mayonnaise and half stiffly whipped cream, mixed lightly together. I think the mayonnaise had a little mustard in it, for I remember the dressing as being vigorous enough to offset its own suavity.

The versatility of vinaigrette

Vinaigrette sauce is perhaps even more versatile than mayonnaise, and can taste like whatever its maker wants to put in it, to bring out the values of what it is then supposed to enhance. A good cook, though, will hold Escoffier's classic keep-it-simple command forever in his mind, and not err on the side of overcomplicating—that is, overseasoning with a mishmash of herbs and bottled sauces.

A plain vinaigrette is the only acceptable dressing to Frenchmen on the clean, crisp leaves of garden salads they eat after the entrée of most good meals. For hors d'oeuvre, the vinaigrette can be made oilier or more tart, according to its purposes. Very thinly sliced mushrooms, for instance, can be tossed before serving in a relatively thick vinaigrette, to coat them well; almost raw green beans, the tiny kind that are almost impossible to find in most American vegetable markets, can be coated with a mustardy vinaigrette with plenty of good wine vinegar in it, since they are still sweet to the taste.

Often a saladlike dish constitutes the first course of a French meal, but it

61

is never the plain mixture of garden greens called a *salade simple* or *verte* which will, at least half the time, follow the entrée. It is, instead, an artful but not too rich concoction—of fresh fish, for instance, from plain poached halibut to lobster, bound with a mayonnaise or a vinaigrette or cream dressing, depending upon the decision of the cook. It may be a hearty mixture of meat or fowl or sausages, bound likewise according to their flavors and textures, and often with cooked potatoes or rice, or a decorative but basically crude *salade Niçoise*. But, hearty or not, this *salade composée* will be served and eaten judiciously, with the basic aim of exciting rather than numbing the appetite.

One of the most popular hors d'oeuvre in its native land and in America is pâté, an artful combination of seasoned meats. A country-style *terrine* (the term means both the earthen baking dish and the food cooked in it) is much coarser in texture than the smoother, richer restaurant version more familiar to Americans.

More often than not in provincial kitchens, several pâtés are made at once, after an especially successful hunting of wild hare or venison, or an unusually rich booty of truffles or thrushes. Some are sent to relatives, some are sold, perhaps to the local butcher, and, depending on the available cool storage space, as many as possible are kept for future enjoyment. Often a pâté, in or out of its original baking dish, is served alone as a first course, especially if it is a very important one, perhaps made last Easter by Aunt Louise or sent from Strasbourg for Christmas.

Country pâtés are strong with the herbs native to the regions in which they are made, and with the alcohols as well: marc in Burgundy, Calvados in the north, Armagnac south of Bordeaux. They are less suave in every way, and much less rich than pâtés served in upper-class restaurants or reserved for special occasions. In *terrines,* more often than not, the taste of a favorite local product will predominate: goose or duck in the Périgord, or pork or ham in Touraine.

The terrine: key to the cuisine

Serious French eaters—which means serious Frenchmen—often gauge the standards of almost any kitchen, whether great or modest, by its *terrine* (or pâté) *maison,* the special product of the house or restaurant. Pâtés are interesting to make, and very rewarding to serve. They need never be what a few of us have termed them after ordering them in inferior restaurants—"nothing but glorified meat loaf!"

Needless to say, bread and wine are on the table for this first course, and the bread is almost always the long, crisp loaf from the nearest bakery. The exception is when oysters are being served. In that case most cooks provide thin slices, buttered or not, of very dark, moist bread. But, when something like an *anchoyade* is being served, there is no need for anything but the crusty bread on which the deliciously loud but subtly seasoned anchovy mixture has been spread and grilled.

As for the wine, it is there, as inevitably as is the air to breathe. The only exception would be if the dish that is to follow the hors d'oeuvre demands a good beer instead. In this case the same beer or a lighter one should come first. The same is true if cider is to be served.

Any wine which accompanies the first course should be lighter and probably younger and less "important" than what will follow with the entrée. In a simple meal, one wine is usually served straight through.

A good cue to what wines will be best to drink with the first (or any) course of the meal is to try to find out what region or province the dish or dishes come from. The wines that are grown in that same place will undoubtedly be the ones which centuries have proved just right for the food flavors involved. With a *quiche lorraine* it would seem entirely natural to drink a cool, light white wine or perhaps a light beer from Alsace, and with a hot, strong, salty *anchoyade*, a thin, sharp white or rosé or red from Provence would be a good and natural foil.

Flattering the taste buds

In any locality, whether in a home or small restaurant, the wines served with the hors d'oeuvre are usually cellar-cool or chilled. And for appetite's sake they are best preceded by more of the same, rather than by strong apéritifs or cocktails. Most of the whites and rosés are too piquant and dainty to try to arouse taste buds that have been deadened by alcohol, and no good red wine will even bother to.

Ideally, the taste buds should come through this part of the meal—the hors d'oeuvre with or without wine—feeling flattered but not content, impressed but still excited about the food that is yet to appear.

Puffed up high above its mold in a golden crown, the perfect soufflé comes out of the oven crisp on the outside and creamy in the center. It must be served at once, for it falls as it begins to cool. Each serving should include some of the crust as well as a generous scoop from the center.

To serve 4

1 tablespoon soft butter
1 tablespoon grated, imported Swiss
  cheese
3 tablespoons butter
3 tablespoons flour
1 cup hot milk
½ teaspoon salt
Pinch of white pepper
4 egg yolks
6 egg whites
1 cup grated, imported Swiss cheese
  or ½ cup each Swiss and freshly
  grated Parmesan cheese

If you use a shallow mold or straight-
sided casserole instead of a soufflé
dish, tie a well-buttered paper collar
around it to hold the soufflé as it rises.

Soufflé au Fromage
CHEESE SOUFFLÉ

Preheat the oven to 400°. Grease the bottom and sides of a 2-quart French soufflé dish or charlotte mold with 1 tablespoon of soft butter, then sprinkle in 1 tablespoon of grated imported Swiss cheese, tipping the dish to spread the cheese evenly on the bottom and all sides. Set the dish aside.

In a 2- to 3-quart saucepan, melt 3 tablespoons butter over moderate heat. When the foam subsides, stir in the 3 tablespoons of flour with a wooden spoon and cook over low heat, stirring constantly for 1 or 2 minutes. Do not let the *roux* (the butter and flour mixture) brown. Remove the saucepan from the heat and pour in the hot milk, beating vigorously with a whisk until the *roux* and liquid are blended. Add the salt and pepper and return to low heat and cook, whisking constantly, until the sauce comes to a boil and is smooth and thick. Let it simmer a moment, then remove the pan from the heat and beat in the egg yolks, one at a time, whisking until each one is thoroughly blended before adding the next. Set the sauce aside.

With a large balloon whisk, beat the egg whites until they are so stiff that they form small points which stand straight up without wavering. (A rotary or electric beater may be used instead, but the whites will not mount as voluminously.) Stir a big spoonful of beaten egg white into the sauce to lighten it; then stir in all but 1 tablespoon of the remaining grated cheese. With a spatula, lightly fold in the rest of the egg whites, using an over-under cutting motion rather than a stirring motion.

Gently pour the soufflé mixture into the prepared dish; the dish should be about three quarters full. Lightly smooth the surface with a rubber spatula and sprinkle the remaining tablespoonful of cheese on top. For a decorative effect make a "cap" on the soufflé with a spatula by cutting a trench about 1 inch deep and 1 inch from the rim all around the dish. Place the soufflé on the middle shelf of the oven and immediately turn the heat down to 375°. Bake for 25 to 30 minutes, or until the soufflé puffs up about 2 inches above the rim of the dish and the top is lightly browned. Serve at once.

SOUFFLÉ AU FROMAGE ET AUX OEUFS MOLLETS (cheese soufflé with boiled eggs): Bring 2 quarts of water to a boil in a heavy 3- to 4-quart saucepan. Gently lower 4 eggs into the water and boil them slowly for 6 minutes (boil them for 7 minutes if they have been refrigerated). Drain immediately and run cold water into the pan. Tap the eggs gently on a hard surface to break their shells, and peel them under a stream of cold water. Preheat the oven to 400°. Prepare the soufflé mixture, following the directions in the recipe above. Scoop about half of it into a buttered and cheese-lined 2-quart French soufflé dish or charlotte mold. Arrange the eggs in a circle on top and cover each with a mound of the remaining soufflé mixture. Dot each mound with a teaspoon of grated cheese and place the soufflé on the middle shelf of the oven. Immediately turn the heat down to 375° and bake for 25 to 30 minutes. When you serve the soufflé, include an egg in each portion.

A tablespoon of grated cheese sprinkled all around the inside of the buttered mold will give the soufflé a delicate cheese-flavored crust.

The secret of a high-rising soufflé is simple: beat the egg whites until they are stiff enough to cling to the beater in firm, unwavering peaks. For best results the egg whites should be at room temperature.

Gently folding, not stirring, the egg whites into the soufflé with a rubber spatula will maintain their volume and ensure a light and airy dish.

After rolling out the *quiche* pastry, lift it gently and roll it onto the pin.

Unroll the pastry over a *quiche* pan and press down along the sides.

Finally, roll hard over the pan rim and trim off the excess pastry.

The *quiche*, with its shell removed from the baking pan, comes to the table a flaky, fragrant round of pastry filled with golden custard.

Quiche au Fromage
OPEN-FACED CHEESE TART

PÂTE BRISÉE: In a large, chilled mixing bowl, combine butter, vegetable shortening, flour and salt. Working quickly, use your fingertips to rub the flour and fat together until they blend and look like flakes of coarse meal. Pour 3 tablespoons of ice water over the mixture all at once, toss together lightly and gather the dough into a ball. If the dough seems crumbly, add up to 2 tablespoons more ice water by drops. Dust the pastry with a little flour and wrap it in wax paper or a plastic bag. Refrigerate it for at least 3 hours or until it is firm.

Remove the pastry from the refrigerator 5 minutes before rolling it. If it seems resistant and hard, tap it all over with a rolling pin. Place the ball on a floured board or table and, with the heel of one hand, press it into a flat circle about 1 inch thick. Dust a little flour over and under it and roll it out—from the center to within an inch of the far edge. Lift the dough and turn it clockwise, about the space of two hours on a clock; roll again from the center to the far edge. Repeat—lifting, turning, rolling—until the circle is about ⅛ inch thick and 11 or 12 inches across. If the pastry sticks to the board or table, lift it gently with a metal spatula and sprinkle a little flour under it.

Butter the bottom and sides of an 8- to 9-inch false-bottomed *quiche* or cake pan no more than 1¼ inches deep. Roll the pastry over the pin and unroll it over the pan, or drape the pastry over the rolling pin, lift it up and unfold it over the pan. Gently press the pastry into the bottom and around the sides of the pan, being careful not to stretch it. Roll the pin over the rim of the pan, pressing down hard to trim off the excess pastry. With a fork, prick the bottom of the pastry all over, trying not to pierce all the way through. Chill for 1 hour.

Preheat the oven to 400°. To keep the bottom of the pastry from puffing up, spread a sheet of buttered aluminum foil across the pan and press it gently into the edges to support the sides of the pastry as it bakes. Bake on the middle shelf of the oven for 10 minutes, then remove the foil. Prick the pastry again, then return it to the oven for 3 minutes or until it starts to shrink from the sides of the pan and begins to brown. Remove it from the oven and set it on a wire cake rack to cool.

CHEESE-CUSTARD FILLING: Preheat the oven to 375°. In a heavy 8- to 10-inch skillet, melt the butter over moderate heat. When the foam subsides, cook the bacon until it is lightly browned and crisp. Remove from the skillet with a slotted spoon and drain on paper towels. With a wire whisk, rotary or electric beater, beat the eggs, extra egg yolks, cream and seasonings together in a large mixing bowl. Stir in the grated cheese. Place the cooled pastry shell on a baking sheet. Scatter the bacon over the bottom of the shell and gently ladle the egg-cheese custard into it, being sure the custard does not come within ⅛ inch of the rim of the shell. Sprinkle the top with dots of butter and bake in the upper third of the oven for 25 minutes or until the custard has puffed and browned and a knife inserted in the center comes out clean. To remove the *quiche* from the pan, set the pan on a large jar or coffee can and slip down the outside rim. Run a long metal spatula under the *quiche* to make sure it isn't stuck to the bottom of the pan, then slide the *quiche* onto a heated platter. Serve hot or warm.

To make an 8- to 9-inch *quiche*

PÂTE BRISÉE (pastry dough or pie crust)
6 tablespoons chilled butter, cut in ¼-inch bits
2 tablespoons chilled vegetable shortening
1½ cups all-purpose flour
¼ teaspoon salt
3 to 5 tablespoons ice water

After the *quiche* is baked, the false-bottomed pan rim is slipped off when the pan is set on a jar or can.

CHEESE-CUSTARD FILLING
1 teaspoon butter
6 slices lean bacon, cut in ¼-inch pieces
2 eggs plus 2 extra egg yolks
1½ cups heavy cream
½ teaspoon salt
Pinch of white pepper
¾ cup grated imported Swiss cheese or Swiss and freshly grated Parmesan cheese combined
2 tablespoons butter, cut in tiny pieces

To serve 4 to 6

1½- to 2-pound uncooked plain or
garlic pork sausage, about 12
inches long and 2 inches in
diameter, fresh or smoked (French,
Italian or Polish)
Water
Pâte brisée (page 67)
1 egg beaten with 1 teaspoon water
Dijon-style prepared mustard

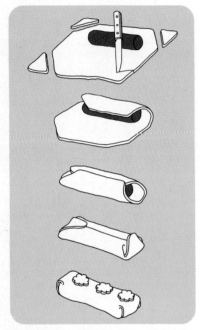

To wrap a sausage in crust, cut the
dough to the shape shown at top, lift
it over the sausage and tuck up the
ends. Then turn it over and decorate
it with pastry shapes.

To serve 1 to 2

3 eggs
Salt
Freshly ground black pepper
1 tablespoon butter
½ teaspoon soft butter

Saucisson en Croûte
SAUSAGE BAKED IN PASTRY CRUST

With the point of a sharp knife, prick the sausage in 5 or 6 places to prevent the skin from bursting, and to release its fat when it cooks. Lay the
sausage flat in a large, deep skillet and add enough cold water to cover it
completely. Bring to a boil over moderate heat and simmer uncovered for
45 minutes. Transfer the sausage to paper towels to drain and cool. Then
split the skin with a sharp knife and peel it off.

Preheat the oven to 375°. Roll the *pâte brisée* out ⅛ inch thick in a
rectangular shape large enough to wrap around the sausage (about 8 inches
long and 15 inches wide). Center the cooled sausage on the rectangle. Cut
triangles of pastry from each corner of the roll and gently, without stretch-
ing the dough, lift the long sides of the pastry up over the sausage. The
pastry should overlap by about an inch on top; trim off anything more than
that with a knife. Brush the lower edge of the pastry with the egg-water
mixture and press the upper edge down upon it firmly to secure it.

Brush the envelopelike flaps at the ends of the roll with a little egg mixture, then lift the flaps up over the ends of the sausage and tuck the edges
in neatly to seal them. Turn the wrapped sausage over and place it seam-side
down on a buttered baking sheet. Cut the pastry scraps into decorative
shapes such as half moons, diamonds or leaves and arrange these on top
of the roll, sealing them in place with the egg-water mixture. With a pastry
brush, coat the whole roll with the rest of the egg mixture. Bake the roll
on the middle shelf of the oven for 45 to 60 minutes or until it is golden
brown. Transfer the roll to a large platter and serve it cut into ¾-inch slices.
Pass the mustard separately.

Omelette
FRENCH OMELET

Break the eggs into a small mixing bowl, season with salt and pepper, and
stir briskly with a table fork 20 to 30 seconds or until the whites and yolks
are blended together. Heat an ungreased 7- to 8-inch omelet pan until it is
very hot, drop in the tablespoon of butter and swirl it in the pan so that it
melts quickly and coats the bottom and sides. When the foam begins to
subside but before the butter browns, pour in the eggs.

Working quickly, stir the eggs with the flat of the fork, at the same time
shaking the pan back and forth vigorously to prevent the eggs from stick-
ing. In a few seconds, the eggs will form a film on the bottom of the pan
and the top will thicken to a light, curded custard. Still shaking the pan
with one hand, gently stir through the top custard with the other hand to
spread the still-liquid eggs into the firmer areas; try not to pierce the bottom film. Then lift the edge closest to you with the fork and roll the omelet
up lightly over to the far side of the pan. Let it rest for a moment on the lip
of the pan, then tilt the pan and roll the omelet out onto a heated plate.
Brush the top with soft butter and serve at once.

NOTE: To make a filled omelet, sprinkle a few tablespoons of grated
cheese, finely chopped herbs or sautéed mushrooms over the eggs before
rolling the omelet up. Do not stir in the filling. To serve more than 1 or 2,
make several individual omelets. Large omelets are rarely successful.

Use the flat of a fork to spread the eggs and make a curded custard.

Use the side of the fork to gather and roll the omelet together.

When the omelet is loosened and lightly rolled to the side of the pan, lift the pan with one hand and a heated plate with the other. Gently tilt the pan up and turn the finished omelet over onto the plate. Brush the top of the omelet with butter and serve while it is piping hot and still just a bit soft inside.

To make 16 stuffed *crêpes*

CRÊPES

1¼ cups all-purpose flour

3 eggs

1 cup milk

¼ cup water

½ teaspoon salt

3 tablespoons butter, melted and cooled

3 tablespoons melted butter combined with 1 tablespoon vegetable oil

DUXELLES

¾ pound fresh mushrooms, finely chopped (about 3 cups)

4 tablespoons butter

4 tablespoons finely chopped shallots or scallions

1 teaspoon finely chopped fresh parsley

1 teaspoon finely cut fresh chives

Salt

Freshly ground black pepper

VELOUTÉ SAUCE

6 tablespoons butter

½ cup all-purpose flour

2½ cups hot chicken stock, fresh or canned

2 egg yolks

1 to 1½ cups heavy cream

1 teaspoon salt

¼ teaspoon white pepper

1 teaspoon lemon juice

THE FILLING AND TOPPING

1 cup sautéed and diced chicken livers (about ½ pound), or 1 cup cooked and diced shrimp (about 1 pound raw shrimp in the shell), or ¼ cup finely chopped defrosted frozen artichoke hearts sautéed in 2 tablespoons butter with ¼ cup diced smoked or boiled ham

1 teaspoon finely chopped fresh parsley or tarragon

Lemon juice

Salt

White pepper

1 cup grated, imported Swiss cheese or Swiss and Parmesan combined

4 tablespoons butter, cut in tiny pieces

Crêpes Fourrées Gratinées
FILLED FRENCH PANCAKES

THE CRÊPES: To make the batter in a blender combine flour, eggs, milk, water, salt and 3 tablespoons melted butter in the blender jar and blend them at high speed for a few seconds. Turn the machine off, scrape down the sides of the jar and blend again for 40 seconds. To make the batter by hand, stir the flour and eggs together in a mixing bowl and gradually stir in the milk, water and salt. Beat with a whisk or rotary or electric beater until the flour lumps disappear, then force through a fine sieve into another bowl and stir in 3 tablespoons of melted butter. The batter should be the consistency of heavy cream; dilute it if necessary by beating in cold water a teaspoon at a time. In either case, refrigerate the batter in the blender jar or bowl for an hour or two before using it.

Now heat a 6-inch *crêpe* pan or skillet over high heat until a drop of water flicked into it evaporates instantly. With a pastry brush, lightly grease the bottom and sides of the pan with a little of the melted butter and oil combination. With a small ladle pour about 2 tablespoons of batter into the pan and tip the pan so that the batter quickly covers the bottom; the batter should cling to the pan and begin to firm up almost immediately. At once tilt the pan over the bowl and pour off any excess batter; the finished *crêpe* should be paper thin. Cook the *crêpe* for a minute or so until a rim of brown shows around the edge. Turn it over with a spatula and cook the other side for a minute longer. Slide the *crêpe* onto a plate. Brush butter and oil on the skillet again and proceed with the rest of the *crêpes*. The *crêpes* should be no more than 1/16 inch thick. Dilute the batter by beating in drops of water if necessary. *Crêpes* may be made hours or even days ahead of time and kept, tightly covered, in the refrigerator or freezer. If you do this, let them return to room temperature before attempting to separate them.

DUXELLES: A handful at a time, place the chopped mushrooms in the corner of a towel and squeeze to extract as much juice as possible. In a heavy 8- to 10-inch skillet, melt 4 tablespoons of butter over moderate heat. Before the foam subsides, stir in the shallots and cook them, stirring constantly, for 1 or 2 minutes or until they are soft but not brown. Stir in the squeezed, chopped mushrooms and cook, stirring frequently, for 10 to 15 minutes or until the moisture they give off has evaporated and they are on the point of browning. Transfer them to a bowl and stir in the parsley and chives. Season with salt and pepper. This makes about 1 cup.

VELOUTÉ SAUCE: In a heavy 2- to 3-quart saucepan, melt the 6 tablespoons of butter, then stir in ½ cup of flour and cook, stirring constantly, over low heat for about a minute. Remove from heat, let cool a moment, and vigorously beat in the hot chicken stock. When the *roux* and liquid are blended, return to moderately high heat, stirring thoroughly until the sauce comes to a boil. Boil, stirring, for 1 minute, then remove from heat. With a clean whisk, blend the egg yolks and ¾ cup of cream together in a bowl. Whisk in the hot sauce, 2 tablespoons at a time, until ½ cup has been added. Still off the heat, reverse the process and slowly pour the egg yolk-cream mixture back into the remaining hot sauce, whisking until it is smooth and creamy. Bring to a boil over moderate heat, still stirring, and boil slowly for 10 seconds. Remove from the heat at once and season with salt, pepper and lemon juice. This makes about 3½ cups of very thick sauce.

THE FILLING AND TOPPING: Preheat the oven to 375°. In a large mixing bowl, combine the chicken livers, shrimp or sautéed ham and artichoke hearts with 1 teaspoon parsley. (Sauté the artichoke hearts in 2 tablespoons of butter for 1 or 2 minutes, then add the ham and cook them for another minute or so.) Stir in the *duxelles* and ½ cup of *velouté* sauce. The mixture should be just thick enough to hold its shape in a spoon; add up to ½ cup more of *velouté* sauce if necessary. Taste and season with lemon juice, salt and pepper. Spoon a scant 2 tablespoons of filling on the lower third of each *crêpe* and roll it up; do not tuck in the ends. Thin the remaining *velouté* sauce with cream until it flows heavily off a spoon. Butter a baking-serving dish large enough to hold all the rolled *crêpes* and spread a film of *velouté* sauce on the bottom. Arrange the *crêpes* side by side in the dish. Mask them with the rest of the sauce and sprinkle the cheese on top. Dot with bits of butter. Bake in the upper third of the oven for 15 to 20 minutes or until the sauce bubbles. The top should be lightly browned; if it isn't, slide the dish under a hot broiler for a few seconds. Serve at once.

Hors d'oeuvre *crêpes* are filled with a combination of *duxelles*, made from mushrooms *(above left)*, with chicken livers, shrimp (shown on tarragon leaves), or ham and artichoke hearts *(right)*. The *crêpes* are then sauced and gratinéed.

71

Cooking the marinade for the vegetables helps to bring out all the flavors of the herbs and other seasonings.

To see if the onions are done, test their softness with the tip of a sharp knife.

After cooling and marinating, the onions, squash, peppers and beans are garnished with a few lemon wedges to make an enticing platter.

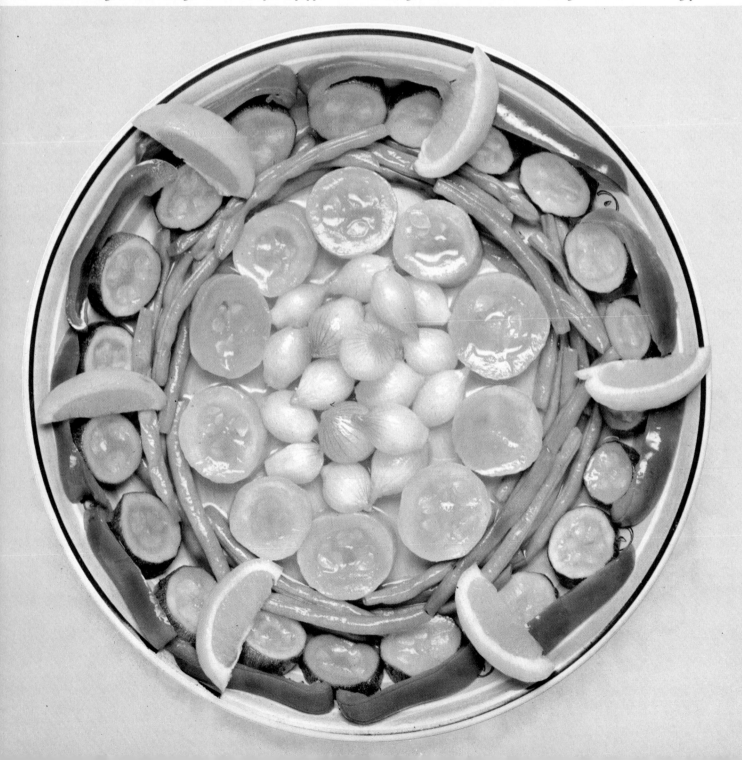

Légumes à la Grecque
MARINATED VEGETABLES, GREEK STYLE

First make the marinade. Stir the ingredients together in a 3- to 4-quart enameled or stainless-steel saucepan, bring to a boil, partially cover the pan and simmer slowly for 45 minutes. Using a fine sieve, strain the marinade into a large bowl, pressing down hard on the ingredients with the back of a spoon to squeeze out their juices before discarding them. Return the marinade to the saucepan and taste it. To be effective, the marinade should be somewhat overseasoned. This makes about 5 cups.

Bring the marinade to a boil and add the onions; cover and cook over moderate heat for 20 to 30 minutes or until the onions are just tender when pierced with the tip of a sharp knife. With a slotted spoon, remove the onions to a large glass or stainless-steel baking dish.

Add the slices of zucchini and yellow squash to the simmering marinade and cook slowly uncovered for 10 to 15 minutes or until they are barely done, then put them in the baking dish with the onions. Finally, add the green-pepper strips and string beans to the marinade and cook them slowly uncovered for 8 to 10 minutes, or until they are just tender. The vegetables must not be overcooked because they will soften as they cool and marinate. Lift the green peppers and string beans out of the pan and add them to the other vegetables. Taste and season the marinade and pour it over the vegetables, making sure that they are all at least partly covered with the hot liquid.

Place the baking dish in the refrigerator to cool the vegetables. Then cover the dish tightly with aluminum foil or plastic wrap and let the vegetables marinate in the refrigerator for at least 4 hours—or overnight if possible—before serving them. To serve, lift the vegetables out of the marinade with a slotted spoon and arrange them attractively on a serving platter. Moisten the vegetables with a little marinade and garnish them with lemon slices.

NOTE: Any other firm vegetable may be added to or substituted for those in the recipe, such as mushrooms, celery hearts, leeks, cucumbers, red peppers and artichoke hearts.

To serve 8 to 10

MARINADE
3 cups chicken stock, fresh or canned
1 cup dry white wine
1 cup olive oil
½ cup lemon juice
6 parsley sprigs
2 large garlic cloves, cut up
½ teaspoon dried thyme
10 peppercorns
1 teaspoon salt

VEGETABLES
24 white onions, 1 inch in diameter, peeled
1 pound small zucchini, unpeeled, sliced 1 inch thick
1 pound small yellow squash, unpeeled, sliced 1 inch thick
3 medium green peppers, seeded and cut lengthwise into ½-inch strips
½ pound whole green string beans, trimmed
2 lemons, cut into ¼-inch slices

Anchoyade
HOT ANCHOVY CANAPÉ

Drain the anchovies of all their oil and place them in a large mortar or heavy bowl with the garlic and the tomato paste. Mash with a pestle, wooden masher or wooden spoon until the mixture is a very smooth purée. Dribble the oil in, a few drops at a time, stirring constantly, until the mixture becomes thick and smooth like mayonnaise. Stir in the lemon juice and a few grindings of pepper.

Preheat the oven to 500° Under the broiler, brown the bread lightly on one side. While the bread is warm, spread the untoasted, soft side with the anchovy mixture, pressing it into the bread with the back of a fork or spoon. Arrange the bread on a baking sheet and bake in the oven for 10 minutes. Sprinkle with parsley and serve at once.

NOTE: For less saltiness, after draining the anchovies soak them for 10 minutes in cold water and then pat them thoroughly dry with paper towels.

To serve 4 to 5

2 two-ounce cans flat anchovy fillets
2 medium garlic cloves, finely chopped
1 teaspoon tomato paste
1 to 1½ tablespoons olive oil
2 teaspoons lemon juice or red-wine vinegar
Freshly ground black pepper
8 to 10 slices fresh French bread (½- to ¾-inch slices)
1 teaspoon finely chopped fresh parsley

To make about 2 cups

3 egg yolks, at room temperature
1 to 3 teaspoons lemon juice or wine
    vinegar
½ teaspoon dry mustard
½ teaspoon salt
⅛ teaspoon white pepper
1½ cups olive oil or vegetable oil or
    a combination of both
2 tablespoons boiling water (optional)

To make about 1½ cups

12 tablespoons butter (1½
    quarter-pound sticks)
3 egg yolks
1 tablespoon lemon juice
1 tablespoon chilled butter
1 tablespoon heavy cream
Salt
White pepper

To make about 1½ to 2 cups

¼ cup tarragon wine vinegar
¼ cup dry white wine
1 tablespoon finely chopped shallots
    or scallions
2 tablespoons finely cut fresh tarragon
    or 2 teaspoons dried tarragon and
    1 tablespoon finely chopped fresh
    parsley
1½ cups *sauce hollandaise* (recipe
    above) made without lemon juice
Salt
White pepper

To make ½ cup

2 tablespoons white or red wine vinegar
Salt
Freshly ground black pepper
¼ teaspoon dry mustard (optional)
6 to 8 tablespoons olive oil

Sauce Mayonnaise

Warm a large mixing bowl in hot water, dry it quickly but thoroughly, and drop the egg yolks into it. With a wire whisk, rotary or electric beater, beat the yolks vigorously for about 2 minutes or until they thicken and cling to the whisk or beater. Add a teaspoon of the lemon juice or vinegar and the dry mustard, salt and pepper. Then beat in the oil, ½ teaspoon at a time; make sure each addition is absorbed before adding more. By the time ½ cup of oil has been beaten in, the sauce should be like thick cream. Add the rest of the oil by teaspoonfuls, beating constantly. Taste and season with lemon juice, salt and pepper if necessary. To make the mayonnaise creamier and lessen the danger of separating, beat in boiling water 1 tablespoon at a time. Keep the mayonnaise in the refrigerator, tightly covered, until ready to use. For *mayonnaise aux fines herbes*, add 2 tablespoons finely chopped parsley and 1 tablespoon each of finely cut fresh chives and fresh tarragon.

Sauce Hollandaise

In a small, heavy pan over low heat, melt 12 tablespoons of butter without letting it brown. Set the butter aside and keep it warm. Off the heat, in a 1½- to 2-quart enameled or stainless steel saucepan, beat the egg yolks vigorously with a wire whisk for 1 minute or until they become thick; the bottom of the pan should show through when the whisk is drawn across it. Beat in the lemon juice. Then place the pan over very low heat and stir in the 1 tablespoon of chilled butter with the whisk. Stir constantly, lifting the pan off the stove occasionally to prevent it from overheating, until the butter has been absorbed and the mixture thickens enough to coat the wires of the whisk lightly. Remove the pan from the heat and beat in the cream. Still off the heat, pour in the warm, melted butter by droplets, stirring constantly with the whisk. The sauce will thicken into a heavy cream. Taste the hollandaise and season with salt and white pepper.

Sauce Béarnaise
HOLLANDAISE WITH TARRAGON AND WHITE WINE

In a small saucepan, briskly boil the vinegar, wine, shallots and 1 tablespoon fresh or 2 teaspoons dried tarragon until reduced to 2 tablespoons. Strain the liquid through a fine sieve into a small mixing bowl, pressing down hard on the herbs with a spoon before discarding them. Then whisk the strained liquid into the *sauce hollandaise* along with 1 tablespoon of fresh tarragon or parsley. Taste and season with salt and pepper.

Sauce Vinaigrette
FRENCH OIL AND VINEGAR DRESSING

With a whisk or fork, beat the vinegar, a little salt and pepper and the mustard (if used) until the salt dissolves. Dribble in the oil a few drops at a time, beating constantly, until it is absorbed. Taste and season.

    NOTE: lemon juice may be substituted for the vinegar, or the sauce may be made with half lemon juice, half vinegar.

Terrine Maison

HOME-STYLE PÂTÉ

Combine the ground meats in a large mixing bowl. In a heavy 8- to 10-inch skillet, melt 3 tablespoons of butter over moderate heat. When the foam subsides, stir in the shallots and garlic and cook, stirring frequently, for 5 minutes, or until soft but not brown. With a spatula, scrape into the bowl of meat.

In the same skillet, melt 2 tablespoons of butter and cook the chicken livers for 3 or 4 minutes or until they have stiffened but are still pink inside. Remove the livers with a slotted spoon and set them aside on a plate. Pour the Cognac into the hot skillet and boil it, stirring and scraping in any browned bits that cling to the bottom or sides of the pan, until it has reduced to about 2 tablespoons. Pour this glaze over the meat and shallots. Set the skillet aside.

Add the cream, lemon juice, flour, egg, spice Parisienne or allspice, salt and a generous grinding of pepper to the meat mixture. Knead vigorously with both hands, then beat with a wooden spoon (or in an electric beater with a pastry arm) until all the ingredients are well blended and the mixture is smooth and fluffy. Lightly fold in the tongue or ham cubes if they are used. Because the mixture contains raw pork, sauté a spoonful of it in the waiting skillet before tasting it for seasoning. Add more seasoning then if needed.

Preheat the oven to 350° and line a deep, rectangular 2-quart mold which has a cover (a *terrine*, or a metal or glass baking pan) with thin strips or sheets of pork fat. Depending on their length, the strips may be arranged lengthwise or crosswise, but they should overlap slightly and completely cover the bottom and sides of the mold. If they are long enough, let them hang over the sides and later lap them back over the top of the filling; otherwise, save enough strips of the fat to cover the top of the *terrine*.

Spoon half of the meat mixture into the lined mold, pressing it down firmly and smoothing it with the back of the spoon or a rubber spatula. Cut the chicken livers into quarters or eighths, depending on their size, and lay them in a row down the center of the mold. Fill the mold with the remaining meat mixture.

Smooth the top with a spoon or spatula and bring the long strips of fat from the sides up over the meat or arrange additional strips over it. Lay a bay leaf on the fat, enclose the top of the mold snugly with foil, then cover tightly.

Place the mold in a large baking pan on the middle shelf of the oven. Pour in enough boiling water to reach at least halfway up the side of the mold and bake the *terrine* for 2 hours or until the fat and juices which will have risen to the top are clear yellow.

Remove the *terrine* from the oven and lift off the cover and aluminum foil. Loosely cover the mold with fresh foil and weight the *terrine* by placing a heavy pan, casserole or cutting board, weighing at least several pounds, on top of it. Let cool to room temperature, then refrigerate the *terrine,* with the weight still in place, until it is thoroughly chilled. To serve, remove the weight and the foil, and cut slices directly from the mold in which the *terrine* baked.

To serve 10 to 12

1 pound fresh pork fat, ground
1½ pounds lean pork, ground
1½ pounds calf's, beef or pork liver, ground
½ pound lean veal, ground
5 tablespoons butter
⅓ cup finely chopped shallots or scallions
½ teaspoon finely chopped garlic
½ pound whole chicken livers
¼ cup Cognac
3 tablespoons heavy cream
2 teaspoons lemon juice
2 tablespoons flour
1 egg, lightly beaten
½ teaspoon spice Parisienne or allspice
1½ tablespoons salt
Freshly ground black pepper
¼ pound cooked smoked beef tongue or baked ham cut in ¼- inch cubes (about 1 cup) (optional)
½ pound fresh pork fat back, the fat from a pork loin or fat salt pork, sliced into ⅛-inch strips or sheets
1 large bay leaf

Traditionally, a *terrine* is baked in a special earthenware mold like the decorated oval one at bottom. But any large baking dish of metal, glass or glazed pottery will serve as well.

Steps to a Perfect Terrine

A savory *terrine* makes an impressive first course and is surprisingly easy to put together. Similar to pâtés, and often called by that name, French provincial *terrines* like this are concocted of finely ground meat, carefully spiced and seasoned, and are baked in a mold lined with pork fat.

1 Line the bottom and sides of the mold with thin strips of pork fat arranged either lengthwise or crosswise.

2 Spread half the meat mixture in the bottom of the mold and smooth it into corners with a rubber spatula.

3 Arrange pieces of sautéed chicken liver along the center of the meat, then add the rest of the mixture.

4 Cover the top of the meat with the remaining pork fat strips, setting them smoothly and overlapping them.

5 Lay a bay leaf on top and seal the *terrine* with a strip of aluminum foil pressed around the edges of the mold.

6 Put the lid on the mold, place it in a large pan and add boiling water to make a *bain-marie*, or double boiler.

7 A *terrine* slice, crusty bread and wine are an hors d'oeuvre treat.

V

Bread: The Crisp and Honest Loaf

It is easy enough to read in statistical surveys, or even to say, that bread is to the Frenchman what rice is to the Chinese and what potatoes are to the Germans, and so on and on. Once a person has been exposed to the mystique of French bread, however, it is hard to class it with any other source of starchy nourishment.

It is true that Chinese would hate to have to accustom themselves to it in place of rice, just as Germans would revolt en masse against substituting it for their infinitude of ways to absorb the potato. But it is fairly safe to say that most normal Frenchmen would rather starve than supplant their daily ration of their own bread by any of the other equally adequate starchy foods.

The French are extremely demanding about what is literally their staff of life. It must be fresh, baked not too long before the time it is to be eaten—except for the grudging concession that the bakery ovens must have one day to cool off each week. On that day somewhat desperate measures are taken: the slightly stale bread (a whole day old!) is toasted to camouflage its antiquity. Or the family may even resort to eating the moister loaves of whole grain flours that are sardonically referred to as "health" bread.

Under ideal circumstances, some people like their loaves very brown and crusty, and some like them comparatively pale but still capable of making razor-sharp crumbs when broken. The loaf must be a certain shape, depending upon the conditioned wishes of the family. Although neighborhood bakeries usually manage to satisfy most of their customers about this structural problem, I have known French housewives to go clear across town to get bread that is perhaps three centimeters wider in the middle, or one foot longer, or an invisible length thinner or shorter, than the ones more readily available.

Most small-town bakers are accommodating enough to put Monsieur Dupont's three loaves aside for an after-work pickup, and even to take old lady Simiot's two morning *croissants* to her very windowsill while she is laid up with that stiff hip.

It is still the custom in little places to take dishes to the bakery to be roasted (a stew, a *cassoulet*, even a suckling pig or turkey), but in general nothing goes into the long ovens but bread and rolls, shoved back and forth artfully on wooden paddles with handles as supple as vaulting poles. The brioches and daintier baked breads, meanwhile, are usually made at different heats and settings in the pastry shops.

Is it as good as it used to be?

It is rare now to find bakers still using wood or coal or charcoal for their fuel, but modern adaptations of their ancient ovens have made breads baked with gas and electricity as palatable to the younger generations as the possibly tastier loaves must have been to their elders. (The last time *I* saw Paris, only once did I find bread as good as what I was sure I remembered from many years before. Was it the new methods, the new qualities of flour—or was it I who had changed since the last visit, perhaps not for the better?)

Bread is usually eaten at all three of the daily meals in France: always in the morning with hot, milky coffee or chocolate; always at noon throughout the main meal, until the final bit of cheese has been finished or the table has been cleared for a dessert; and often at night, with a good bowl of hearty soup.

Leftover bread, which is treated with the respect due any part of such an intrinsic design for living, is fairly rare, for most housewives know almost to the last crumb what their families will eat on one day. When there is any bread left over, it goes into stuffings or puddings, or forms a delicate and simple dessert that is often eaten for breakfast in American homes and called French toast. The Americans put maple syrup or honey on it and order it instead of pancakes or waffles. In France the crisply golden slices are often flavored judiciously with a little liqueur like Grand Marnier, and served with a sprinkling of sugar or a bit of jelly or butter at the end of the meal. Any way at all, it is best made with slices of honest French bread.

A good source of the exactly right, crisp, honest loaf is hard to locate, but once found, it is worth that trip across town, no matter what the bread's shape, height, width or length. A Frenchman's whole meal can hinge upon it, just as will his whole day—and, in fact, his existence, at least by his own reckoning.

Fresh Loaves in Many Shapes, Sizes and Flavors

A few of the many varieties of French bread are shown in the photograph on pages 82 and 83, and in the key diagram below. By far the most popular kind in France is the *baguette* (5), a golden, rod-shaped loaf about two feet long. Next comes the *petit parisien* (3), which is shorter and fatter than the *baguette* and is usually softer in the center. Many of the breads now common throughout France originated in the provinces or even in foreign countries (the French, sometimes a bit disdainful of foreign cooking, are quick to recognize and adopt a good bread, no matter what its origin). Most of the whole-grain breads, like the black rye *tourte d'Auvergne* (8), are provincial in origin. The *natte ordinaire* (20) and the *natte aux cumins* (28) are borrowed from Austria, and the *pain espagnol* (13) is, as the name suggests, from Spain. In addition to the traditional loaves, many French bakers invent their own specialties, in which they take particular pride. The sunburst-shaped *petit Saint-Ouen* (21) is a specialty of the Paris bakery that assembled this display and is named after the proprietor, M. Saint-Ouen. Another bread that deserves special mention is the light, buttery roll known as *croissant*, or crescent (23, 24). The *croissant* along with the *brioche* (26) is sacred to breakfast and is floated down on rivers of hot chocolate or coffee.

NOTE: There are no recipes for bread in this chapter for two reasons: traditionally and almost universally, the French do not bake their bread at home but buy it; and to bake it successfully without having French flour and other French ingredients on hand is most difficult.

Breads in the photograph on the next two pages are listed below:

1. Épi de Charente
2. Couronne Tressée
3. Petit Parisien
4. Palette
5. Baguette
6. Pain de Campagne Bis
7. Pain de Seigle
8. Tourte d'Auvergne
9. Couronne Sarthoise
10. Soleil
11. Pain au Levain (various sizes)
12. Pain Alsacien
13. Pain Espagnol
14. Pain Cuit au Bois
15. Fendu de Gruau
16. Sarthoise
17. Cassadière Corse
18. L'Empereur
19. Bagnat
20. Natte Ordinaire
21. Petit Saint-Ouen
22. Petit Pain Ordinaire
23. Croissant au Beurre
24. Croissant Ordinaire
25. Natte aux Pavots
26. Brioche
27. Main Provençale
28. Natte aux Cumins

VI

Soups: Hearty and Light

There is a legend, still firmly fixed in many of our romantic and therefore somewhat impractical minds, that an enormous black kettle sits at the back of every provincial French stove, continuously brewing its own delectable botulism day after day. Bones, crusts, carcasses are tossed into it, simmering "a simple little soup of the country."

Anyone who has ever tried to make this dream come true, even on paper, knows differently. A good soup must be fresh. As was first said about *all* good food by Curnonsky, "prince of gastronomes," a good soup must taste of the things it is made of.

As a possible comfort to the dewy-eyed dreamers of that old black soup kettle fuming away, it is safe to say that most French family cooks do not discard flavorful chicken carcasses or other good bones and leavings. Instead they simmer them with a few herbs, strain the juice and save it to use for stock.

They do not stick a sauté pan automatically under the hot-water faucet, but instead swirl a little red or white wine in it after the eggplant or lamb chop (or almost anything else) has been removed to the serving dish. The enriched natural juices are then either poured over the dish that is ready for the table or are put aside for future use. The stock is usually used as a base for soup, artfully made dignified by some quickly chopped fresh vegetables tossed in a little butter, the rescued richness of the pan broth, a handful of noodles, and some fresh parsley added at the last.

In the great numbers of provincial families that eat their main and soupless meal at noon, the soup is served for supper, with perhaps a light egg

A hearty soup like one of these can serve as a meal in itself. From top: split pea soup; vegetable soup with garlic, basil and tomato sauce; and French onion soup—all in the sturdy pots they cooked in. An evening meal in France is frequently such a substantial soup, served just with bread.

dish or vegetable to follow, and an equally simple dessert like custard or stewed fruits.

In simple French fare, a soup is kept simple: since it is meant to be eaten at the end of the day, it should lead to easy sleep unhindered by a too-active digesting of rich or unaccustomed ingredients. If there is no stock, the soup will be based, usually, on water, or on broth left from some dish like boiled beef, or occasionally on milk. The whole family will eat it, with the last of the daily bread, and then go to bed.

Occasionally soup is served at noon. When a good *pot-au-feu* or *poule-au-pot* is to be the main dish, the broth from it may be served first. More rarely, and usually on formal occasions, a clear soup will be served at the midday meal, either hot or cold. When cold it is never stiffened with gelatin, but is wobbly with its own textures.

A comparatively complex dish like a *bouillabaisse* is seldom served at night, being rich and in other ways eminently unsuited to peaceful slumber. In this same category of main-dish soups, usually served in the middle of the day, are such regional dishes as *cotriade*, which is a pungent Breton *bouillabaisse; bourride*, a garlicky fish stew; and *soupe au pistou*, a spicy vegetable soup. Each of these soups has a complementary sauce, in some cases mixed into the soup itself to enhance the flavor, and in all cases offered on the side to reinforce the pungency of the dish.

Rouille, a peppery concoction suited to the taste of *bouillabaisse,* is served separately from the soup to be ladled in at the discretion of the individual diner. The *aïoli* for *bourride* is a strong, garlicky mayonnaise, part of it blended into the broth to make it a smooth, egg-yolk yellow, and the rest offered for those insatiable for garlic. The *soupe au pistou,* a vegetable mélange of Provence, gains its name from the *pistou,* a blend of garlic, herbs, tomato paste and cheese which is added to the soup.

Many soups that evolved through the centuries in the French provinces are based more on vegetables than on meats or even meat stocks, and are frankly described as "healthy": *potages de santé.* Their recipes are ancient, as basic as the need for cabin-bound men to go out with their livestock in the first days of spring and gather the grasses and roots of the awakening meadows.

These soups depend upon spinach and sorrel, and all the herbs, and mushrooms, and fresh milk and cream and butter, all tasting perennially and incredibly delicious after the long dark months of eating stored roots like turnips and potatoes, and cabbages and onions and garlic. The ways of preparing these dependables for the best possible survival are good too, in a country that has survived as long as France.

It is impossible, of course, to try to change the modern American pattern of dining at home or in public at night, with snack-lunch or "business lunch" at noon. But a hearty soup in the winter after a long day, or a light one with fresh herbs and vegetables in the summer, bears out the saying that "soup's enough, if there's enough soup."

Light soups that can serve as the first course of a formal dinner are, from top, cream of asparagus, leek and potato (called vichyssoise if served cold), and purée of carrot.

Potage Purée de Pois Cassés
SPLIT PEA SOUP

To serve 4 to 6

2 cups dry green split peas
5 cups water or fresh or canned chicken stock
Bouquet garni, made of 2 parsley sprigs, 2 chopped celery tops and 1 bay leaf, tied together
¼ teaspoon dried thyme
Ham bone (optional)
2 tablespoons butter
¼ pound salt pork, finely diced
½ cup finely chopped carrots
½ cup finely chopped onions
1 large leek, chopped (white part plus 2 inches of green) or 1 extra onion, finely chopped
1 cup coarsely chopped spinach or lettuce leaves
½ cup shelled fresh green peas (about ½ pound, unshelled) or substitute defrosted frozen peas
Salt
Freshly ground black pepper
½ pound baked ham, cut in ½-inch cubes (about 2 cups)
2 tablespoons soft butter

Wash the split peas thoroughly under cold running water. In a heavy 4- to 5-quart saucepan or a soup kettle, bring 5 cups of water or chicken stock to a boil and drop in the peas. Add the *bouquet garni*, the thyme and the ham bone, if you use it. Reduce the heat and simmer half covered for 30 minutes to 1 hour, or until the peas are tender but not mushy.

While the peas simmer, melt 2 tablespoons of butter in a heavy 8- to 10-inch skillet, and brown the diced salt pork until it is crisp and renders its fat; remove the pork and discard it. In the fat remaining in the skillet, cook the carrots, onions, leek and spinach or lettuce leaves uncovered over moderate heat for 5 minutes, or until the onions are soft and the leaves have wilted. When the split peas are tender, add all of the vegetables including the fresh green peas to the soup and simmer uncovered for another 30 minutes. Remove and discard the *bouquet garni* and the ham bone. Purée the soup through a food mill into a large bowl, and then rub it through a fine sieve back into the saucepan. Taste and season with salt and freshly ground black pepper, add the ham cubes and bring the soup to a simmer over low heat. If the soup seems too thick, thin it with a little chicken stock or water.

Before serving, remove the pan from the heat and stir in the soft butter, 1 tablespoon at a time. Ladle the soup into a large tureen or soup bowls.

Soupe à l'Oignon
FRENCH ONION SOUP

To serve 6 to 8

4 tablespoons butter
2 tablespoons vegetable oil
2 pounds onions, thinly sliced (about 7 cups)
1 teaspoon salt
3 tablespoons flour
2 quarts beef stock, fresh or canned, or beef and chicken stock combined

CROÛTES
12 to 16 one-inch-thick slices of French bread
2 teaspoons olive oil
1 garlic clove, cut
1 cup grated, imported Swiss cheese or Swiss and freshly grated Parmesan cheese combined

In a heavy 4- to 5-quart saucepan or a soup kettle, melt the butter with the oil over moderate heat. Stir in the onions and 1 teaspoon salt, and cook uncovered over low heat, stirring occasionally, for 20 to 30 minutes, or until the onions are a rich golden brown. Sprinkle flour over the onions and cook, stirring, for 2 or 3 minutes. Remove the pan from the heat. In a separate saucepan, bring the stock to a simmer, then stir the hot stock into the onions. Return the soup to low heat and simmer, partially covered, for another 30 or 40 minutes, occasionally skimming off the fat. Taste for seasoning, and add salt and pepper if needed.

While the soup simmers, make the *croûtes*. Preheat the oven to 325°. Spread the slices of bread in one layer on a baking sheet and bake for 15 minutes. With a pastry brush, lightly coat both sides of each slice with olive oil. Then turn the slices over and bake for another 15 minutes, or until the bread is completely dry and lightly browned. Rub each slice with the cut garlic clove and set aside.

To serve, place the *croûtes* in a large tureen or individual soup bowls and ladle the soup over them. Pass the grated cheese separately.

ALTERNATIVE: To make onion soup *gratinée*, preheat the oven to 375°. Ladle the soup into an ovenproof tureen or individual soup bowls, top with *croûtes*, and spread the grated cheese on top. Sprinkle the cheese with a little melted butter or olive oil. Bake for 10 to 20 minutes, or until the cheese has melted, then slide the soup under a hot broiler for a minute or two to brown the top if desired.

Fonds de Cuisine
HOMEMADE BEEF AND CHICKEN STOCKS

Good soups depend on good stocks—and so do stews, casseroles, braised meats and vegetables, and many sauces. Here are recipes for three stocks (or *fonds de cuisine*) that are basic to French cooking.

SIMPLE STOCK: Place the beef and bones, or the chicken backs and necks in a soup pot or kettle, and add enough cold water to cover them by 1 inch. Bring to a boil over high heat, skimming off the scum that rises to the surface. Add the vegetables, *bouquet garni* and salt. Bring to a simmer, skimming if necessary, then partially cover and cook very slowly for 4 hours. Remove the bones and strain the stock through a fine sieve into a large bowl, pressing down hard on the vegetables and herbs before discarding them. Taste and season. Skim any fat from the surface or refrigerate until the fat solidifies on the top and can be removed. The stock will keep refrigerated for 3 or 4 days or can be frozen for future use. For richer taste boil down the strained and degreased stock until its flavor has concentrated.

BROWN BEEF STOCK: Preheat the oven to 450°. Roast the beef bones, onions and carrots in a shallow pan for 30 to 40 minutes, turning them occasionally. Transfer the bones and vegetables to a soup pot. Then discard the fat from the roasting pan, add 2 cups of water and bring to a boil over high heat, scraping in any browned bits clinging to the pan. Pour this into the soup pot and add the celery, *bouquet garni*, salt and cold water to cover. Proceed with the stock, following the directions above.

BROWN POULTRY STOCK: Over high heat, brown the chicken backs and necks in 2 tablespoons of vegetable oil in a large skillet. Transfer them to the soup pot and deglaze the skillet with a little water. Add this to the soup pot with the onions, carrots, celery, *bouquet garni*, salt and cold water to cover. Proceed with the stock, following the directions for simple stock.

Soupe au Pistou
VEGETABLE SOUP WITH GARLIC, BASIL AND TOMATO SAUCE

Bring 3 cups of water to a boil in a 2- to 3-quart saucepan. Drop in the dry beans and boil them for 2 minutes. Remove from the heat and let the beans soak for 1 hour. Return the pan to low heat and simmer uncovered for 1 to 1½ hours, or until the beans are tender. Drain the beans and reserve the cooking liquid. In a heavy soup pot or kettle, heat 4 tablespoons of olive oil. Stir in the diced onions and cook over moderate heat until limp and golden, then add the tomatoes and cook for 3 or 4 minutes longer. Pour in 3 quarts of water and bring to a boil over high heat. Add the carrots, potatoes, leeks, celery leaves, salt and a few grindings of pepper; reduce the heat and simmer uncovered for 15 minutes. Stir in the white beans, their cooking liquid, the green beans, zucchini, spaghettini and saffron, and simmer for 15 minutes, or until the vegetables are tender. Taste and season. Meanwhile, prepare the *pistou*. With a mortar and pestle (or a wooden spoon and heavy bowl), mash the garlic and basil to a paste. Work in the tomato paste and ½ cup of the cheese, then beat in six tablespoons of olive oil, 1 tablespoon at a time. Ladle the soup into a tureen. Thin the *pistou* with ½ cup of soup stock and stir as much of the *pistou* as you like into the soup. Sprinkle in the crumbled bread. Pass the rest of the cheese separately.

To make 3 to 4 quarts

2 pounds beef shank and 4 pounds beef bones or 6 pounds chicken backs and necks
4 to 5 quarts cold water
2 onions, peeled
2 carrots, peeled
2 celery stalks with leaves, cut up
Bouquet garni, made of 6 parsley sprigs, 1 bay leaf, 2 garlic cloves and ½ teaspoon dried thyme, wrapped together in cheesecloth
1 tablespoon salt

To serve 10 to 12

3 cups water
¾ cup dry white beans (Great Northern, marrow or navy)
4 tablespoons olive oil
1 cup diced onions
1 pound tomatoes, peeled, seeded and coarsely chopped (about 1½ cups)
3 quarts water
1½ cups diced carrots
1½ cups diced boiling potatoes
1 cup coarsely chopped leeks (optional)
½ cup coarsely chopped celery leaves
1 tablespoon salt
Freshly ground black pepper
1½ cups sliced fresh green string beans
1½ cups diced, unpeeled zucchini
½ cup broken pieces of spaghettini
2 pinches crumbled saffron threads

PISTOU
5 garlic cloves, finely chopped
½ cup finely cut fresh basil or 5 tablespoons dried basil
2 tablespoons tomato paste
½ cup freshly grated Parmesan cheese
6 tablespoons olive oil
1 small slice stale French bread, finely crumbled (optional)
1½ cups freshly grated Parmesan cheese

Potage Crème d'Asperges
CREAM OF ASPARAGUS SOUP

To serve 4 to 6

2 pounds fresh asparagus
6 cups chicken stock, fresh or canned
1 teaspoon salt
7 tablespoons butter
6 tablespoons flour
2 tablespoons finely chopped shallots
    or scallions
2 egg yolks
¾ cup heavy cream
2 tablespoons soft butter
Salt
White pepper

With a small sharp knife (*not* a vegetable peeler), peel each asparagus stalk of its skin and tough outer flesh. At the butt end the peeling may be as thick as ¹⁄₁₆ inch, but it should gradually become paper thin as the knife cuts and slides toward the tip. Cut off the tips where the scales end and trim away any oversized scales. Trim off and discard about ¼ inch from the butt ends and cut the rest of the stalks into ½-inch lengths; set aside. In a 3- to 4-quart saucepan, bring the chicken stock and the salt to a boil over moderate heat. Drop in the asparagus tips and boil slowly for 5 to 8 minutes, or until they are just tender. Drain the stock into a bowl and set the tips aside in another.

In the same saucepan, melt 5 tablespoons of the butter over moderate heat. Stir in the 6 tablespoons of flour, then cook over low heat, stirring constantly, for 1 or 2 minutes. Do not let this *roux* brown. Remove the pan from the heat, let it cool for a few seconds, then pour in the stock, beating constantly with a wire whisk to blend the stock and the *roux*. Return the pan to moderate heat and stir until this cream soup base comes to a boil, thickens and is perfectly smooth. Turn the heat down and let the soup base simmer very gently.

Melt the remaining 2 tablespoons of butter in an 8- to 10-inch enameled or stainless-steel skillet. When the foam subsides, stir in the cut-up asparagus stalks and the shallots, and toss them in the butter over moderate heat for 3 minutes. Stir the stalks and shallots into the simmering soup base and cook over low heat, stirring occasionally, for 15 minutes or until the asparagus is tender.

Purée the soup through a food mill into a mixing bowl and then again through a fine sieve back into the pan. With a wire whisk, blend the egg yolks and cream together in a medium-sized mixing bowl. Whisk in the puréed soup, 2 tablespoons at a time, until ½ cup has been added. Then reverse the process and slowly whisk the now-warmed egg-yolk-and-cream mixture into the soup. Bring to a boil, and boil for 30 seconds, stirring constantly. Remove the pan from the heat and stir in the 2 tablespoons of soft butter, 1 tablespoon at a time. Taste the soup and season it with salt and white pepper. Add the reserved asparagus tips and ladle the soup into a tureen or into individual soup bowls.

Potage Crécy
PURÉE OF CARROT SOUP

To serve 4 to 6

2 tablespoons butter
¾ cup finely chopped onions
3 cups finely chopped carrots
1 quart chicken stock, fresh or canned
2 teaspoons tomato paste
2 tablespoons plain white raw rice
Salt
White pepper
½ cup heavy cream
1 tablespoon soft butter
8 to 12 carrot curls (optional)

In a heavy 3- to 4-quart saucepan, melt the butter over moderate heat. Stir in the onions and cook, stirring occasionally, for 5 minutes, or until they are soft but not browned. Add the carrots, chicken stock, tomato paste and rice, and simmer gently, uncovered, for 30 minutes. Purée the soup through a food mill into a clean saucepan. Season it with salt and white pepper, and stir in the cream.

Before serving, return the soup to low heat and bring it to a simmer. Remove the pan from the heat and stir in the tablespoon of soft butter. Ladle the soup into a tureen or into individual soup bowls and garnish with carrot curls if desired.

Potage Parmentier; Vichyssoise
LEEK OR ONION AND POTATO SOUP

To serve 6 to 8

In a heavy 6-quart saucepan or a soup kettle, simmer the potatoes, leeks, chicken stock and salt partially covered for 40 to 50 minutes or until the vegetables are tender. Force the soup through a food mill or sieve into a mixing bowl and then pour back into the pan. Season the soup with salt and a few grindings of pepper, and stir in the cream. Before serving, return the soup to low heat and bring it to a simmer. Ladle the soup into a tureen or individual soup bowls. Serve garnished with fresh chives or finely chopped fresh parsley.

VICHYSSOISE: When Louis Diat was chef at the Ritz-Carlton Hotel in New York City half a century ago, he devised vichyssoise—a cold version of *potage Parmentier*. To make it, force the soup through a food mill or sieve, then through a fine sieve back into the pan. Season and stir in 1½ cups of heavy cream. (Do not use a blender; the mixture will be too smooth.) Chill the soup until it is very cold. Serve it garnished with finely cut fresh chives.

4 cups peeled and coarsely chopped potatoes
3 cups thinly sliced leeks (white part plus 2 inches of green) or substitute 3 cups thinly sliced onions
2 quarts chicken stock, fresh or canned, or substitute water or a combination of chicken stock and water
1 teaspoon salt
Freshly ground black pepper
½ cup heavy cream
3 tablespoons finely cut fresh chives or finely chopped fresh parsley

Potage Crème de Champignons
CREAM OF MUSHROOM SOUP

To serve 4 to 6

Separate the mushroom caps and stems. Then slice half the mushroom caps about ⅛ inch thick and coarsely chop the remaining caps and all the stems. In an 8- to 10-inch enameled or stainless-steel skillet (iron or aluminum will discolor the mushrooms), melt 2 tablespoons of the butter over moderate heat.

When the foam subsides, add the sliced mushrooms and cook them, tossing them constantly with a wooden spoon, for 2 minutes or until they are lightly colored. With a slotted spoon, transfer them to a bowl and set them aside. Melt an additional 2 tablespoons of butter in the same skillet and cook the chopped mushroom caps and stems and the shallots for 2 minutes. Set them aside in the skillet.

In a heavy 4- to 6-quart saucepan, melt the remaining 5 tablespoons of butter over moderate heat. Remove the pan from the heat and stir in the 6 tablespoons of flour, then cook over low heat, stirring constantly, for 1 or 2 minutes. Do not let this *roux* brown. Remove the pan from the heat, let cool a few seconds, then pour in the chicken stock, beating constantly with a wire whisk to blend stock and *roux*. Return to heat and stir until this cream soup base comes to a boil, thickens and is perfectly smooth. Then add the chopped mushrooms and shallots and simmer, stirring occasionally, for 15 minutes.

Purée the soup through a food mill into a mixing bowl and then again through a fine sieve back into the saucepan. With a wire whisk, blend the egg yolks and the cream together in a bowl. Whisk in the hot puréed soup, 2 tablespoons at a time, until ½ cup has been added. Then reverse the process and slowly whisk the now-warm egg-yolk-and-cream mixture into the soup.

Bring to a boil, and boil for 30 seconds, stirring constantly. Remove the pan from the heat. Taste and season with salt and white pepper. Add the reserved sliced mushrooms and serve the soup from a tureen or individual soup bowls.

1½ pounds fresh mushrooms
9 tablespoons butter (1 quarter-pound stick plus 1 tablespoon)
2 finely chopped shallots or scallions
6 tablespoons flour
6 cups chicken stock, fresh or canned
2 egg yolks
¾ cup heavy cream
Salt
White pepper

Fish for a *bourride* should be firm-fleshed white fish such as the haddock *(top)*, section of cod and porgy shown in this picture, or halibut, sole or perch.

Bourride should be served in a large bowl *(bottom)* with the soup *(top)* ladled over a *croûte* (toasted French bread) and the fish. A dab of *aïoli* sauce *(right center)* goes on top.

To serve 8 to 10

COURT BOUILLON
2 pounds fish heads, bones and
    trimmings
6 cups water
1 cup dry white wine
2 onions, thinly sliced
2 leeks, white part only, thinly sliced
    (optional)
2 tablespoons wine vinegar,
    preferably white
2 three-inch strips fresh orange peel
2 bay leaves
1 teaspoon fennel seeds
2 teaspoons salt

AÏOLI
1 tablespoon fine, dry bread crumbs
1 tablespoon wine vinegar
6 garlic cloves, coarsely chopped
7 egg yolks
½ teaspoon salt
⅛ teaspoon white pepper
1½ cups olive oil
1 tablespoon lemon juice

FISH
2 pounds each of three kinds of firm,
    white fish fillets or steaks such as
    haddock, porgy, cod, sole, perch,
    rockfish, pollack or halibut, cut in
    2-inch serving pieces

CROÛTES
12 *croûtes* (see recipe for *soupe à*
    l'oignon, page 88)

Bourride
PROVENÇAL FISH SOUP WITH GARLIC MAYONNAISE

In a 4- to 6-quart saucepan, bring the court bouillon ingredients to a boil, partially cover the pan, and cook over low heat for 30 minutes. Meanwhile, make the *aïoli.* Soak the bread crumbs in 1 tablespoon of wine vinegar for 5 minutes, then squeeze the crumbs dry in the corner of a towel. With a large mortar and pestle or a small, heavy mixing bowl and wooden spoon, vigorously mash the crumbs and garlic to a smooth paste. Beat in 3 egg yolks, one at a time and, along with the third yolk, add the salt and pepper. When the mixture is thick and sticky, begin to beat in the olive oil a few drops at a time. As soon as the mixture resembles thick cream, transfer it to a large mixing bowl. With a wire whisk, rotary or electric beater, beat in the rest of the oil, 1 teaspoon at a time. The sauce will be like a thick mayonnaise. Season it with lemon juice, salt and pepper if needed. Spoon ⅔ cup of *aïoli* into a small sauceboat and cover with plastic wrap. Put the rest of the sauce (about 1⅓ cups) into a 3- to 4-quart saucepan.

Strain the court bouillon through a sieve into a bowl, pressing down hard on the vegetables and trimmings with a spoon before discarding them. Wash the pan and return the court bouillon to it. Add the fish, bring to a boil and simmer uncovered for 3 to 8 minutes, or until the fish is just firm to the touch. Watch the fish carefully; different kinds and thicknesses cook at different speeds. With a slotted spatula or spoon, transfer the pieces to a heated platter as soon as they are done. Cover the platter loosely to keep the fish warm.

Off the heat, beat the 4 remaining egg yolks, one at a time, into the *aïoli* in the saucepan. Add 1 cup of hot fish broth, beating constantly, then gradually beat in the remaining broth. Cook over low heat, stirring, until the soup is thick enough to coat the whisk lightly. Do not let it come to a boil. Season with salt, pepper, and lemon juice if needed.

To serve, pour the soup into a large tureen and bring it to the table with the platter of fish, the sauceboat of *aïoli,* and the *croûtes.* Place a *croûte* in the bottom of each individual soup bowl, lay one or several pieces of fish on top of the *croûte,* and ladle in the soup. Top with a dab of *aïoli* and pass the remaining sauce separately.

Fish for *bouillabaisse* are, clockwise from the top, red snapper, eel, lobster, sea bass, fish heads and tails, and on the chopping board, halibut steak, mussels and scallops.

To serve 8 to 10

COURT BOUILLON
2 cups thinly sliced onions
1 cup thinly sliced leeks
¾ cup olive oil
8 cups water or 2 cups dry white wine
  and 6 cups water
2 pounds fish heads, bones and
  trimmings
3 pounds ripe tomatoes, coarsely
  chopped (about 6 cups)
½ cup fresh fennel or ½ teaspoon dried
  fennel seeds, crushed
1 teaspoon finely chopped garlic
1 three-inch strip fresh orange peel
1 teaspoon dried thyme
2 parsley sprigs
1 bay leaf
¼ teaspoon crushed saffron threads
Salt
Freshly ground black pepper

ROUILLE
2 small green peppers, seeded and
  cut in small squares
1 dry chili pepper or a few drops of
  Tabasco added to the finished sauce
1 cup water
2 canned pimientos, drained and dried
4 garlic cloves, coarsely chopped
6 tablespoons olive oil
1 to 3 tablespoons fine dry bread
  crumbs

Bouillabaisse

MEDITERRANEAN FISHERMAN'S SOUP WITH HOT PEPPER SAUCE

In a heavy 4- to 6-quart saucepan, cook the onions and leeks in the oil over low heat, stirring frequently, for 5 minutes, or until they are tender but not brown (additional onions may be substituted for the leeks). Add the water or wine and water, the fish trimmings, tomatoes, herbs and seasonings, and cook uncovered over moderate heat for 30 minutes.

THE ROUILLE: Meanwhile, prepare the *rouille*. In a 6- to 8-cup saucepan, simmer the green peppers and chili pepper in 1 cup of water for 10 minutes, or until they are tender. Drain them thoroughly and dry them with paper towels. Then, with a large mortar and pestle, or a mixing bowl and wooden spoon, mash the peppers, pimiento and garlic to a smooth paste. Slowly beat in the olive oil and add enough bread crumbs to make the sauce thick enough to hold its shape in a spoon. Taste and season with Tabasco if you have omitted the chili pepper.

A quicker but less authentic way to make *rouille* is to combine the sim-

mered peppers, the pimiento, garlic and the olive oil in an electric blender. Blend at low speed until they are smooth, adding more oil if the blender clogs. With a rubber spatula, transfer the sauce to a bowl and stir in enough bread crumbs to make it thick enough to hold its shape in a spoon. Taste and season with Tabasco if you have omitted the chili pepper. Set aside.

ASSEMBLING THE SOUP: When the court bouillon is done, strain it through a large fine sieve into a soup pot or kettle, pressing down hard on the fish trimmings and vegetables with the back of a spoon to extract their juices before discarding them. Bring the strained stock to a boil over high heat and add the lobster. Boil briskly for 5 minutes, then add the fish and the eel, if you wish, and cook another 5 minutes. Finally, add the mussels and scallops (optional) and boil 5 minutes longer. Taste for seasoning.

To serve, remove the fish and seafood from the soup with a slotted spoon and arrange them on a heated platter. Ladle the soup into a large tureen. Thin the *rouille* with 2 or 3 tablespoons of soup and pour it into a sauceboat. At the table, place a *croûte* in each individual soup bowl, ladle in the soup over it, and arrange fish and seafood on top. Pass the *rouille* separately.

FISH AND SEAFOOD

2 two-pound live lobsters, cut up and cracked (see directions in recipe for *homard à l'américaine*, page 116)

1½ pounds each of three kinds of firm, white fish cut into 2-inch serving pieces: halibut, red snapper, bass, haddock, pollack, hake, cod, yellow pike, lake trout, whitefish, rockfish

1 eel, cut in 2-inch pieces (optional)

2 pounds live mussels (optional)

2 pounds fresh or frozen sea scallops, cut in halves or quarters (optional)

12 *croûtes* (see *soupe à l'oignon*, page 88)

Bouillabaisse, a hearty fisherman's stew, is best brought to the table in a tureen, with *rouille* on the side.

VII

Fish: The Exotic and Familiar

People who are not French have long been astonished by the behavior of people who are. This is especially true of table habits: a Frenchman will look for, and then prepare and eat with enjoyment, certain foods which to Anglo-Saxon palates are plain outlandish. Yet gradually we grow accustomed to the strange-seeming things in nature that are prepared so delectably in France. By now there are few traveled Westerners who have not tasted, and for the most part really enjoyed, French foods that are still not on their daily lists at home.

Snails are a good example. Once scorned, they recently were, ironically, a bootleg item. The tourist and export demands for them became so great that at one point they were actually threatened with extermination, and were shamelessly smuggled across Swiss and Italian borders into French kitchens. To meet the insatiable demand, two thirds of the snails consumed must be imported, from all over Western and Eastern Europe.

Snails are usually prepared in the Burgundian style, served in their shells in butter heavily flavored with garlic and herbs. Unless one has a gastric block about this seasoning, or an unconquerable prejudice against consuming mollusks in general and creepy-crawly ones in particular, they are a delicious thing indeed.

They are generally served at noon as an hors d'oeuvre, six or 12 on a sizzling, dimpled plate. They are rich, because of the sauce, every drop of which is carefully mopped up with bread by a real snail-eater, but in Dijon I have seen hearty Burgundians on a cold market day engulf four or five dozen of them at a sitting, and then follow them with an equally lusty stew

Fresh from the waters around Marseilles, carefully arranged shellfish await the morning's buyers at a market in the city's ancient Vieux-Port area. The shop is named for its proprietress, "Pascaline, The Queen of Shellfish."

SERVING SNAILS

Snails, available canned in many groceries, are an acquired taste, but one relished by devotees. The shells are sold separately. The proper serving equipment, also widely available, is shown below.

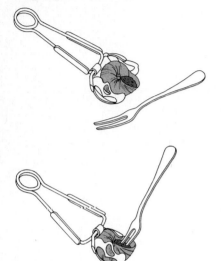

Snails are picked up and held in a clamp *(above);* a small-tined fork is used to reach the meat of the mollusk. *Below:* A pan with round indentations to hold the snails upright is used for both baking and serving.

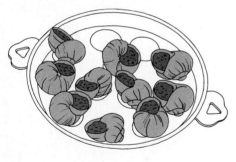

ESCARGOTS À LA BOURGUIGNONNE
TO SERVE 2. Drain a can of 24 snails. Cream together ¼ pound soft butter, 1 tablespoon finely chopped shallots or scallions, 1 teaspoon finely chopped garlic, 2 tablespoons finely chopped fresh parsley, salt and pepper. Put some of the mixture into each shell, insert the snails and the rest of the mixture. Place the shells in pans and bake in a 450° oven for 10 minutes, or until the butter sizzles.

or *ragoût*, a salad and a good fruit tart. Needless to say, such a performance takes centuries of practice.

Another creature that the French have raised to a lordly place on any table is the frog. Not long ago, Englishmen became so upset by this exotic taste that they called Frenchmen, whom they were peeved at anyway, "frog-eaters" or plain "frogs." By now the tone has changed, thanks partly to the diplomacy of good digestion, and although the legs are not as frequently served in England as in America, one often sees them on restaurant menus.

In the United States frogs' legs are large, and are prepared and eaten rather like chicken legs. I have seen these large legs a few times in Switzerland, but they cannot compare with the delicate morsels found in almost any part of France where there are lively cold streams and lakes, and which are called *cuisses de grenouilles.*

They are perhaps two inches long, and are skinned and prepared in such a way that the two little legs stay fastened together, so that one can eat them with the fingers (always extra-flavorful that way), picking up the two tiny ankle bones with both hands and pulling off in one bite the delicious little thighs. These tidbits are served hot from the butter in which they were quickly browned, with lemon and parsley alongside. Or they can be prepared as in the recipe *(page 112)* for *coquilles St. Jacques à la provençale.* Or, they can be used instead of mussels, I have found, in any of the good French recipes for them: *à la crème, marinière,* and so on.

Plainly almost anything that lives is edible, in France at least. Another delectable proof of this Gallic theory is what happens there to *les goujons.* A *goujon,* across the Channel, is a gudgeon or a smelt. Across the Atlantic it is, quite simply, a minnow.

Dictionaries say that the minnow is a small fresh-water fish used for bait, but on the excellent premise that what is good enough for a salmon or a pike is good enough for a two-legged creature, the French can cook "minnies" as they never seem to be cooked elsewhere—which is to say, to perfection. In many of the regions rushing with brooks and rivers, *goujons* are as much a specialty of the kitchens as *pâté de foie gras* or Bar-le-Duc jelly may be in others, and are cooked simply, rapidly and in gargantuan quantities, so that an order of *petite friture* (a "fry" of tiny fish), heaped on a hot platter and ringed with quarters of lemon, can start off any good Sunday dinner in a country inn, or make the main course of a simple supper, served under the trees beside a lake in twilight, or in front of a good winter fire.

Usually the tiny fish are dipped in a simple batter (of flour and beer in the North), and deep fried while they are kept separated with a fork for the few seconds it takes to brown them. In some provinces they are combined with thin strips of potato, a delicate and subtle variation on the classical fish-and-chips theme of English beach resorts. When at their best, they can be eaten from tip to toe, but longer than three inches they are usually held by the head or tail or both, and only the tender middle is bitten out, with no thought of its almost invisible bones.

Tiny fish are fried and served in this way along the coasts of France as well as in its rivery regions. I have often eaten them in Marseilles, in the best as well as the most modest restaurants: bigger than true whitebait, smaller than sardines, crisp and amusing to nibble from their platters.

One fish as much accepted in England as in France, and for centuries, is the eel, which is not served in America except in certain regions, or in ethnic pockets where it can be caught and prepared in ways brought from more ancient countries. It is hard to find in markets. It is hard to find people who would cook it if they could find it.

In England, on the other hand, it has been savored for centuries in pies, in stews, in soups, and its delicate white flesh has been smoked, roasted, fried, broiled and boiled, but never with the regional variations of the adventuresome French cooks. As in all other true provincial cooking, the recipes for preparing eel are the natural result of what there is to prepare them with. In Provence I have eaten eel stewed with saffron and served with the same *rouille* that often accompanies a *bouillabaisse*, as wildly hot as anything called *salsa fuerte* in Mexico, while in Touraine, far to the north and east, the famous *matelote* of eel or other fresh-water fish is made with prunes in it, and in Burgundy it is dark and fumy with red wine. Perhaps canned eel meat, like snails and frogs' legs, will soon be a popular export for the enterprising housewives of other countries.

Many Americans feel uneasy about foods that have long been savored by people who have more tolerant or venturesome palates. Once a fisherman in northern California told me that over 150 kinds of delicious sea creatures were caught and eaten around Monterey, but perhaps 10 kinds went to market.

"Then who eats. . . ?" I asked.

"*We* do," he said with triumph and amusement, and he took me home for one of the best fish soups that I have ever tasted anywhere. It had tiny squid in it. It had paper-thin slices of abalone tossed in at the last minute. It had a few small crabs, cleaned in their shells, and some thick slices of a kind of bass not popular in the market, and a handful of whole, little, unidentifiable things like whitings. Of course there were also garlic and herbs, and the touch of a cook who respects what Providence has put in his hands.

In France oysters are usually eaten raw, but clams and scallops and mussels find their way into all kinds of delicious cooked hors d'oeuvre, or fish dishes proper for the second course of a long dinner, or as a light main course. Depending upon the regions where they are found, these shellfish may be prepared with butter and cream, as in the north, or with olive oil, garlic, herbs and tomatoes in the south.

A l'armoricaine vs. à l'américaine

An interesting confusion in this regional pattern has been the cause of heated arguments for a long time, over a notable lobster dish. Should it be called *homard à l'armoricaine*, after Armorica, as Brittany once was known, or *à l'américaine*, after America? Some believe it cannot possibly be a true creation of Brittany but is more Provençal in its use of tomatoes, garlic, herbs and oil. Others attribute its alternate name, *à l'américaine*, to the American patrons who first enjoyed it in a Paris restaurant now long gone. Whatever the origin of the name, the resultant dish *(page 116)* can be eaten as happily in Brittany as in Massachusetts, as one of the countless ways to cope with that extraordinary-looking sea beast, the lobster, and its many local representatives, such as the *langouste*.

The spreading knowledge of freezing techniques and of how to use frozen products makes it possible for many Americans to have excellent crab, lobster and scallops at their command, although not as they would be fresh off the boat in Nantes or Kennebunkport, of course. The fresh shellfish are best steamed to be eaten with drawn butter, or boiled to serve cold with a bowl of good mayonnaise. But fresh or frozen, they are amenable to many of the simple methods of French provincial cooking. Scallops can be baked in the Parisian way, or sautéed *à la provençale;* crabs and lobsters and crayfish are treated any way at all, whether simply cooked in a court bouillon and served with mayonnaise, or elaborately combined with one another and complicated with flavors and sauces native to their provinces and their cooks. Shellfish are eminently available in the market, and as eminently desirable on the plate, plain or fancy.

As for the boundless ocean and fresh-water fish like sturgeon, halibut, cod, carp, pike and trout that bless the kitchens of France, it is safe to say that they are usually cooked very simply, with any inventiveness expressed in the sauces that may be a part of the dish or the accompaniment. Depending on the other resources of the region in which they are caught and cooked, the fish will be poached in a court bouillon, or boiled, as in a *bouillabaisse* from Provence or a *cotriade* from Brittany or a *matelote* from Champagne. For special occasions, fish will be served whole, poached and cooled, or stuffed and baked to be eaten hot.

The treatment and mistreatment of fish

In country inns perched along the wild streams of the Jura Mountains, as well as in great restaurants in Paris or Lyon, fish may be served *au bleu:* trout usually, killed and cleaned in an expert flash, then cooked in a court bouillon made with white wine, and served in five or six minutes, with melted butter and small, steamed potatoes. In some regions a sauce made of the broth and eggs is poured over a fish, laid on a bed of little fresh carrots. The fish gazes up with some rebuke for its speedy demise, but one can only hope that it might be pleased, philosophically at least, by ending so deliciously. All fish do, in France. I have eaten some that were better prepared than others. I have eaten some that I thought could have been left more to their own flavors than to the overenthusiasm of their cooks. This is especially so in Provence, where basically delicate seafood like lobster is subjected to unmerciful onslaughts of herbs and sauces. Or the natural flavor is so masked by rich, complicated coatings and the additions of crayfish tails, mussels, and on and on, that the original tastes of the creatures are literally stifled.

Never, anywhere but in my own country, however, have I eaten fish, any and every kind of it, as insulted as it can be by the misuse of the word *meunière,* which calls for the fish to be lightly floured and sautéed in butter. In much the way that a fastidious traveling salesman I knew sniffed out good coffee shops by how they baked apples for his breakfast, so I find myself ordering sole or any other fish listed as *meunière* in America, to see whether the establishment will damn itself or live to see me again. More often than not it does the former, serving fish, from the most delicate to the coarsest, coated in a heavy batter and then fried in deep and happily unanalyzed fat. Of course it makes an appearance with a garnish of tartare sauce in a little paper cup, and several almost unrecognizable vegetables which I did not ask for and which should never show their overboiled faces on the same plate with anything trying even hopelessly to retain its natural fishy flavor. The mistreated flesh within this odious envelope of grease-soaked starches is often quite tender and honest. But, usually I reach it too late.

Instead, I think resolutely of the next time I go back to France; back, quite literally, to any restaurant in France which I have ever had the money to set foot in, from the simplest student hostel to the most elegant place in Paris. I will order, to soothe my outraged inner palate, *sole meunière*.

I will wait for it without a qualm. In a simple restaurant I will bone it myself: I miss that small exercise of my deftness in a larger place where the waiter likes to exercise his own. The fish will be hanging its crisp brown tail over the side of the plate, quite often. (I eat the tail too, the last nutty mouthful.) It will be innocent of anything but the fresh butter it was quickly fried in, and unlike a properly prepared trout it will be headless. What butter is left in the pan will be poured over it, golden-dark and delicately flavored, unchallenged by anything like herbs, or slivered almonds, or even a rinsing of white wine.

There will be a cut lemon at hand. The two sections along the back will fall cleanly before my fish-knife, and the browned sidebones, so dainty, will be pulled ruthlessly away, although I always regret not being able to eat them too. And once I have finished topside, I can flip out the spine of the dainty creature and tackle the other half, still hot and somewhat more buttery.

It will happily erase from memory all meaner *soles meunière*.

Sea urchins, those porcupines of the ocean, so dreaded by barefooted bathers, are offered as food delicacies along with pink starfish from the stern of this fisherman's boat at a dock in Marseilles. The sea urchins' coral-tinted flesh is scooped out with a teaspoon and eaten raw, flavored with a few drops of lemon juice.

This boat serves as a floating display case for a catch of eels, red mullet and sardines sold by the fishermen's wives.

The Many-hued Markets of Marseilles' Waterfront

As France's biggest city next to Paris and the oldest next to none, Marseilles makes its living as a seaport, shipping everything from oil and soap to semolina flour. It makes a contribution to gastronomy through its fishing fleet. Every morning except Sundays, small craft from the fishing grounds crowd into the waterfront as they have for centuries, bearing cargoes that are sold right off the boats or in nearby fish markets, soon to land on tens of thousands of French dinner tables. Marseilles' port district is one of the world's most colorful marketplaces, where delicate pink shrimp nestle alongside blue mussels, white clams, red mullet, inkfish—whatever the sea has yielded, a vast *bouillabaisse* in the raw.

Marseilles businessmen in their dark city suits bargain with fishermen for mullet that were caught the night before.

At an outdoor shop near the waterfront, trays are filled with shellfish ready to be eaten as is, with a squirt of lemon.

Bar Poché au Beurre Blanc
POACHED BASS WITH WHITE BUTTER SAUCE

In a 6- to 8-quart enameled or stainless-steel pot or soup kettle, bring all the ingredients for the court bouillon to a boil over high heat. Partially cover the pot, reduce the heat and simmer for 30 minutes. Strain through a large, fine sieve into a fish poacher or a large, deep roasting pan which has a cover, and set aside to cool.

When the court bouillon is lukewarm, wash the fish inside and out under cold running water. Without drying it, wrap the fish in a long, double-thick piece of damp, washed cheesecloth, leaving at least 6 inches of cloth at each end to serve as handles for lifting the fish in and out of the pan. Twist the ends of the cloth and tie them with string, then place the fish on the rack of the poacher or roasting pan and lower the rack into the court bouillon. (If you are using a roasting pan, tie the ends of the cheesecloth to the handles of the pan.) The court bouillon should cover the fish by 1½ to 2 inches; add water if necessary.

Cover, and bring to a slow simmer over moderate heat; immediately reduce the heat and cook barely at a simmer for 15 minutes. Remove the pan from the heat and leave the fish in it for another 15 minutes. Then, using the ends of cheesecloth as handles, lift the fish from the pan and lay it on a large cutting board or platter. Open the cheesecloth and skin the fish with a small, sharp knife by making a cut in the skin at the base of the tail and gently pulling off the skin in strips from tail to gill. Holding both ends of the cheesecloth, carefully lift the fish and turn it over onto a heated serving platter. Peel off the skin on the upturned side. Garnish the fish with sprigs of fresh parsley and cover the platter loosely to keep the fish warm. (Court bouillon can be refrigerated or frozen and used again as stock.)

BEURRE BLANC: In a 1½- to 2-quart enameled saucepan, bring the vinegar, wine, shallots, salt and pepper to a boil over high heat and cook uncovered, stirring occasionally, until the liquid is reduced to about 1 tablespoon—just a film on the bottom of the pan. Remove the pan from the heat and with a wire whisk immediately stir in 3 tablespoons of chilled butter, beating constantly until the liquid completely absorbs the butter.

Return the pan to the lowest possible heat and add the rest of the chilled butter 1 piece at a time, whisking constantly; and making sure that each piece is absorbed before adding the next. The finished sauce will be a thick, ivory-colored cream. Serve it at once in a warm, not hot, sauceboat.

To de-bone the fish for serving, divide the top layer into individual portions with a fish server without cutting through the spine. Leave the head and tail intact. Lift the portions with the fish server and a fork and arrange them on another platter. Then gently lift out the backbone in one piece, discard it and divide the bottom layer of fish into individual portions.

ALTERNATIVE: To serve poached bass cold, cook and skin it as described above. Cover the fish with plastic wrap or with aluminum foil and refrigerate it until it is thoroughly chilled. Serve the fish with *mayonnaise aux fines herbes (page 74),* and garnish it with sprigs of fresh herbs, whole cherry tomatoes and lemon slices.

To serve 6

COURT BOUILLON
2 quarts water
2 cups dry white wine
¼ cup wine vinegar
3 onions, thickly sliced
2 carrots, cut in 1-inch chunks
4 celery stalks with leaves, cut in 1-inch chunks
4 parsley sprigs
2 bay leaves
1 teaspoon finely cut fresh tarragon or ½ teaspoon dried tarragon
1 teaspoon finely cut fresh thyme or ½ teaspoon dried thyme
2 tablespoons salt
10 peppercorns

FISH
A 3- to 3½-pound whole striped bass, cleaned and scaled, but with head and tail left on (or substitute such firm, white-meat fish as red snapper, haddock, cod, pollack, rockfish, whitefish or lake trout)
Fresh parsley sprigs

BEURRE BLANC
⅓ cup white-wine vinegar
⅓ cup dry white wine
2 tablespoons finely chopped shallots or scallions
½ teaspoon salt
⅛ teaspoon white pepper
½ pound butter, cut into 16 tablespoon-sized pieces and thoroughly chilled

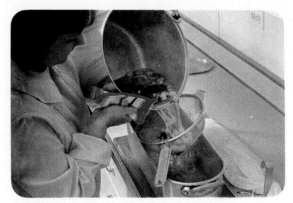

A Basic Technique: Poaching a Bass

1. Combine the ingredients for a rich court bouillon (*see recipe on preceding page*) in a pot, bring to a boil and simmer uncovered for about 30 minutes.

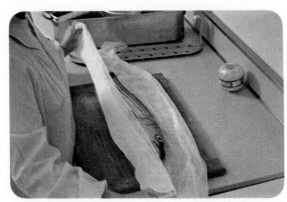

2. Strain through a fine sieve into a fish poacher and let the broth cool until lukewarm. A deep roasting pan with a cover will do if you don't have a fish poacher.

3. Press down hard on the vegetables with the back of a spoon so as to extract every bit of their flavor into the court bouillon before discarding them.

4. After washing the bass under cold water, wrap it loosely in a double layer of damp cheesecloth and tie the ends of the cloth to secure the wrapping.

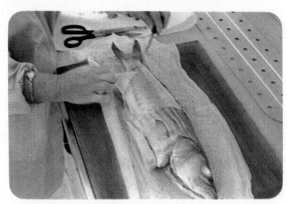

5. Lay the fish on the tray of the poacher and lower into the liquid. If using a roaster, tie the ends of the cloth to the pan handles to suspend the fish in the pan.

6. To skin the fish after poaching, slit it at the base of the tail and cut along the sides. Lift the skin with the tip of a sharp knife and gently peel it away.

7. Cold poached bass is brought to the table garnished with lemon slices, sprigs of watercress, cucumber slices and cherry tomatoes.

8. In serving the fish, cut the portions down to the backbone, but do not sever the backbone.

9. Lift the individual portions from the top layer of the fish with a flat fish knife or with a spatula.

10. After the top layer has been served, the backbone and ribs can be loosened and removed in one piece.

107

To serve 6 to 8

SPINACH STUFFING
4 tablespoons butter
3 tablespoons finely chopped shallots
    or scallions
½ cup finely chopped, cooked fresh
    spinach, squeezed dry and firmly
    packed (about ½ pound), or 1
    ten-ounce package frozen,
    chopped spinach, defrosted and
    squeezed completely dry
2½ cups fresh white bread crumbs
    made in the blender from home-
    made-type bread (about 6 slices)
2 to 4 tablespoons heavy cream
¼ teaspoon lemon juice
½ teaspoon salt
Freshly ground black pepper

FISH
A 4- to 5-pound whole red snapper,
    cleaned and scaled, with the
    backbone removed but the head
    and tail left on (or pollack, lake
    trout, cod, rockfish, whitefish,
    salmon or mackerel)
6 tablespoons melted butter
1 cup dry white wine
1 tablespoon soft butter
Watercress sprigs, decoratively cut
    lemons

To serve 4

GARLIC AND HERB BUTTER
8 tablespoons soft butter (one
    quarter-pound stick)
1 tablespoon finely chopped shallots
    or scallions
1 teaspoon finely chopped garlic
2 tablespoons finely chopped fresh
    parsley
Salt
Freshly ground black pepper

FISH
4 salmon steaks, cut 1-inch thick and
    each weighing about ¾ pound
¼ cup butter, melted
Salt
Freshly ground black pepper
2 lemons, cut in quarters or slices

Poisson Farci à la Florentine
BAKED FISH WITH SPINACH STUFFING

SPINACH STUFFING: Using a heavy 6- to 8-inch stainless-steel or enameled skillet, melt 4 tablespoons of butter over moderate heat and in it cook the shallots for 2 minutes, or until they are soft but not brown. Add the spinach and cook over high heat, stirring constantly, for 2 or 3 minutes to evaporate most of the moisture. Transfer to a large mixing bowl. Add the bread crumbs, cream, lemon juice, salt and a few grindings of pepper, and gently toss them all together. Season with more lemon juice, salt or pepper if needed.

BAKING THE FISH: Preheat the oven to 400°. Wash the fish inside and out under running water, and dry it thoroughly with paper towels. Fill the fish with the stuffing, close the opening with small skewers, and crisscross kitchen string as you would lace a turkey. Brush 2 tablespoons of melted butter on the bottom of a shallow baking-and-serving dish large enough to hold the fish. (If you prefer to serve the fish from a platter, line the dish with a long piece of foil oiled or buttered on both sides to make it easy to handle later.) Place the fish in the dish, brush the top with another 2 tablespoons of melted butter, and salt and pepper it. Combine the rest of the melted butter with the wine and pour it around the fish. Bring to a simmer on top of the stove, then bake uncovered on the middle shelf of the oven, basting the fish every 5 to 7 minutes with the juices that will accumulate in the pan. If the wine evaporates, add up to ¾ cup more as needed.

In 40 to 50 minutes the fish should be just firm when pressed lightly with a finger. Remove the pan from the oven and, if the fish will be served from the baking dish, use a bulb baster to transfer the juices to a small pan. If the fish will be served from a platter, carefully lift the foil and fish from the baking dish, using the long ends of foil as handles. Gently slide the fish from the foil to the platter. Then pour the juices into a small pan.

Boil the juices down over high heat until they are syrupy. Remove from the heat, stir in 1 tablespoon of soft butter, and pour the sauce over the fish. Serve the fish alone or with *beurre blanc (page 105)* or hollandaise sauce *(page 74)*. Garnish it with watercress and decoratively cut lemons.

Darnes de Saumon Grillées au Beurre d'Escargots
BROILED SALMON STEAKS WITH GARLIC AND HERB BUTTER

GARLIC AND HERB BUTTER: Cream the soft butter by beating it against the side of a small bowl with a wooden spoon until it is fluffy. Beat in the shallots, garlic, parsley, salt to taste and a few grindings of pepper.

SALMON STEAKS: Preheat the broiler to very hot for 15 minutes. Dry the salmon thoroughly with paper towels. With a pastry brush, spread both sides of each steak with melted butter. Arrange the steaks on the rack of the broiling pan, and broil them with the top surface of the steaks 3 to 4 inches from the heat for 3 minutes on each side. Then baste them with any remaining melted butter or with the butter from the bottom of the broiling pan. Salt and pepper them and broil another 3 minutes. Then turn them over, baste again, and broil, basting once, for 5 to 8 minutes more, or until firm to the touch. With a spatula, transfer the steaks to a heated serving platter and garnish with lemon quarters or slices. Spread the garlic and herb butter over the steaks, or serve it separately in a sauceboat.

108

 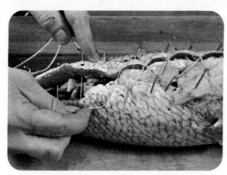 

1. Since the stuffing swells in baking, do not stuff the fish tightly.

2. Secure the cavity with roasting pins and lace it firmly with string.

3. After baking, pull the pins out gently to remove the lacing.

A whole fish, such as this red snapper with spinach stuffing, makes an impressive dish garnished with lemon halves and parsley sprigs.

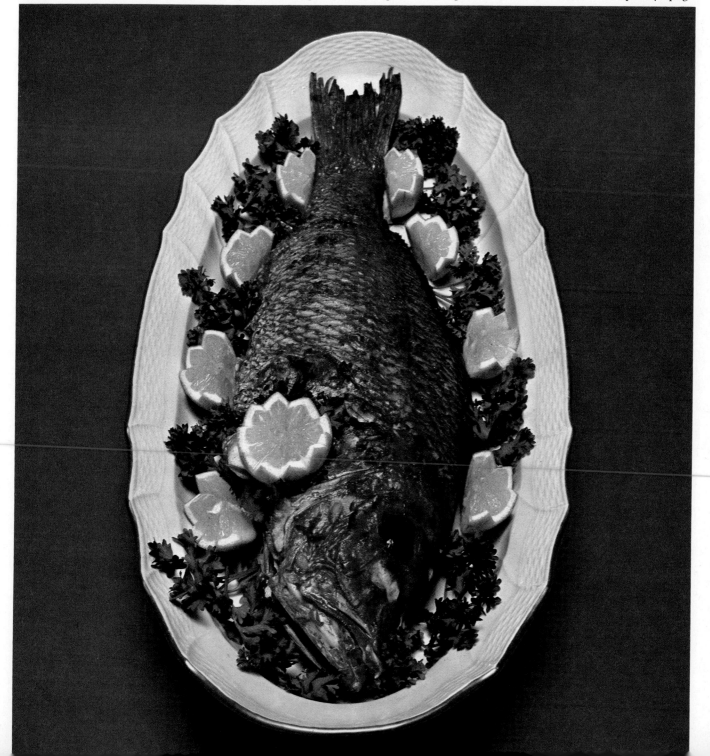

To serve 6 to 8

¾ pound fresh mushrooms
4 tablespoons butter
2 tablespoons vegetable oil
1 tablespoon finely chopped shallots
    or scallions
1 teaspoon lemon juice
3 pounds gray, lemon, or petrale sole
    or flounder fillets, skinned and cut
    into serving pieces all of the same
    size
Salt
Freshly ground black pepper
¾ cup dry white wine
Water

Filets de Soles Bonne Femme
FILLETS OF SOLE WITH MUSHROOM AND WINE SAUCE

Preheat the oven to 350°. Remove the caps from 12 to 16 of the mushrooms and slice all the stems and the rest of the caps. In a 6- to 8-inch enameled or stainless-steel skillet, melt 2 tablespoons of the butter with 1 tablespoon of the oil over moderate heat. Toss the whole mushroom caps in the hot fat for 1 or 2 minutes or until lightly browned, then set them aside in the skillet. In an 8- to 10-inch enameled or stainless-steel skillet, melt 2 tablespoons butter with 1 tablespoon oil over moderate heat. Add the sliced mushrooms and cook them, stirring constantly, for 2 minutes. Stir in the shallots, and cook for 1 minute. Then stir in the lemon juice.

Butter a shallow flameproof baking-and-serving dish large enough to hold the fillets in one layer. Lay the fillets in it side by side, folding them in half if they are less than ¼ inch thick. Salt and pepper the fillets and spread with the mushroom-shallot mixture. Pour in the wine and enough water to come barely to the top of the fish. Bring to a slow simmer on top of the stove, cover with buttered wax paper, and then cook on the middle shelf of the oven for 8 to 10 minutes or until the fillets are just firm to the touch. Remove from the oven and discard the wax paper. With a bulb baster,

Draw off the liquid formed during poaching fillets of sole, using a bulb baster. Strain the broth through a sieve into a saucepan. The liquid, when reduced, becomes the base for *sauce crème*.

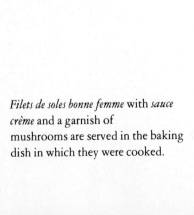

Filets de soles bonne femme with *sauce crème* and a garnish of mushrooms are served in the baking dish in which they were cooked.

draw up all the liquid from the dish and strain it into a 1½- to 2-quart saucepan. Set the baking dish aside, lightly covered to keep the fish warm. Boil the poaching liquid over high heat until it has reduced to 1 cup.

SAUCE CRÈME: In a heavy 2- to 3-quart saucepan, melt 4 tablespoons of butter over moderate heat. When the foam subsides, remove from the heat and stir in the flour. Return to low heat and cook, stirring, for a minute or two. Remove from the heat and slowly add the reduced poaching liquid, whisking constantly. Then return to high heat and cook, stirring with a whisk, until the sauce comes to a boil. It will be very thick. Whisk in ½ cup of cream and bring to a simmer again, stirring. Then thin it gradually with more cream added by spoonfuls until the sauce coats the spoon with a creamy layer. Season with lemon juice, salt and white pepper.

Just before serving, reheat the mushroom caps. Draw off with a bulb baster any juices which have accumulated in the baking dish. Remove the sauce from the heat and, by tablespoons, beat in as much of the soft butter as you wish. Spoon the sauce over the fish and arrange the mushroom caps on top. Serve at once.

SAUCE CRÈME
4 tablespoons butter
4 tablespoons flour
⅔ to ¾ cup heavy cream
1 tablespoon lemon juice
1 teaspoon salt
White pepper
4 to 8 tablespoons soft butter

Coquilles Saint-Jacques à la Parisienne
SCALLOPS WITH MUSHROOMS IN WHITE WINE SAUCE

To serve 6

1½ cups thoroughly degreased
   fresh or canned chicken
   stock, or water
1½ cups dry white wine
3 sliced shallots or scallions
3 celery tops with leaves, cut in
   2-inch pieces
4 parsley sprigs
1 bay leaf
10 whole peppercorns
2 pounds whole bay scallops, or sea
   scallops cut into ½-inch slices
¾ pound fresh mushrooms, sliced

SAUCE PARISIENNE
4 tablespoons butter
5 tablespoons flour
¾ cup milk
2 egg yolks
¼ to ½ cup heavy cream
A few drops of lemon juice
1 teaspoon salt
White pepper
¼ cup grated imported Swiss cheese

Preheat the oven to 375°. In a heavy 3- to 4-quart saucepan, bring the stock, wine, shallots, celery, parsley, bay leaf and peppercorns to a boil over high heat. Reduce the heat, and simmer uncovered for 20 minutes. Strain this court bouillon through a sieve into a 10- to 12-inch enameled or stainless-steel skillet. Add the scallops and mushrooms, cover and simmer for 5 minutes. Transfer the scallops and mushrooms to a large mixing bowl. Quickly boil the remaining court bouillon down to 1 cup.

SAUCE PARISIENNE: In a 2- to 3-quart enameled or stainless-steel saucepan, melt 4 tablespoons of butter over moderate heat. When the foam subsides, lift the pan from the heat and stir in the flour. Return to low heat and cook, stirring constantly, for a minute or two. Do not let this *roux* brown. Remove the pan from the heat and slowly pour in the reduced poaching liquid and the milk, whisking constantly. Then return to high heat and cook, stirring the sauce with a whisk. When it thickens and comes to a boil, reduce the heat and let it simmer slowly for 1 minute. Mix the egg yolks and ¼ cup cream together in a small bowl, and stir into it 2 tablespoons of the hot sauce. Add 2 more tablespoons of sauce, then whisk the now-heated egg-yolk-and-cream mixture back into the remaining sauce in the pan. Over moderate heat bring the sauce to a boil, stirring constantly, and boil for 30 seconds. Remove from heat and season with lemon juice, salt and pepper. The sauce should coat a spoon fairly thickly; if it is too thick, thin it with more cream.

With a bulb baster, draw up and discard any juices that may have accumulated under the scallops and mushrooms. Then pour in about ⅔ of the *sauce parisienne* and stir together gently. Butter 6 scallop shells set on a baking sheet or in a broiler pan, or 6 shallow 4-inch baking dishes, and spoon the scallop mixture into them. Mask with the remaining sauce and sprinkle with cheese. Bake the scallops in the top third of the oven for 10 to 15 minutes or until the sauce begins to bubble, then slide them under a hot broiler for 30 seconds to brown the tops if desired. Serve at once.

Coquilles Saint-Jacques à la Provençale
SCALLOPS SAUTÉED WITH GARLIC BUTTER SAUCE

To serve 4

2 pounds whole bay scallops, or sea
   scallops cut into ¼-inch slices
Salt
White pepper
Flour
2 tablespoons butter
3 tablespoons vegetable oil

GARLIC BUTTER
8 tablespoons unsalted, or "sweet,"
   butter (1 quarter-pound stick)
1 teaspoon finely chopped garlic
2 tablespoons finely chopped fresh
   parsley
1 lemon, quartered

Wash the scallops in cold water and dry them with paper towels. Season them with salt and pepper; then dip them in flour and shake them in a sieve or colander to remove all but a light dusting of flour. In a 10- to 12-inch enameled or stainless-steel skillet, melt 2 tablespoons of butter with the oil over moderate heat. When the foam subsides, sauté the scallops in two batches so they are not crowded in the pan, shaking the skillet and stirring the scallops until they are lightly browned. With a slotted spoon or spatula, transfer the scallops to a heated platter.

GARLIC BUTTER: In a 1½- to 2-quart saucepan, clarify 8 tablespoons of butter by melting it slowly, skimming off the foam. Spoon the clear butter on top into a 6- to 8-inch skillet and discard the milky solids at the bottom of the pan. Heat the butter until it sizzles, but do not let it brown. Remove it from the heat and quickly stir in the garlic. Pour the garlic butter over the scallops and serve at once, garnished with parsley and lemon quarters.

Scallops *à la parisienne* are presented with each individual portion set in a shell. The dish is accompanied by a dry white wine.

Cook vs. Lobster: A Winning Technique

Dissecting and cleaning a lobster is not a difficult job once you have learned the technique. But for *homard à l'américaine (page 116)* or any lobster dish, the taste is best if the lobster is freshly killed —by you, if necessary. Just remember that there is a first time for everything. Three tips that will make the task easier: use a towel to get a better grip, be sure the claws are pegged when you buy the live lobster, and pierce the shell by using a hammer to tap the knife. The operation only seems formidable; it can be mastered in your own kitchen by following these step-by-step photographs.

1 With a heavy knife, cut through the lobster behind the head. This severs the spinal cord and kills the lobster.

4 The lobster's intestinal tract should be removed, though it is not harmful if eaten.

5 Wrench or cut the claws from the body of the lobster: a towel helps you grip the body firmly.

8 Cut the body section in half lengthwise, again using a hammer if more force is needed.

9 Remove and discard the gelatinous sac in the head. It is the one inedible part of the lobster.

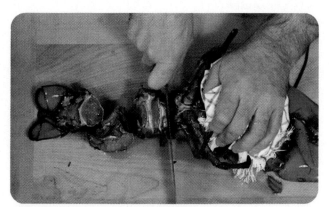

2 Cut across the tail at the natural ridges to make wedges. These are called medallions. Or . . .

3 . . . An alternate method to (2) is to cut the tail lengthwise down the center into two halves.

6 Crack the flat underside of each large claw with a sharp blow to make it easier to extract the meat.

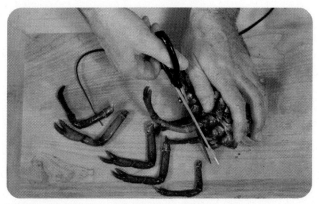

7 Separate the joints or feelers from the body. Reserve them to garnish the finished dish if you wish.

10 Scoop out and save two delicacies—the brownish-green tomalley and the black coral, if there is any.

11 This arrangement of the lobster parts shows what you end up with, ready for cooking (see next page).

To serve 4 to 6

8 tablespoons butter (1 quarter-pound
    stick)
¼ cup finely chopped carrots
½ cup finely chopped onions
2 tablespoons finely chopped fresh
    parsley
1 teaspoon dried thyme
1 bay leaf
2 live lobsters, each 2 to 2½ pounds,
    cut into serving pieces
2 teaspoons salt
6 tablespoons olive or vegetable oil
⅓ cup Cognac
5 large tomatoes, peeled, seeded and
    coarsely chopped (about 3 cups)
¼ cup finely chopped shallots or
    scallions
1 cup dry white wine
1 cup chicken stock, fresh or canned
1 tablespoon tomato paste
1 teaspoon bottled meat extract
1 tablespoon flour
½ teaspoon lemon juice
1 tablespoon finely cut fresh tarragon
    or 1 teaspoon dried tarragon,
    crumbled
Salt
Freshly ground black pepper

Homard à l'Américaine

LOBSTER SIMMERED WITH WINE, TOMATOES AND HERBS

In a heavy 3- to 4-quart flameproof casserole, melt 4 tablespoons of the butter over moderate heat. When the foam subsides, stir in the carrots and onions, and cook, stirring, for 5 to 8 minutes, or until they are soft but not brown. Remove from the heat, stir in 1 tablespoon of the parsley, the thyme and bay leaf.

Remove and discard the gelatinous sac near the head of each lobster, if the fish dealer did not. Scoop out the greenish-brown tomalley (or liver) and set aside. If there is black roe (or coral) save it. Sprinkle the lobster with 2 teaspoons salt. Then heat the oil almost to the smoking point in a heavy 10- to 12-inch skillet, and sauté the lobster over high heat, turning frequently, for 4 or 5 minutes, or until the shells are red.

Remove all but a film of oil from the skillet and, off the heat, flame the lobster with Cognac. Warm the Cognac in a small saucepan over low heat, ignite it with a match, and pour it flaming over the lobster a little at a time. Shake the skillet gently until the flame dies. Using tongs, transfer the lobster pieces to the casserole. Pour the juices from the skillet over them, and stir in the tomatoes and shallots.

In the same skillet, combine the wine, stock, tomato paste and meat extract. Bring this sauce to a boil, stirring constantly; boil for 2 minutes, then pour it over the lobster. Stir the contents of the casserole together until all the lobster pieces are coated with the sauce. Bring to a boil over high heat; immediately reduce the heat, cover the casserole tightly, and simmer for 30 minutes, basting 2 or 3 times with the juices.

Meanwhile cream the remaining 4 tablespoons of butter by beating it vigorously against the sides of a small bowl with a wooden spoon until it is fluffy. Beat in the coral, tomalley, flour, lemon juice, tarragon, 1 tablespoon of parsley and a little salt and pepper. Press through a sieve and set aside. When the lobster is done, arrange the pieces on a large, heated platter and cover loosely to keep the lobster warm, or set the platter in a 250° oven.

Strain the entire contents of the casserole through a fine sieve into a 2- to 3-quart saucepan, pressing down on the vegetables with a spoon before discarding them. Boil the juices over high heat until reduced by about ½. Turn the heat to low and beat in the creamed butter mixture, 1 tablespoon at a time. Cook the sauce over low heat for 5 minutes; do not let it boil. Taste for seasoning. To serve, pour the sauce over the lobster.

CUTTING THE LOBSTERS: If the fish dealer does not cut up the lobsters, make sure the claws are pegged and do the cutting yourself. Wash the lobsters in cold water and drain them. Then lay one lobster at a time on its underbelly on a chopping board and, with a towel wrapped around one hand for protection, grasp the lobster firmly. With a large, heavy, sharp knife, cut through the lobster behind the head; this severs the spinal cord and kills the lobster. Slice the tail into 4 or 5 crosswise pieces or cut it lengthwise in half. (This and all the other cutting steps are easier if you put the knife into position and hit the back of it sharply with a hammer.) Then cut the claws from the lobster and separate the joints from the claws. Crack the flat side of each large claw. Remove the feelers, then cut the body section in half lengthwise. Don't forget to remove and discard the gelatinous sac near the head, but scoop out and save the tomalley and the coral.

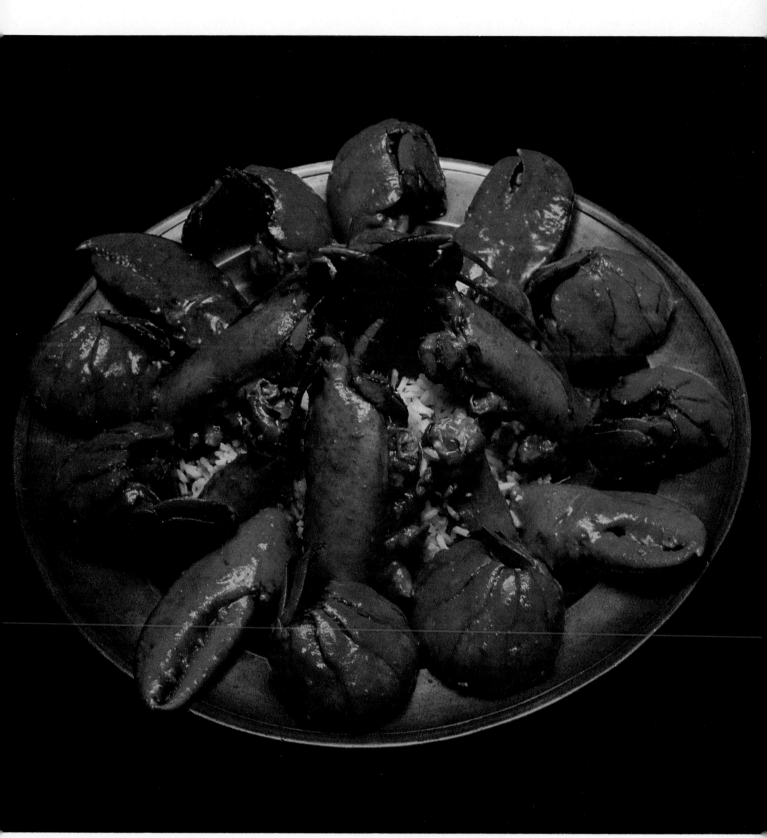

The lobster parts may be served on a mound of
rice. Pour the sauce over it and, for a
different color effect, garnish with chopped parsley.

VIII

Poultry: Those Foolproof Fowl

Within the memory of many Americans, a Presidential campaign was distinguished by the promise that votes cast for one of the parties would put a chicken in every pot in the country.

This strategic appeal to man's love of good food was not original in 1928. Somewhat the same idea was expressed several hundred years before in a more warmhearted way by a French king, Henry IV of Navarre. After eating a *poule-au-pot* he said fervently that he wished every subject in his realm might do the same, every Sunday of the year. (A kind heart came with the coronet in his case. But then, he did not have to count votes every four years, or phrase personal wishes as political promises.)

The royal dish is made today exactly as it was then, and is as much a part of provincial cooking throughout France as is the chicken that goes into it: a fine, plump hen, stuffed with fresh pork sausage and herbs, poached with vegetables—regally simple.

In its delicately flavored richness the *poule-au-pot* is a far cry from the stewed chicken that our grandmothers learned to make from their Victorian manuals. Those were days of stern disregard of French fripperies and non-sense, and a hen plainly past her prime was considered the only requisite to the dish. Fortunately for France, although Queen Victoria influenced the politics and even the hair styles across the Channel, her impact upon French cooking was practically nil.

In France the *poule-au-pot*, whether stuffed or not, simmers very gently in ample water. Then the bird is removed to a platter with the vegetables and kept hot, while the broth is served to the diners. The chicken is then

In the tiny Basque village of Peyrehorade, Wednesdays are market days, and the fowl and game are sold alive. At this shopper's feet are a quintet of Muscovy drakes *(left)* and a basket of rabbits—their legs tied so they won't get away.

carved and eaten with any number of sauces, often made with butter and cream *à la normande,* or with a base consisting of some of the broth and eggs.

Other versions of King Henry's dish are legion, generally varying in accordance with the province they spring from. But they always call for a fine, plump hen, not a stringy dowager that is best passed over. To average American housewives, whose repertoire of cooked chicken is limited to roasted, Southern fried or barbecued, the lists of French ways to treat this common barnyard fowl may seem almost stupefying. Sautéing, or pan-frying, is surely one of the simplest ways. However, once chicken is prepared *à la bordelaise (page 123),* interestingly accompanied by artichoke hearts, or garnished with eggplant or olives, or any of a hundred other things—the delicious but potentially monotonous Sunday fried chicken in its crisp coating of batter will become simply part of the repertory instead of "the only way to do it."

And there are ways housewives have evolved, from Picardy to Perpignan, to make fricassees: unctuous white ones, rich with cream, savorous with little mushrooms and onions; heady dark ones, firm with the flavors of wine and herbs. Best of all, perhaps, are the chickens simply roasted, always with good butter, sometimes deliciously flavored with fresh tarragon in the summer, or a little lemon juice and a dusting of parsley. They are served, tender and succulent and crackly skinned, with nothing but the juices they have made. They are exactly what Escoffier said everything should be: "Simple."

Of course all these methods will work, with a modicum of common sense,

To produce the most savory possible *poule-au-pot,* the French housewife —like this Basquaise—favors starting with an unquestionably fresh chicken, still feathered and squawking.

on any domesticated fowl. A duck or goose, much fatter than a chicken, must have its additional richness coped with, as is clear in any recipe for these birds (such as the one for braised duck with turnips, on page 126).

Wild birds, because of their diet and the strenuous lives they lead, are tougher, dryer and more flavorsome than most tame ones, and they must be cooked somewhat differently, in a fashion likely to involve slow simmerings rather than roastings. They seem to survive home-freezing better than the fatter barnyard poultry, which is convenient for housewives with hunters in the family. But in France most game that is not eaten almost at once is made into pâtés and *terrines,* to be savored later.

Tender squabs and even somewhat older pigeons are treated like young pullets and fryers and are roasted with butter. Cockerels are treated with the dignity of full-fledged roosters and are cooked in hearty wine sauces, as are the more plentiful hens, which function as male impersonators in many an otherwise honest *coq au vin.* In the same general pattern, young turkeys, which are increasingly common today in France (their popularity died out after an almost hysterical passion for them that swept the country in the 18th Century), are cooked more like chickens, depending upon their age and apparent succulence.

There are regions in France like Bresse where chickens of a certain breed seem to attain a special delicacy. The recipes adapted to them bring out all this extra-ness and will help most fowl with less distinguished origins. In America, many cooks still feel that the best way to get a good chicken is to

In bigger cities, fowl is more likely to be sold oven-dressed than in full plumage. Here in a Paris shop are counters of *première qualité* chickens—some already roasted.

buy it from a local grower who has proved his knowledge in feeding and caring for his hens. Many equally good but somewhat desperate cooks believe that the only way to buy decent chicken from supermarkets, where most of the so-called fresh birds are packed in chopped ice for countless hours and days, is to buy frozen whole birds and defrost them. At least, the birds have not lost half their precious vapors and flavors, lying in hundreds of pieces in the frigid air of a market counter.

And on this point, any French housewife will agree—cut-up chicken, from no matter how good a market, cannot possibly have the flavor of a whole fowl: some of its juices will be lost. If it is to be sautéed in sections, it should be cut up by the cook, and none other.

Whole or in pieces, young or even "of a certain age," a chicken will be a reward if it is cooked the way French provincial housewives do it, simply and with loving respect.

CHAPTER VIII RECIPES

Poulet Rôti
ROAST CHICKEN

To serve 4

A 3½- to 4-pound roasting chicken
2 tablespoons soft butter
½ teaspoon lemon juice
Salt
Freshly ground black pepper
3 tablespoons melted butter
1 tablespoon vegetable oil
1 onion, sliced
1 carrot, cut in ½-inch chunks
1 celery stalk, cut in ½-inch chunks
1 cup chicken stock, fresh or canned

Preheat the oven to 450°. Wash the chicken quickly under cold running water and dry it thoroughly inside and out with paper towels. Cream the soft butter, beating it vigorously against the side of a bowl with a wooden spoon until it is fluffy. Beat in the lemon juice, ¼ teaspoon salt and a few grindings of pepper. Spread the seasoned butter inside the chicken. Truss the chicken with kitchen string. Combine the melted butter and oil and brush about half of it over the outside of the chicken.

Place the chicken on its side on a rack in a shallow roasting pan just large enough to hold it comfortably—about 9 by 12 inches—and place on the middle shelf of the oven. After 10 minutes, turn the chicken onto its other side. Brush with butter and oil and roast for another 10 minutes. Reduce the oven heat to 350°. Turn the chicken on its back, brush it with butter and oil and salt it lightly. Spread the vegetables in the bottom of the pan. Roast the chicken, basting it every 10 minutes with butter and oil while they last, then use a bulb baster or spoon to baste it with pan juices. After 60 minutes, test the chicken for doneness by lifting it with a wooden spoon inserted in the tail opening. When the juices that run out are yellow, it is done. If they are pink, cook a few minutes longer. Transfer the bird to a carving board, cut off the trussing strings, and let it rest for 5 minutes or so before serving.

Meanwhile, make the sauce. Stir the chicken stock into the roasting pan and bring to a boil over high heat, stirring and scraping in any browned bits clinging to the pan. Boil briskly for 2 or 3 minutes until the sauce has the desired intensity of flavor. Strain through a sieve, pressing the vegetables with the back of a spoon before discarding them. Skim off as much surface fat as possible, and taste for seasoning. The chicken may be carved in the kitchen or at the table. Serve the sauce separately.

Poulet Sauté à la Bordelaise
SAUTÉED CHICKEN WITH SHALLOTS AND ARTICHOKE HEARTS

To serve 4

A 2½- to 3-pound frying chicken, cut up
6 tablespoons butter
2 tablespoons vegetable oil
16 to 24 large whole peeled shallots,
    or 16 one-inch peeled white onions
Salt
Freshly ground black pepper
2 bay leaves
1 teaspoon lemon juice
1 nine-ounce package frozen
    artichoke hearts, defrosted and
    drained
½ cup chicken stock, fresh or canned

Wash the chicken quickly under cold running water and dry the pieces thoroughly with paper towels; if they are damp, they won't brown well. In a heavy 10- to 12-inch enameled or stainless-steel skillet or sauté pan, melt 4 tablespoons of the butter and the 2 tablespoons of oil over moderately high heat. When the foam begins to subside, brown the chicken a few pieces at a time, starting them skin side down and turning them with tongs. As the pieces become a rich golden brown, remove them to a plate.

When all the chicken is browned, add the shallots or onions to the skillet and cook them, shaking the pan to color them lightly and as evenly as possible. Pour off all but a thin film of fat and return the chicken to the skillet. Season with salt and pepper, lay the bay leaves on top and cover the pan. Cook over high heat until the fat splutters. At once reduce the heat and cook the chicken slowly, using a bulb baster or spoon to baste it with pan juices every 7 or 8 minutes.

Meanwhile, melt the remaining 2 tablespoons of butter in an 8- to 10-inch enameled or stainless-steel skillet. When the foam subsides, stir in the lemon juice. Add the artichoke hearts and toss them in the lemon butter until they glisten. Season them with salt, cover the skillet, and cook over low heat for 10 to 15 minutes or until the artichoke hearts are tender.

After the chicken has cooked for about 30 minutes it should be done, and its juices will run yellow when a thigh is pierced with the tip of a sharp knife. Remove the chicken from the skillet and arrange the pieces attractively on a large heated platter with the shallots or white onions and the artichoke hearts around them. Discard the bay leaves.

Pour the chicken stock into the juices remaining in the skillet and bring to a boil over high heat, scraping in any browned bits clinging to the bottom and sides of the pan. Boil for 2 or 3 minutes until the sauce is reduced to about ⅓ cup. Pour it over the chicken and serve at once.

ALTERNATIVE: If you like, you may cook the artichoke hearts with the chicken. In that case, omit the 2 tablespoons of butter and the lemon juice from the recipe. Add the artichoke hearts to the chicken after it has cooked with the shallots for 15 minutes and baste them well with the pan juices. Cover and cook, basting every 7 or 8 minutes, for 15 minutes longer, or until the chicken is done and the artichoke hearts are tender.

First the chicken is browned, starting each piece skin side down.

Next shallots are swirled in the same skillet until they are golden.

Then the chicken and shallots are combined, covered and simmered.

The sautéed chicken—cooked in butter and oil and its own juices—comes to the table garnished with the whole shallots and

halved artichoke hearts. The flavors of the chicken and vegetables complement each other in this *poulet sauté à la bordelaise*.

To serve 4

A 5-pound duck
1 teaspoon salt
2 tablespoons vegetable oil
1 tablespoon butter
1 onion, thinly sliced
1 carrot, thinly sliced
Salt
Freshly ground black pepper
¼ teaspoon dried thyme, crumbled
Bouquet garni made of 4 parsley
    sprigs and 1 bay leaf, tied together
1½ pounds peeled white turnips, cut
    in quarters or 2-inch-long olive
    shapes
¾ cup boiling brown duck stock
    (recipe below) or fresh or canned
    chicken stock
A few drops of lemon juice
1 tablespoon finely chopped fresh
    parsley

BROWN DUCK STOCK

2 tablespoons vegetable oil
1 onion, coarsely chopped
1 carrot, coarsely chopped
1 celery stalk, coarsely chopped
Duck neck, gizzard, heart and liver,
    cut up
2 cups chicken stock, fresh or canned

Caneton aux Navets

DUCK WITH TURNIPS

Preheat the oven to 325°. Wash the duck and giblets under cold running water and dry with paper towels. Set the giblets aside. Rub the cavity of the duck with 1 teaspoon salt, then truss the duck neatly. In a heavy 10- to 12-inch skillet, heat the oil almost to the smoking point and in it brown the duck on all sides, turning it with tongs or two spoons.

In a heavy enameled casserole, just large enough to hold the duck comfortably, melt 1 tablespoon butter over low heat. In it, cook the sliced onions and carrots over low heat, stirring occasionally for about 10 minutes, or until they are limp and lightly colored. Place the duck on top of them, season with salt and pepper, and add the thyme and *bouquet garni*. Cover the casserole, draping a piece of foil over the duck if the cover isn't snug, and braise it on the middle shelf of the oven for 1 hour.

Remove the duck from the casserole and strain the braising juices and vegetables through a fine sieve into a small mixing bowl, pressing down hard on the vegetables with a spoon to extract their juices before discarding them. Let the juices settle, then skim off as much surface fat as possible. Return the duck to the casserole and arrange the turnips around it. Pour in the strained juices and either boiling brown duck stock or chicken stock. The liquid should almost cover the turnips; if it doesn't, add more boiling stock. Bring to a simmer on top of the stove, cover the casserole and return it to the oven for 15 to 20 minutes or until the turnips are tender when they are pierced with the tip of a sharp knife.

Remove the casserole from the oven and increase the heat to 500°. Transfer the duck to a rack set in a shallow roasting pan and return it to the oven for 10 minutes to glaze to a deep brown. (Glazing isn't essential, but it improves the appearance of the duck and crisps the skin. This step can be omitted.) Cut off the trussing strings and place the duck on a heated platter. Arrange the turnips around the duck or at one end of the platter. Skim as much fat off the braising sauce as possible; taste and season with lemon juice, salt and pepper. Carve the duck in the kitchen or at the table and serve the braising sauce in a bowl, sprinkled with parsley.

BROWN DUCK STOCK: While the duck is roasting, heat 2 tablespoons of oil in a heavy 2- or 3-quart saucepan. When the oil is very hot, brown the chopped onion, carrot and celery over moderate heat, stirring occasionally for about 10 minutes, or until they are lightly colored. Add the duck neck, gizzard, heart and liver and cook, stirring frequently, until they are deep brown. Pour in 2 cups of chicken stock, bring to a boil, reduce heat and simmer partly covered for 1 hour. Strain the stock through a fine sieve into a bowl, then skim off the fat on the surface. There should be at least 3/4 cup of stock when you are through.

VARIATION I: WITH OLIVES. Simmer 2 dozen ripe green olives (often called California-style) uncovered in 1 quart of boiling water for 2 or 3 minutes. Drain. Braise them with the duck in place of the turnips.

VARIATION II: WITH PEAS. Simmer 1½ pounds of shelled fresh green peas uncovered in 1 quart of boiling salted water for 5 minutes. Drain the peas in a sieve or colander and plunge them into cold water to stop their cooking. Braise them with the duck in place of the turnips.

Browned, braised and then glazed, this duckling is crackling crisp outside, tender and juicy on the inside. The turnips that garnish it are a traditional accompaniment.

IX

Meat: Cause to Be Different

When William the Norman conquered England in 1066, he brought much more than armed law to that island. His knights, and the ladies and households they soon installed in the hostile Saxon country, lived in a gracious and deliberate manner that at first outraged and finally won the half-wild chiefs, who still celebrated great events by roasting an ox whole and providing oceans of ale to drink with its carcass.

The Normans, in the comparatively comfortable new castles they built throughout England, ate their meals in courses, often to music, and they drank wine, and made "cooked dishes" of their meats instead of tearing them from the bones half-raw. They also ate puddings and sweetmeats.

To native Britons, the Normans' table manners seemed hilariously dainty at first. But gradually such customs became as acceptable as the French language itself, and the upper classes in England, almost a thousand years later, still reflect the more elegant aspects of the Norman invasion. Until the Industrial Revolution in Queen Victoria's time, however, the lower classes seemed impervious to all this. They kept their own old names and dialects, and their inborn dependence upon beef, bread and ale for life itself.

In millions of English homes the "joint," or roast, is still the symbol of a robust meal. But there has never been any culinary English conquest of France. A large piece of roasted beef is seldom served in French provincial homes as it would be in England and America, on Sunday or for a treat. The special dish in France is more likely to be lamb, veal or pork, roasted simply to bring out its best flavor, and helped a bit with additions of garlic and herbs that would be ignored by most Anglo-Saxon cooks.

On market day at Villeneuve de Marsan in southwestern France, cattle raisers and meat dealers trade gossip as they haggle over prices. The cattle are brought to the market live in vans and sold to retail butchers for slaughter.

If a good piece of beef is to be served, it will be browned briefly on top of the stove and then braised, or stewed in its own juices, in the oven, imparting its own flavor at the same time to a few vegetables that share the pot. Served hot, and garnished with these vegetables, the roast is called *boeuf à la mode (page 136)*. Served cold, the meat remains tender and flavorful, and can be made into a most elegant main dish by arranging slices of the meat on a bed of aspic, artfully surrounded with glazed vegetables.

During the last few decades there has been an increasing tendency in France among young people, especially in university towns, to eat rare beef, usually cut as a small steak and served with "French" fried potatoes and watercress. Honestly made, it is good, simple, quick nourishment, and more dependable than the dubious stews fobbed off on hungry students by many cheap restaurants, which flourish today as they did in Rabelais' time wherever there is hunger for both books and food.

Older Frenchmen, with more time to enjoy what they have already learned, incline toward loyalty to the classical, slow dishes they were raised on, and in general do not like the rare-to-bloody-to-blue beefsteaks now considered modishly healthful. Mainly, they like sauces and stews. And a sauce or stew that was good five hundred years ago is good today, as any collection of provincial recipes will prove.

It seems illogical to many Americans who abhor well-done beef that lamb, more often than not, is served pink in France, while at home they seldom see it that way. Once a leg of real, truly young lamb has been roasted in the French way, though, it will be high on any family's list of favorite recipes. Like many essentials of provincial cooking, it is a more seasonal food than in the United States, where we have a heavier, more strongly flavored meat at our disposal all year round.

In praise of spring lamb

Lamb is a springtime dish, traditionally ready for the Easter feasting, but still lamb for another three months or so. During this judiciously prolonged season, in France, everyone who can will eat it, at home or in the restaurants, prepared in an infinity of ways, but always tasting unmistakably and simply like spring lamb.

One favorite way of cooking lamb, which springs from Brittany, is to braise it and then serve it with little white beans. This makes, as its cooks would say, a perfect marriage, and one that I have never tasted in America. The best dish of this kind I ever ate in France was at the opposite end of the country from Brittany, near Vence and the Italian border, and the leg of lamb was not braised in the oven but was roasted vertically before a kind of barbecue. It was very dramatic to see as it dangled there under a disciplined dousing of its own juices, administered by an agile and apparently fireproof young apprentice cook. The meat was served with day-fresh, shelled white beans, not the dried kind used in the Breton recipe: they were as tender and sweet as tiny grapes exploding in my mouth, and delicately reminiscent of onions.

Beans are important in another great and much more famous regional French dish, the *cassoulet (page 148)*. They must be *good* beans—the best—not stale, tired ones. Any American housewife raised in the baked-beans tradition ascribed to New England, especially to Boston, will agree with this dictum, and while the majority of Frenchmen prefer to eat dried white beans cooked in a *cassoulet*, they give a gastronomical salute to its Yankee grandnephew, once they have tasted an honest version of it.

Cassoulets: Not always simple but always sturdy

Like any form of long-cooked stew which has evolved through centuries of use in country kitchens, a *cassoulet*, given its fundamental ingredients of beans and meat, can vary according to the family tastes and the availability of materials. But whatever is put into it, simple or complex, it will remain a sturdy dish, meant to warm and fill the belly, and to be enjoyed and digested without any other richness. A few cold oysters first, a green salad and a piece of fruit after (here is one time when even a morsel of good cheese seems too heavy): that is the general pattern of a meal built cautiously around the impact of a *cassoulet*.

Anatole France once asserted that the best *cassoulets* in the world were made by a chef named Clemence, whose dish, he said, had been simmering

A mother, son and grandmother in Villeneuve de Marsan leave the market after buying two brace of prime live rabbits, which will go into the stew pot for a *ragoût de lapin*, a traditional family dish.

for 20 years. This was somewhat exaggerated, but it is the slowest possible cooking that makes the indescribable juices of a good *cassoulet*. Most recipes advise at least five hours in the oven, but this can be shortened by precooking most of the ingredients.

Among the best French cooks it is considered heinous to open the oven or create any kind of draft until the crumbs on top are golden brown and the *cassoulet* is ready to eat. (One good story, among dozens about this dish, is of a locked and shuttered little cobbler's shop with a sign posted on the front door: "Closed against currents of air—*cassoulet* in oven. Please return tomorrow.")

Moreover, a number of good cooks feel that no *cassoulet* should be considered fit for its rightful place of honor on the table until *two* browned layers of crumbs have been gently folded down into the pot, and yet a third layer has reached its proper color. You pays your money (and a *cassoulet* can be costly or quite inexpensive, of everything but time, that is) and you takes your choice. Fortunately, such is the prerogative of a provincial cook, who is not bound by the rigorous discipline and measurements of haute cuisine.

Innards: Disdained here, honored there

An interesting facet of the common-sense thriftiness of the French is their attitude toward what Anglo-Saxons refer to more or less disdainfully (or disgustedly) as "livers-and-lights," or "innards." We are inclined to think of them as economy meats, to be coped with gastronomically, if at all, when the next paycheck seems dangerously far off. In France, however, innards are treated as respectfully as any other part of the almost totally edible animals raised for the table. Indeed, the French often regard as special delicacies those meat parts which in England or America would meet unnamable ends in the stockyards rather than clutter a butcher's counter, to

His ears cocked, a young porker peers through a fence on an Alsatian farm. When fattened, he and his brothers will be transformed into the local smoked ham and blood sausage— both served with sauerkraut.

be stared at with revulsion by young housewives buying the Thursday staple of two pounds of ground chuck.

A spirit of adventure is called for in getting reoriented to innards. Kidneys, if cooked correctly, need not be tough and smelly. Sweetbreads and brains need not be soft, sickish reminders of our puzzling glands and cerebral confusion. Liver need not be considered solely as a revolting remedy for anemia. And tripe, fixed almost any way at all, but especially as it is done in the Norman region around Caen, need not be thought of as simply the lining of a cow's second stomach!

A typical charcuterie, or processed-meat shop, in Alsace displays pork, veal, beef and garlic sausages, homemade pâtés and cooked meats. The shop is busiest on Mondays, when butchers are closed.

A dozen hours of baking—but worth it

The best proof of this is to try all the parts for oneself. It is true that *tripes à la mode de Caen* must bake for at least 12 hours, and that an economical housewife may feel shocked to have to throw away all the carefully assembled ingredients except the juices and the tripe itself, once the dish is done. But when *tripes à la mode* is served, piping hot and in hot soup plates, with plenty of crusty bread (and for me a soup spoon please), it lays to rest the ghost of that "second stomach" forever.

Like the meat from wild game, which is stringier, tougher and stronger in flavor than that of domesticated creatures, the parts we call innards were created for specialized duties, and demand different and often more complicated treatment *(page 140)* than, say, a grilled steak or a roasted hen.

Once rid of inherited prejudices, however, any family will find a whole new treasury of enjoyment in the recipes that French country housewives have shaped over hundreds of years. Most provincial recipes fit the tastes of their diners to the materials their localities have provided for them. Butter and cream are abundant here, pork fat there, olive oil someplace else; there are wild mountain herbs and rough wine for the asking in one region, leeks and carrots and strong cider in another. It is a pure case of "the proof of the pudding."

The hop from greeting card to menu

Another unfortunate but easily corrected prejudice common in America (and only a little less so in England) is against the common rabbit, which people feel is perhaps suitable for Easter greeting cards, but a treacherous insult to the chicken it is supposed to substitute for in any pot. In France it is a poor family indeed that cannot support at least one fecund doe in a neat hutch somewhere behind the cottage. And it is a common sight to see workingmen on their way home jump off their bicycles to pull some especially succulent herbs from the ditch or meadow, for the family's gentle producer of regularly delivered litters of delicious table-victuals.

Ways of preparing rabbit are legion, of course, and often depend upon the supplies of other things at hand. In Picardy, up north, the dish may include crushed juniper berries and mushrooms. Farther south prunes and dried raisins are added to the pots. In Provence the pieces of rabbit are sautéed in olive oil, not butter, and simmered in garlic (of course) and onions, thyme, tomatoes and white wine.

Because of the prejudice against rabbit, this delicious meat is not easy to find everywhere in America, but most butchers will seek it out on request, and even frozen rabbit, when you can find it, is worth attention. Perhaps the best method of obtaining good rabbit, like good chicken, is to know an honest farmer, who feeds his animals with care to give them flavor and texture. Then, cooked with knowledge and respect, the dish will wipe out with one delicious forkful one's deepest distrust, and prove that 50 million Frenchmen are right again.

Taking the Mystery out of French Meat Dishes

When the Normans invaded England, they brought with them their own names for meat. The French *boeuf, porc, mouton* and *veau* have almost letter for letter dictated the English names beef, pork, mutton and veal, and *longe* and *cotelette* became loin and cutlet.

Helpful as such similarities may be, they leave many French meats something of a mystery. For one thing, the French tend to describe each variation of the same cut with a different name. A loin chop is a *côte,* the word for rib; but when it is boned the same chop is a *noisette*—which means "nut" but has come to stand for boneless meat. There are several names for steaks cut from the tenderloin: the largest part of the tenderloin sliced 2 inches thick is a *Chateaubriand* (named for a 19th Century nobleman whose chef invented the dish); sliced 1 inch thick it is a *filet* (the word connotes delicacy); the upper "tail" of the tenderloin produces *tournedos* (sometimes called *médaillons*); *filets mignons,* the daintiest and tenderest of all, are cut from the extreme end of the tail.

From such cuts as these, cooks will discover that in France meats are butchered differently. Where American butchers usually cut across the grain, leaving in the bones, the French cut along the muscles to make boneless chops and roasts; prime rib roasts and Porterhouse steaks are not to be found in a typical *boucherie.* Nor are the basic meats themselves like those found in the U.S. The cattle of France, even the famous white Charolais, are usually grass-fed and their beef is lean. Larding a roast with additional fat (using the method shown at right) turns out to be a necessity rather than a nicety.

On the small farms of France, newborn calves are often kept on a milk diet for three months or more. From them comes the delicately flavored and almost white veal that is prized and popular in France but rare in the U.S. American calves' meat is pinker because they generally feed not on milk but on grasses and grains.

Pork is eaten at French tables as often as beef, and it is cooked and cured in hundreds of ways; the *charcuterie,* or processed-meat store, is an important market in every provincial town. Lamb is the greatest of delicacies—especially the tiny Pauillac, or milk-fed lamb 6 to 8 weeks old, which may weigh only 15 pounds dressed. (In the U.S., lamb is slaughtered at up to 8 months and a leg may weigh 7 pounds.) With such very young animals, it is possible for the French to serve roasts like the *baron*: two whole hind legs with the double loin or saddle between. But mutton —the meat of sheep a year or more old—is also a French favorite.

Fortunately, in the kitchen, such differences—of cut and even of quality —can be set aside. The recipes in this book take the differences into account, and in the end most French meat dishes translate smoothly. Some of the techniques may sound unfamiliar, and some names may be difficult to pronounce, but the French flavor will be unmistakable.

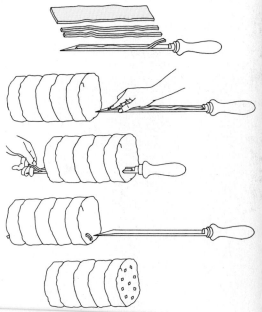

LARDING MEAT
Larding is a technique used in France to enrich lean roasts. First, pork fat is cut into thin sheets, or *bardes de lard (top),* and then into strips, or *lardons.* Each strip, held in a larding needle, is threaded through the roast and the needle is withdrawn. The number of strips used depends on the size and cut of the meat. Larding is less common in the U.S. because most American meat, unlike French meat, is already rich in fat content.

Braising Beef: a Skill Worth Learning

Braising beef—cooking a roast in its own juices with stock or wine, in a covered casserole in the oven—is a useful technique for every cook to master. It takes time, which serves to tenderize the tough, range-fed beef of some countries. It also turns a secondary cut of meat, such as chuck, into a main dish that will impress and please any dinner party.

Boeuf à la mode, described on the following pages, is a perfect example of the braising technique. It is equally suited for serving hot *(below)* or cold, as an elegant leftover *(below right)*. In England and in the United States, cooks often bring the roast to the table as the center of attention and serve the vegetables separately, but the French present the meat on the same platter with the vegetables that have been cooked with it.

The cold braised beef on the opposite page benefits from another kitchen process perfected by the inventive French: glazing vegetables and leftover meats with aspic *(en gelée)* to transform a mundane meal into a festive one. It is not difficult to make and handle aspic, and once you have learned how, you can use the skill to create many culinary works of art.

Hot *boeuf à la mode* is served as a roast on a platter covered with its pan juices. Around it are arranged the onions and carrots that have cooked with it. Additional thickened pan juice is passed separately.

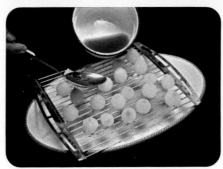

Vegetables to garnish meat are glazed with aspic that has been chilled almost to the point of thickening.

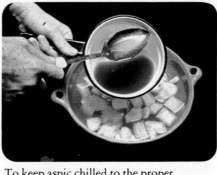

To keep aspic chilled to the proper degree, work with the pan set in a larger container filled with ice.

Aspic may be pressed through a pastry tube with a plain tip to produce scrolls or other designs.

Alternatively, aspic may be chilled more firmly in a shallow pan, then cut in diamond shapes or diced.

Cold *boeuf à la mode en gelée* may be as simple or as decorative as you like. Here the meat is covered with aspic and dotted with carrot stars, with glazed vegetables arranged around it; aspic shapes trim the platter.

To serve 10 to 12

THE BEEF

1 tablespoon salt

1 teaspoon coarsely ground black
pepper

A 5-pound boneless beef chuck or
bottom round roast at least 5
inches in diameter, trimmed and
tied

THE MARINADE

3 cups red Burgundy or other dry red
wine

1 cup thinly sliced onions

¾ cup thinly sliced carrots

1 teaspoon finely chopped garlic

2 bay leaves, crumbled

2 tablespoons finely chopped fresh
parsley

1 teaspoon dried thyme, crumbled

THE ONIONS AND CARROTS À BRUN

½ pound fresh pork fat, diced

20 to 24 white onions, about 1 inch
in diameter, peeled

6 to 8 carrots, peeled and cut into
1½-inch cylinders or olive shapes

THE BRAISING STOCK

4 tablespoons butter

⅓ cup Cognac

2 calf's feet and / or 1 large veal
knuckle, sawed into pieces

2 medium tomatoes, peeled, seeded
and coarsely chopped

Bouquet garni made of 6 parsley
sprigs, 1 bay leaf and the white
part of 1 leek, tied together

3 cups beef stock, fresh or canned

Salt

Freshly ground black pepper

½ cup finely chopped fresh parsley

Boeuf à la Mode

POT ROAST OF BEEF BRAISED IN RED WINE

MARINATING THE BEEF: Press 1 tablespoon of salt and 1 teaspoon of pepper into the surface of the beef. In a large glass, porcelain or stainless-steel bowl, mix the marinade ingredients. Add the beef and turn it in the marinade until it is well moistened on all sides. Let it marinate for at least 6 hours at room temperature or 12 to 24 hours in the refrigerator, turning it over every few hours.

THE ONIONS AND CARROTS À BRUN: Preheat the oven to 350 °. In a heavy 10- to 12-inch skillet, sauté the diced pork fat over moderate heat, stirring constantly, until crisp and brown. Remove the diced pork fat and reserve it. In the fat left in the skillet, brown the whole onions and the carrots lightly over moderately high heat, shaking the pan occasionally to roll them around and color them as evenly as possible. Transfer them to a shallow baking dish large enough to hold them in one layer, and sprinkle them with about 3 tablespoons of pork fat. (Set the skillet aside, without removing the remaining fat.) Bake the onions and carrots uncovered on the middle shelf of the oven, turning and basting them once or twice, for 30 minutes, or until they are barely tender. Remove from the oven, pour out the cooking fat and set the vegetables aside.

BRAISING THE BEEF: While the vegetables bake or when they are done, remove the beef from the marinade and dry it thoroughly with paper towels. Strain the marinade into a small bowl, and drain the vegetables on paper towels. Heat the pork fat remaining in the skillet to the smoking point and brown the beef over moderate heat until it is richly colored on all sides. While the beef is browning, melt 4 tablespoons of butter in a heavy, 6-quart flameproof casserole or Dutch oven. Add the marinated vegetables and cook over low heat, turning frequently, until most of their moisture has boiled away and they are lightly colored. When the beef is browned, use a bulb baster to draw off all but a thin film of fat from the skillet.

The next step is to flame the beef. Experts simply flame the beef with Cognac directly in the pan. But a more reliable way is to warm the Cognac first in a small saucepan over low heat, ignite it with a match, and pour it flaming over the beef a little at a time, shaking the skillet gently until the flame dies. Transfer the beef to the casserole and surround it with the pieces of calf's feet and / or veal knuckle, the chopped tomatoes, the diced pork fat and the *bouquet garni*.

Pour the strained marinade and 3 cups of beef stock into the skillet, and bring them to a boil over high heat, stirring and scraping in any browned bits that cling to the pan. Boil briskly for 1 or 2 minutes, then pour it into the casserole. The liquid should come about halfway up the side of the meat; add more beef stock if needed. Bring the casserole to a boil on top of the stove, then cover tightly and place on the middle shelf of the oven. Regulate oven heat so the beef simmers slowly, and turn and baste the meat 2 or 3 times during the cooking. After 2½ to 3 hours the meat should be tender when pierced with the tip of a sharp knife.

To serve the beef and the vegetables hot, transfer the beef from the casserole to a plate. Remove and discard the bones and *bouquet garni* and strain the rest of the contents of the casserole through a large, fine

138

sieve into a 3- to 4-quart saucepan, pressing down hard on the vegetables before discarding them. Let the strained braising liquid, or sauce, settle for a few minutes, then skim as much fat as possible from the surface. Boil the sauce briskly over high heat until it has been reduced to half its original quantity (about 3 to 4 cups). Taste and season with salt and pepper. Return the meat and sauce to the casserole and add the baked onions and carrots. Simmer slowly on top of the stove to heat the beef and vegetables thoroughly. Transfer the beef to a carving board to remove the strings. Then arrange the roast on a large heated platter, surrounded with the onions and carrots. Spoon some of the sauce over it, and serve the rest separately in a warm sauceboat.

BOEUF À LA MODE EN GELÉE (cold pot roast of beef in aspic): To prepare the cold version of *boeuf à la mode*, let the beef cool for an hour in the braising liquid, turning it once or twice. Transfer the beef to a platter, let it cool to room temperature, then wrap and refrigerate it. Strain the braising liquid; cool, cover and refrigerate it. Cool, cover and refrigerate the baked onions and carrots.

When the braising liquid is thoroughly chilled, carefully remove and discard all of the fat that has solidified on the surface. In a 2- or 3-quart saucepan, melt the braising liquid over low heat and then measure it. Add enough beef stock to make 5 cups in all, and return it to the pan. Soften the gelatin in an additional 1 cup of cold fresh stock, and add it. Beat the egg whites to a froth with a wire whisk, and stir them into the stock, together with the lemon juice, thyme, bay leaf, peppercorns and salt. Bring to a boil over moderate heat, stirring constantly. When the aspic begins to froth and rise, remove the pan from the heat. Let it rest off the heat for 5 minutes, then strain it into a deep bowl through a fine sieve lined with a dampened kitchen towel. Allow the aspic to drain without disturbing it at any point. When it has drained completely through, add the Madeira, and taste and season the aspic with more salt if needed. Pour a thin layer of aspic—about ⅛ inch thick—into the bottom of a large serving platter, and refrigerate it until the aspic is set. Then carve the cold beef into ¼-inch slices and arrange the meat, onions and carrots attractively on the platter. Heat about ¾ cup of the aspic in a small pan just until it melts, then set it in a bowl filled with crushed ice or ice cubes immersed in water. Stir the aspic gently with a metal spoon until it thickens almost to the point of setting. Working quickly, spread a thin glaze of aspic over the sliced beef and vegetables. Chill until the aspic sets. Repeat this process two more times to make three coatings of aspic—melting and chilling the aspic for each layer. Refrigerate the platter until the glaze is firm. Meanwhile, melt the remaining aspic and pour it into a large flat roasting pan to make a sheet or film no more than ¼ inch deep; chill it.

When all the aspic is very firm, remove the roasting pan from the refrigerator, and score the sheet of aspic into diamonds with the tip of a sharp knife by cutting crossing diagonal lines about 1 to 1½ inches apart. Arrange the diamonds decoratively around the aspic-covered beef. Chop any scraps into fine dice, and garnish the platter with it as fancifully as you like. You can even put the chopped aspic into a pastry bag with a plain tip and press the aspic out in scrolls on the beef.

THE ASPIC FOR BOEUF À LA MODE EN GELÉE
2 to 4 cups beef stock, fresh or canned
3 envelopes unflavored gelatin
3 egg whites
½ teaspoon lemon juice
½ teaspoon dried thyme, crumbled
½ bay leaf
10 peppercorns
1 teaspoon salt
½ cup dry Madeira

Innards

Typical innards, sometimes called variety meats, are tripe, brains, sweetbreads and kidneys. Inexpensive and delicious when properly prepared, these meats need careful cleaning. Although some are available frozen, they are best when absolutely fresh.

TRIPE, frozen in a block, can be sliced for cooking. When bought fresh, it comes in ready-to-cook strips.

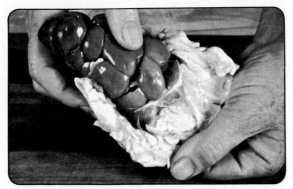

KIDNEYS may come encased in a layer of fat, which should be loosened with a sharp knife and then carefully

peeled back and discarded *(left)*. On the underside *(right)* is a pocket of fat which should also be removed.

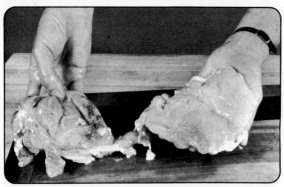

SWEETBREADS are first soaked in cold water, then the tube *(left, center)* connecting the two lobes of each

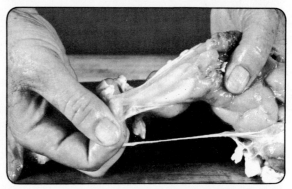

sweetbread is cut off with a knife. Finally, the filament covering the meat is delicately pulled away *(right)*.

BRAINS must be treated gently. Soak them *(left)* for three hours in several changes of cold water, adding

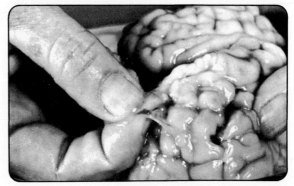

vinegar to the last change. Then pull off as much membrane as possible *(right)* without tearing the meat.

Rognons en Casserole
SAUTÉED KIDNEYS WITH MUSTARD SAUCE

In a heavy, shallow flameproof casserole about 10 inches across, or in a chafing dish, melt the 6 tablespoons of butter over moderate heat. When the foam subsides, sauté the kidneys in the butter, uncovered, turning them frequently, until they are lightly browned. (Sauté veal kidneys for 10 minutes, lamb kidneys for 4 to 5.) With tongs, transfer the kidneys to a heated platter and cover loosely to keep them warm.

Stir the shallots into the butter remaining in the casserole and cook, stirring, for 1 minute. Then add the wine and bring to a boil, stirring constantly and scraping in any brown bits or coagulated juices that cling to the pan. Boil briskly for 4 to 5 minutes or until the wine is reduced to ¼ cup. Remove the casserole from the heat. Cream the butter by beating it vigorously with a wooden spoon until it is fluffy, then beat in the mustard, salt and a few grindings of pepper. Off the heat, swirl spoonfuls of the seasoned butter into the casserole.

Working quickly, cut the kidneys into crosswise slices ⅛ inch thick. Return them to the casserole, sprinkle with lemon juice and parsley, and toss over low heat for 1 or 2 minutes to heat them through. Serve at once.

To serve 4 to 6

6 tablespoons butter
3 or 4 whole veal kidneys or 12 whole lamb kidneys, peeled and trimmed of fat
2 tablespoons finely chopped shallots or scallions
¾ cup dry white wine
4 tablespoons soft butter
2 tablespoons Dijon-style prepared mustard
½ teaspoon salt
Freshly ground black pepper
2 teaspoons lemon juice
3 tablespoons finely chopped fresh parsley

Ris de Veau ou Cervelles au Beurre Noir
SWEETBREADS OR BRAINS IN BROWN BUTTER SAUCE

Soak the sweetbreads or brains in several changes of cold water for 2 hours; then soak them for another hour in acidulated cold water, using one tablespoon of vinegar for each quart of water. Gently pull off as much of the outside membrane as possible without tearing the brains or sweetbreads. Trim the sweetbreads by cutting the two lobes from the tube between them with a small sharp knife; discard the tubes. Trim the brains by cutting off the white, opaque bits at the base. Place the sweetbreads or brains in an enameled saucepan with enough water to cover by 2 inches, add the salt (1 teaspoon per quart of water) and lemon juice (1 tablespoon per quart of water), and cook uncovered just below a simmer for 15 to 20 minutes. Spread the sweetbreads or brains on paper towels to dry.

Clarify 12 tablespoons of the butter in a small heavy saucepan or skillet by melting it slowly, skimming off the surface foam. Spoon the clear butter on top into a clean pan and discard the milky residue. Pour the vinegar into the pan in which the butter melted and boil it briskly until it has been reduced to 1 tablespoon. Over moderate heat, brown the clarified butter. Stir in the reduced vinegar, taste and season with salt and pepper.

If the sweetbreads or brains are to be served whole, add them to the brown butter sauce and, basting periodically, heat through. If they are to be sliced and sautéed, set the brown butter sauce aside. Dip the slices in flour, then shake off all but a fine dusting of flour. In a heavy 10- to 12-inch skillet or sauté pan, melt the remaining 3 tablespoons of butter with the oil over moderate heat. When the foam subsides, sauté the sliced sweetbreads or brains 3 or 4 minutes on each side, or until lightly browned. If all the slices don't fit into the skillet easily, sauté them in two batches. Arrange the slices neatly on a heated platter. Reheat the brown butter and pour it over them. Sprinkle with chopped parsley and serve at once.

To serve 6

1½ pounds calf's sweetbreads or brains
Water
Vinegar
Salt
Lemon juice
15 tablespoons butter (almost ½ pound)
¼ cup wine vinegar or lemon juice
Freshly ground black pepper
Flour
3 tablespoons butter
1 tablespoon vegetable oil
2 tablespoons finely chopped fresh parsley

141

Foie de Veau Sauté
SAUTÉED CALF'S LIVER

To serve 6

6 slices of calf's liver, cut ½ inch
thick (about 1½ pounds)
Salt
Freshly ground black pepper
Flour
4 tablespoons butter
2 tablespoons vegetable oil
½ cup beef or chicken stock, fresh or
canned
1 tablespoon soft butter
A few drops of lemon juice
2 tablespoons finely chopped, fresh
parsley

Season the liver slices with salt and a few grindings of pepper. Dip the slices in flour, then vigorously shake off all but a fine dusting. In a heavy 12-inch skillet or sauté pan, melt the butter with the oil over high heat. When the foam subsides, sauté the liver quickly for 2 or 3 minutes on each side, turning the slices with kitchen tongs. Remove the liver to a heated platter and cover loosely to keep warm.

Working quickly, pour off almost all the fat from the skillet, leaving just enough to film the bottom. Add the chicken stock and cook over high heat, stirring constantly and scraping in any brown bits that cling to the pan.

Continue to cook until the stock is syrupy and has been reduced to about ¼ cup. Remove the pan from the heat and swirl in 1 tablespoon of soft butter and a few drops of lemon juice. Pour the sauce over the liver, sprinkle with parsley and serve at once.

Tripes à la Mode de Caen
CASSEROLE OF TRIPE

To serve 8 to 10

5 pounds ready-to-cook tripe
4 ready-to-cook calf's feet, split in
half and boned, or 2 sawed veal
knuckles and an 8- by 3-inch piece
of fresh or salt pork rind
3 onions, peeled and cut in half
3 carrots, peeled and cut in chunks
4 leeks, whites plus 2 inches of green,
split, or substitute 2 more onions,
cut in half
Bouquet garni made of 6 parsley
sprigs, 2 bay leaves, 5 peeled garlic
cloves, 1 teaspoon dried thyme and
15 peppercorns, tied together in
washed cheesecloth
1½ tablespoons salt
3 cups dry white wine
3 cups chicken stock, fresh or canned
1½ cups Calvados or applejack
½ pound beef fat, sliced in ⅛-inch
sheets
2 tablespoons finely chopped fresh
parsley

With a sharp knife, cut the sheets of tripe into 1½-inch squares. Wash them in a large bowl set under a slow trickle of cold tap water until the water in the bowl is clear. Drain thoroughly in a colander or large sieve. Meanwhile, blanch the calf's feet (or veal knuckles and pork rind) in a large saucepan or soup kettle by covering them with cold water, bringing the water to a boil over high heat and cooking them briskly for 2 minutes. Drain the feet in a colander and rinse thoroughly in cold water.

Preheat the oven to 250°. Spread the onions, carrots, leeks and *bouquet garni* in the bottom of a heavy flameproof 6- to 8-quart casserole that has a tight cover. Lay the tripe over them and salt it. Place the calf's feet (or veal knuckles and pork rind) on top and pour in the wine, stock and Calvados. (Unsweet cider, instead of wine, is traditional in Caen. If your liquor store has it, you may substitute imported dry hard cider—not apple juice or sweetened cider—for the wine.) Add more stock or water if necessary to cover the ingredients. Drape the sheets of beef fat loosely over the top. Seal the casserole with a double layer of aluminum foil folded down over the sides and tied in place, then cover the casserole. Bring to a simmer on top of the stove; set the casserole in a large roasting pan to catch any overflow and place it on the middle shelf of the oven to bake for at least 12 hours—up to 16 hours if you wish.

When the tripe is done, remove the casserole from the oven, uncover it and peel off the foil. With tongs, remove and discard the calf's feet (or veal knuckles and pork rind), vegetables and *bouquet garni;* pour the tripe and all its juices into a fine sieve set over a large mixing bowl. After the tripe has drained, transfer it to a 3- to 4-quart casserole. Let the sauce from the tripe settle for 5 minutes, then skim as much fat as possible from the surface. Taste the sauce for seasoning, pour it over the tripe and bring the casserole to a simmer on top of the stove. Sprinkle with parsley and serve at once. It is important that tripe be served on heated plates because the sauce will thicken to a jelly if the plates are the slightest bit cool.

Gigot d'Agneau Rôti
ROAST LEG OF LAMB

Preheat the oven to 500°. Make 6 or 8 quarter-inch incisions on the fatty side of the lamb, and insert a sliver of garlic in each cut. Brush the leg with oil and pat salt all over it. Insert a meat thermometer into the thickest part of the leg, being careful not to touch a bone. Place the leg, fat side up, on a rack in a shallow roasting pan and roast it uncovered for 20 minutes on the middle shelf of the oven. Then reduce the heat to 375°, scatter the vegetables around the rack and roast the lamb for another 40 to 60 minutes, or until done to your liking. For rare lamb, roast it until the meat thermometer reads 130° to 140°, for medium, 140° to 150°; for well done, 150° to 160°. Transfer the lamb to a heated platter and remove the thermometer; let it rest 10 minutes before carving.

Meanwhile, skim off the fat from the roasting pan, add the stock to the vegetables and boil briskly on top of the stove for 4 or 5 minutes, scraping in any browned bits clinging to the pan. When the sauce has reached the intensity of flavor desired, strain it through a fine sieve into a saucepan, pressing down hard on the vegetables before discarding them. Skim the sauce of its surface fat; taste the sauce and season it with lemon juice, salt and pepper. Reheat the sauce and serve it with the lamb.

Sauté de Lapin au Vin Blanc
RABBIT STEWED IN WHITE WINE SAUCE

Wash the rabbit under running water and dry it with paper towels. Combine ½ cup of the wine, 1 tablespoon wine vinegar, olive oil, the sliced onion, thyme, bay leaf, parsley, salt and pepper for the marinade in a shallow baking dish or casserole. Marinate the rabbit 6 hours at room temperature, 12 to 24 hours refrigerated. Turn the pieces every few hours.

Simmer the pork dice in 2 cups of water for 5 minutes; drain and pat dry with paper towels. In a heavy 10- to 12-inch skillet, melt 1 tablespoon of butter over moderate heat and in it brown the pork dice until they are crisp and golden. Set the pork aside and pour most of the fat into a bowl, leaving just a film on the bottom of the skillet. Brown the onions in the fat left in the skillet, then transfer them to a bowl.

Remove the rabbit from the marinade and dry it with paper towels. Reserve the marinade. Brown the rabbit in the skillet, adding more fat as needed, then transfer the pieces to a heavy flameproof 2- to 3-quart casserole. Pour off almost all the fat from the skillet, add the shallots and garlic and cook, stirring constantly, for 2 minutes. Stir in the flour and cook, stirring over low heat 1 minute. Remove from heat and pour in the remaining ½ cup wine and stock, stirring constantly. Cook over moderate heat, stirring, until the sauce thickens. Pour it over the rabbit and add the *bouquet garni,* reserved marinade and pork dice. Preheat the oven to 350°.

Bring the stew to a boil on top of the stove, cover, and cook on the middle shelf of the oven for 40 minutes. Gently stir in the onions and cook for another 20 minutes, or until the rabbit is tender when pierced with the tip of a sharp knife. Just before serving, stir the remaining 1 tablespoon of vinegar into the sauce and taste for seasoning. Serve the stew directly from the casserole.

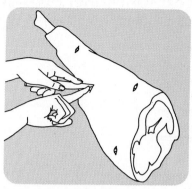

Make small slits in the leg of lamb to insert slivers of garlic.

To serve 6 to 8

A 5- to 6-pound leg of lamb trimmed of excess fat but with the fell (or parchmentlike covering) left on
1 garlic clove, cut in slivers
3 tablespoons vegetable oil
2 tablespoons salt
2 onions, thinly sliced
2 carrots, thinly sliced
1½ cups fresh or canned beef or chicken stock
½ teaspoon lemon juice
Salt
Freshly ground black pepper

To serve 4 to 6

A 2½- to 3-pound fresh rabbit or defrosted frozen rabbit, cut in serving pieces
1 cup dry white wine
2 tablespoons white wine vinegar
¼ cup olive oil
1 onion, thinly sliced
½ teaspoon dried thyme
1 bay leaf, crumbled
2 teaspoons finely chopped fresh parsley
½ teaspoon salt
Freshly ground black pepper
¼ pound lean salt pork, diced
2 cups water
1 tablespoon butter
12 to 16 peeled white onions, about 1 inch in diameter
3 tablespoons finely chopped shallots
½ teaspoon finely chopped garlic
2 tablespoons flour
1½ cups beef stock, fresh or canned
Bouquet garni made of 4 parsley sprigs and 1 bay leaf, tied together

The five most popular kinds of innards are *(clockwise from top right)*: brains, cooked in brown butter sauce; casserole of tripe; sweetbreads in brown butter sauce; sautéed calf's liver, served in a chafing dish with cherry tomatoes and peas; at center are sautéed kidneys with mustard sauce, served with mushroom slices. The tripe and liver are ready to serve as shown here; the other meats are usually sliced and cooked further before they are served *(page 141)*.

These foods are well adapted to chafing-dish cooking—or for serving at the table in a chafing dish, which keeps them warm. Care should be taken that the delicate meats do not dry out over the low, steady heat from the chafing-dish burner.

MARCHAND DE VINS SAUCE

2 tablespoons butter

½ cup finely chopped shallots or
   scallions

1½ cups dry red wine

½ bay leaf

¼ teaspoon dried thyme

4 parsley sprigs

2 teaspoons meat extract combined
   with 3 tablespoons hot water

12 tablespoons soft butter (1½
   quarter-pound sticks)

1 tablespoon lemon juice

1 teaspoon flour

2 tablespoons finely chopped fresh
   parsley

THE STEAK

A 3- to 3½-pound sirloin, porterhouse
   or T-bone steak, cut 1 to 1¼
   inch thick and trimmed of excess
   fat

1 tablespoon butter

2 tablespoons vegetable oil

Salt

Freshly ground black pepper

To serve 4

6 quarts water

Salt

3 pounds cabbage, finely chopped
   (about 12 cups)

3 tablespoons butter

½ cup finely chopped onions

½ teaspoon finely chopped garlic

Freshly ground black pepper

8 center-cut loin pork chops, about
   ¾ inch thick

3 tablespoons oil

½ cup dry white wine

1 cup heavy cream

1 bay leaf

4 teaspoons freshly grated Parmesan
   cheese mixed with 2 teaspoons
   fine, dry bread crumbs

Bifteck Marchand de Vins
SAUTÉED STEAK WITH RED WINE SAUCE

MARCHAND DE VINS SAUCE: In a 1- to 2-quart enameled saucepan, melt 2 tablespoons of butter over moderate heat. When the foam subsides, cook the shallots, stirring constantly, for 2 minutes, or until they are soft but not brown. Pour in the wine, add the bay leaf, thyme and parsley sprigs and simmer over moderate heat until reduced to ¾ cup. This process may take 10 to 15 minutes. Strain the reduced wine through a fine sieve into a small bowl, pressing down hard on the shallots and herbs with the back of a spoon before discarding them. Return the wine to the saucepan, add the thinned meat extract and bring to a boil. Set the pan aside.

Cream 12 tablespoons of soft butter, beating it vigorously against the side of a small bowl with a wooden spoon until it is fluffy. Beat in the lemon juice, flour and parsley. Set the bowl aside.

THE STEAK: Pat the steak thoroughly dry with paper towels. Cut small incisions every inch or so around the outside of the steak so the fat won't curl as it cooks. In a heavy 12- or 14-inch skillet or sauté pan, melt 1 tablespoon of butter with the 2 tablespoons of vegetable oil over high heat. Add the steak and brown it quickly for 1 or 2 minutes on each side, turning it with tongs. Then reduce the heat to moderate and sauté the steak for about 5 minutes on each side, or until it is done to a medium-rare degree.

Experts test a steak by pressing it with a finger. It should be slightly resilient, neither soft nor firm. If that method seems tricky, make a small incision near the bone with the tip of a sharp knife and judge by the meat's color. Transfer to a heated platter and season with salt and pepper.

Pour the reduced wine mixture into the skillet and bring it to a boil over moderate heat, stirring constantly and scraping in any browned bits that cling to the bottom and sides of the pan. Remove from the heat and blend in the creamed butter mixture, 2 tablespoons at a time. To serve, slice the steak and offer the sauce separately.

ALTERNATIVE: *Sauce béarnaise (page 74)* can take the place of the *marchand de vins* sauce. In this case, the name of the dish becomes *bifteck béarnaise.*

Côtes de Porc à l'Auvergnate
PORK CHOPS BAKED WITH CABBAGE

In a soup pot or kettle, bring the water and 3 tablespoons of salt to a bubbling boil. Drop in the cabbage and boil for 5 minutes. Drain the cabbage thoroughly in a sieve or colander. In a 10- to 12-inch skillet, melt 2 tablespoons of the butter over moderate heat. When the foam subsides, cook the onions and garlic, stirring constantly, for 3 or 4 minutes, or until they are soft but not brown. Stir in the cabbage, ½ teaspoon salt and a few grindings of pepper, and cook, stirring frequently, for 5 minutes, or until almost all of the moisture in the pan has evaporated. With a rubber spatula, transfer the contents of the skillet to a bowl; set aside.

Pat the pork chops dry with paper towels, and season them with salt and a few grindings of black pepper. In the skillet, melt the remaining 1 tablespoon of butter with the oil over moderate heat. When the foam subsides, brown the chops for about 3 minutes on each side, or until they are a rich golden color. Remove them from the skillet with tongs and set them aside.

Pour off almost all the fat from the skillet, leaving only a thin film on the bottom. Add the wine and boil rapidly, stirring frequently and scraping in any brown bits that cling to the bottom and sides of the pan, until the wine is reduced to ¼ cup. Mix the reduced wine into the cabbage. Spread about ⅓ of the cabbage in the bottom of a heavy flameproof casserole at least 4 inches deep, and large enough to hold 4 chops in a single layer. Lay 4 chops on top of the cabbage, then add another layer of cabbage, 4 more chops, and finish with the rest of the cabbage. The casserole should be firmly packed. Preheat the oven to 350°.

In a small saucepan, scald the cream by heating it over moderate heat until tiny bubbles form around the edge of the pan. Pour the hot cream into the casserole and place a bay leaf on top of the cabbage. Bring the casserole to a simmer on top of the stove, then set it into a larger pan to catch any juices that may spill over during cooking, cover it tightly, and bake it on the middle shelf of the oven for 1½ hours. Remove the cover, discard the bay leaf and check the seasoning. Sprinkle the cabbage with cheese and crumbs. Bake the casserole for 30 minutes longer, or until the top is browned and crusty. Serve directly from the casserole.

Côtes de Veau à l'Ardennaise
BRAISED VEAL CHOPS WITH HAM AND PARSLEY DRESSING

To serve 4

5 tablespoons butter
½ cup finely chopped onions
¼ cup finely chopped carrots
10 juniper berries
½ teaspoon dried basil
½ teaspoon salt
Freshly ground black pepper
3 tablespoons vegetable oil
4 veal loin chops, cut 1 to 1½ inches thick
1 cup dry white wine
½ cup chicken stock, fresh or canned
¾ cup fresh white bread crumbs, made in a blender from about 3 slices of white bread with crusts removed
1 tablespoon finely chopped boiled ham
2 tablespoons finely chopped fresh parsley
½ teaspoon lemon juice
1 tablespoon butter, cut in tiny pieces

Preheat the oven to 350°. In a heavy shallow flameproof casserole or baking dish that is large enough to hold the chops in one layer and has a cover, melt 2 tablespoons of the butter over moderate heat, and in it cook the chopped onions and carrots, stirring occasionally, for 8 to 10 minutes, or until limp and lightly colored. Set aside.

With a mortar and pestle or a wooden spoon and small, heavy mixing bowl, crush the juniper berries and pound in the basil, salt and a few grindings of pepper. Press the juniper-berry seasoning into both sides of the chops, forcing it into the meat as much as possible.

Melt 1 tablespoon of the butter with the oil in a heavy 10- to 12-inch skillet over moderate heat. When the foam subsides, brown the chops to a rich golden color on both sides, turning them carefully to avoid dislodging the seasoning. Transfer the browned chops to the casserole. Pour off all but 1 or 2 tablespoons of fat from the skillet and add the wine. Boil briskly, stirring and scraping in any browned bits that cling to the pan, until the wine has been reduced to ½ cup; then stir in the stock and pour the mixture around the veal chops. In a 6- to 8-inch skillet, melt the remaining 2 tablespoons of butter over low heat, and cook the bread crumbs until they are lightly browned. Off the heat, stir in the ham, parsley and ½ teaspoon of lemon juice. Divide the mixture into quarters, and spoon a portion onto each chop. Dot the topping with butter.

Bring the casserole to a boil on top of the stove, cover tightly and bake for 40 minutes. Then transfer the veal to a heated platter, preferably one with a well to catch the sauce. Working quickly, strain the contents of the casserole through a fine sieve into a small saucepan, pressing down hard on the vegetables with the back of a spoon before discarding them. Boil down the liquids over high heat until they are reduced to about ½ cup. Taste the sauce for seasoning, pour it around the chops and serve at once.

To serve 10 to 12

THE BEANS AND SAUSAGE

4 quarts chicken stock, fresh or
    canned
2 pounds or 4 cups dry white beans
    (Great Northern, marrow, or navy)
1 pound lean salt pork, in one piece
½ pound fresh pork rind (optional)
1 quart water
1 pound uncooked plain or garlic pork
    sausage, fresh or smoked (French,
    Italian or Polish)
3 whole peeled onions
1 teaspoon finely chopped garlic
1 teaspoon dried thyme, crumbled
Bouquet garni, made of 4 parsley
    sprigs, 3 celery tops, white part of
    1 leek, and 2 bay leaves, wrapped
    and tied in cheesecloth
Salt
Freshly ground black pepper

THE DUCK

4 tablespoons soft butter
1 tablespoon vegetable oil
A 4- to 5-pound duck, quartered

THE PORK AND LAMB

½ pound fresh pork fat, diced
1 pound boned pork loin, cut in
    2-inch chunks
1 pound boned lamb shoulder, cut in
    2-inch chunks
1 cup finely chopped onions
½ cup finely chopped celery
1 teaspoon finely chopped garlic
1 cup dry white wine
1½ pounds firm ripe tomatoes, peeled,
    seeded and coarsely chopped (about
    2 to 2½ cups) or substitute 2 cups
    chopped, drained, canned
    whole-pack tomatoes
1 bay leaf
½ teaspoon salt
Freshly ground black pepper

THE GRATIN TOPPING

1½ cups fine, dry bread crumbs
½ cup finely chopped fresh parsley

Cassoulet
CASSEROLE OF WHITE BEANS BAKED WITH MEATS

THE BEANS AND SAUSAGE: In a heavy 6- to 8-quart pot or soup kettle, bring the chicken stock to a bubbling boil over high heat. Drop the beans in and boil them briskly for 2 minutes. Remove the pot from the heat and let the beans soak for 1 hour. Meanwhile, simmer the salt pork and optional pork rind in 1 quart of water for 15 minutes; drain and set aside.

With the point of a sharp knife, pierce 5 or 6 holes in the sausage; then add the sausage, salt pork and pork rind to the beans. Bring to a boil over high heat, skimming the top of scum. When the stock looks fairly clear, add the whole onions, garlic, thyme, *bouquet garni,* salt and a few grindings of black pepper. Reduce the heat and simmer uncovered for 45 minutes, adding stock or water if needed. With tongs, transfer the sausage to a plate and set it aside. Cook the beans and salt pork for another 30 to 40 minutes, or until the beans are tender, drain and transfer the salt pork and rind to the plate with the sausage; discard the onions and *bouquet garni.* Strain the stock through a large sieve or colander into a mixing bowl. Skim the fat from the stock and taste for seasoning. Then set the beans, stock and meats aside in separate containers. If they are to be kept overnight, cool, cover and refrigerate them.

THE BROILED DUCK: Preheat the oven to 350°. Cream the butter by beating it vigorously against the sides of a small bowl with a wooden spoon until it is fluffy, then beat in the oil. Dry the duck with paper towels, and coat the quarters with creamed butter and oil. Lay them skin side down on the broiler rack, and broil them 4 inches from the heat for 15 minutes, basting them once with pan juices, and broil 5 minutes more. Then increase the heat to 400° and broil for 15 minutes, basting the duck once or twice. With tongs, turn the quarters over, baste, and broil skin side up for 10 minutes. Increase the heat to 450°, baste again, and broil for 10 minutes more. Remove the duck to a plate and pour the drippings from the broiler into a bowl, scraping in any browned bits that cling to the pan. Let the drippings settle, then skim the fat from the top and save it in a small bowl. Pour the degreased drippings into the bean stock. When the duck is cool, trim off the excess fat and gristle, and use poultry shears to cut the quarters into small serving pieces. If they are to be kept overnight, cool and cover the duck and bowl of fat and refrigerate them.

THE PORK AND LAMB: Preheat the oven to 325°. In a heavy 10- to 12-inch skillet, sauté the diced pork fat over moderate heat, stirring constantly, until crisp and brown. Remove the dice and reserve. Pour all but 2 or 3 tablespoons of rendered fat into a small mixing bowl. Heat the fat remaining in the skillet almost to the smoking point, and in it brown the pork and the lamb, 4 or 5 chunks at a time, adding more pork fat as needed. When the chunks are a rich brown on all sides, transfer them with tongs to a 4-quart Dutch oven or heavy flameproof casserole.

Now discard all but 3 tablespoons of fat from the skillet and cook the chopped onions over low heat for 5 minutes. Scrape in any browned bits clinging to the pan. Stir in the celery and garlic and cook for 2 minutes. Then pour in the wine, bring to a boil and cook over high heat until the mixture has been reduced to about half. With a rubber spatula, scrape the contents of the skillet into the casserole. Gently stir the tomatoes, bay leaf, salt and a few grindings of pepper into the casserole. Bring to a boil on top of the stove, cover, and bake on the middle shelf of the oven (adding a little stock or water if the meat looks dry) for 1 hour, or until the meat is tender. With tongs, transfer the meat to a bowl. If it is to be kept overnight, cool, cover and refrigerate. Skim the fat from the juices in the casserole, then strain the juices into the bean stock and discard the vegetables.

ASSEMBLING THE CASSOULET: Preheat the oven to 350°. Peel the sausage and cut it into ¼-inch slices; cut the salt pork and pork rind into 1-inch squares. In a heavy flameproof 6- to 8-quart casserole at least 5 inches deep spread an inch-deep layer of beans. Arrange half of the sausage, salt pork, pork rind, diced pork fat, duck, braised pork and lamb on top. Cover with another layer of beans, then the rest of the meat, finally a last layer of beans, with a few slices of sausage on top. Slowly pour in the bean stock until it almost covers the beans. (If there isn't enough stock, add fresh or canned chicken stock.) Spread the bread crumbs in a thick layer on top and sprinkle them with 3 or 4 tablespoons of duck fat. Bring the casserole to a boil on top of the stove, then bake it uncovered in the upper third of the oven for 1¼ hours, or until the crumbs have formed a firm, dark crust. If desired, the first gratin, or crust, can be pushed gently into the *cassoulet*, and the dish baked until a new crust forms. This can be repeated two or three times if you wish. Serve directly from the casserole, sprinkled with parsley.

Skim foam from boiling beans and meat.

Wrap *bouquet garni* to add to pot.

Prick sausage to release excess fat.

Broil duck to prepare it for pot.

Sauté lamb and pork chunks until brown.

Arrange the ingredients in layers.

Crusty and golden brown, the *cassoulet* should look moist when the surface is broken and the meat and bean flavors should be well blended. Although time-consuming to prepare, the *cassoulet* can be cooked in easy stages, assembled and refrigerated for a day or so before final baking. Among the most famous of provincial dishes—it originated in Languedoc—the *cassoulet* is a full meal in itself. The one shown here, made from the recipe on the preceding pages, is a fairly complex dish, calling as it does for duck, lamb, pork and sausage. But many French housewives create delicious *cassoulets* with only two or three meats.

X

Vegetables: Not So Lowly

In a village on the outskirts of Strasbourg, an old wooden cart filled with plump white cabbages is a familiar harvest-time sight, its load of cannon-ball-sized *choux* destined to be shredded into sauerkraut for *choucroute garnie*.

The soil of France, which includes some of the most productive acreage in the world, has been cultivated by men for many hundreds of years and, when treated with respect, has never failed them. During the first 500 years or so of the Christian era, vast stretches of French forest were set afire to make room for the human newcomers who moved over from Celtic Britain and up from the Mediterranean. The ashes of these colossal bonfires still influence the earth. Instinctively the French have fed back into their soil the elements it needs to make harvests of high quality. Today, as a thousand years ago, no reputable French gardener works without a good compost pit as his ally, one cannily layered with vegetable matter, from dead leaves to wilted lettuces or wormy apples, droppings from the hen house or the rabbit hutches, and an occasional forkful of good, fresh manure. The aged product of this ripe mixture is everything that the modern usage of the word "organic" implies, and it is employed as carefully as it is prepared: a sparse spading-in here, a generous spreading there, sometimes on top of the first snow, which will pull down the precious elements as it melts into the soil.

A good example of French care and prudence in dealing with the nation's limited amount of arable land is the comparatively new use of the salty marshes in the Camargue, in Provence. In 1942, when a war-bound France found its colonial supplies of rice threatened, it swiftly utilized the vast watery stretches of this strange region, which until then had supported little except flamingoes and wild horses. Paddies were made, and men were trained to work them. By now Camarguais rice is sought out by lovers of good food for its special, salty firmness.

153

In America we live for the most part on virgin soil. The first we ever knew of organic fertilizers was when the Pilgrims saw the Indians lay one or two dead fish in each hummock of earth where they would plant their corn. Many of the Indian tribes were not even faintly agrarian; if they did cultivate certain crops they simply moved to a more fertile place when they had exhausted the resources of their camp sites. The white settlers evidently shared the Indians' notion that the land was limitless. When they "wore out" soil they moved on, and New England was dotted with their abandoned farms even before the 19th Century began. There are still people who remember the vast stretches of wild buffalo grass that once grew like a protective fur on the hills of the Dakotas. It was ruthlessly stripped off to make wheat fields, and later blew down into the Dust Bowl, that hideous punishment to our nation in the '30s. One result of the widespread exploitation of our soil is that we have had to force its productivity to give us the foods we need. In the 20th Century, the obvious way has been through fast-acting chemicals rather than through the long, patient feeding that has kept European farms, pastures and orchards rich and generous.

Vive la différence in vegetables, too

The difference in vegetable flavors in France and in the U.S. is one of the first things a fairly sophisticated palate will notice. However, the key ingredient to taste in vegetables on either side of the Atlantic is freshness. Garden-fresh vegetables, in the prime of their growing season, cooked simply to retain that unfaded quality, are unmatchable.

The French housewife's way of holding the newness and greenness of the fresh vegetables is simplicity itself: boil (or blanch, in cooking terminology) green things like beans in a large quantity of rapidly boiling water. Then plunge them when barely done into an equally large amount of very cold water. This second process is called "refreshing" and the end result reflects the name. Drained, the beans will have kept all their flavor and color, and will be ready for last-minute preparation such as reheating in butter in a skillet, before they are served. This procedure, familiar to anyone who has prepared summer garden produce for the home freezer, is the one used for all green vegetables by the technicians of the frozen-food companies. Done properly, it can make dishes that will be almost like the ones remembered with misty nostalgia from "that little bistro near Les Halles."

Another French kitchen trick is braising vegetables, which means cooking them in a covered casserole in very little water. The process will please health-seekers who count their vitamins as gone down the drain if even a teaspoonful of the water is discarded; it can be done in advance of the meal; and every bit of the juice can be reduced and then poured over the vegetables to enhance the full flavor.

A third technique, particularly successful when applied to freshly picked carrots, is glazing. Carrots are cooked in a little stock, to which sugar is added, to give them a syrupy, shiny coating.

I once ate a most delicious and refreshing supper, served to me by a friend who was about as poor as one would ever want to become. She had bought a whole box of lettuces from a storekeeper who was discarding them for being plainly beyond their first beauty. She got rid of what seemed

like another boxful of outer leaves, and then braised the hearts whole, and served them with some little crisp sausages on top. The platter looked bountiful, which was what my near-penniless friend needed to make her feel rich, and with a bottle of extremely *ordinaire* white *vin ordinaire*, and a loaf of bread, we made a most satisfactory meal indeed; we later went our ways convinced that Fate could not harm us, for we had dined well that day.

Vegetables also can make a delicious hors d'oeuvre (or a separate course after the entrée, as is more customary in France) or they can add interest to the innumerable dishes which they accompany. Asparagus, for instance, is used in more ways by French cooks than the average American housewife imagines, and at every point in the meal from the soup right through to the moment of clearing the table for cheese or dessert.

Artichokes in the hands of the French are even more versatile. They seem to grow as enthusiastically as weeds in some parts of France, and in Provence can be found almost the year around, in dozens of sizes and colors. Artichokes from the northern provinces are as round as tennis balls, as tender as butter. When properly prepared, with the clipped leaves spread out and the center freed of its "choke" and filled with a simple mayonnaise (or with a hollandaise if hot), they are like some rare, delectable flower.

In the warm, rocky lands to the south artichokes are tougher and more pungent. One of the best artichokes in Provence, for instance, is almost purple in color, and long and pointed. When it is very young it has no hairy center, and is often eaten whole, with only its outer leaves pulled off. I have eaten the same artichoke raw. The young plant was simply cut into quarters at the table for an hors d'oeuvre; the stalk-end was dipped in a little salt and then was eaten with some bread and sweet butter to offset the peculiar tantalizing bitterness of the nutlike flesh.

Long braids of garlic bulbs, essential to the cuisine of Provence, are stacked at the market in Cavaillon. Such decorative strings, which assure the cook an ample supply, hang on the walls of many rural French kitchens.

Baskets of tomatoes, fresh from the field, are as necessary to Provençal cooking as are garlic and olive oil.

Cooked artichoke bottoms, the large rich ones, are often used as garnishes for meat dishes, or are stuffed or filled with little peas in season, for a separate course. The so-called hearts, which are blanched and used in many dishes, are now available almost everywhere both canned and frozen and, treated carefully, can add interest to any meal: cold and *à la grecque,* for an hors d'oeuvre, or seasoned simply to make a salad; or braised; or seasoned and used as a garnish or accompaniment to many entrées. They are a cook's faithful ally in preparing distinctive meals at all seasons.

A dish that's always good next day

Besides the near-primitive boiling, braising and refreshing of vegetables, there are countless other ways of making them into dishes that are hardly less ancient. A *ratatouille* from Provence, for instance, has been served for many years in most of the countries of the Near East and the Mediterranean basin and is made from the same basic ingredients: eggplant, tomatoes, onions, olive oil. It will vary a little not only with the cook but with the herbs and materials available, but it is rare to find an end result that is not highly edible. A *ratatouille* improves with age, unlike most vegetable concoctions, and can be reheated or served cold for several days.

This gift of happy reappearance at the table is common to many dishes made by French housewives (and increasingly by good restaurants, which are conscious of the reassuring simplicity of regional cooking, the increasing costs of the classical haute cuisine—and the lack of trained men capable of practicing it). There are countless dishes like *tomates à la provençale,* for instance, which are inexpensive when in season, easy to prepare, and if possible even more refreshing and delicious cold than hot.

The characteristically French way of stuffing things in order to use several different textures and flavors in one combination, always to their mutual good, may be applied to almost any vegetable that is vaguely shaped to hold a mixture of crumbs, eggs, finely chopped meats and herbs. Zucchini, eggplants and cucumbers can be hollowed and filled. Mushrooms, better shaped by nature to hold a stuffing, may be cast in any part from baked appetizers in the first course to a garnish for meats or an elegant solitary course after the entrée *(page 162).* Artichokes are hollowed, stuffed and baked with the same general results (though they are somewhat messier to eat). Either lettuces or cabbage may be blanched, stuffed and served as a truly honorable entrée. Often their filling will be based on some kind of sausage meat, skillfully combined with bread crumbs and such.

In Alsace, this dish can be a red cabbage stuffed with a purée of chestnuts and simmered in red wine and plenty of butter. Down near Grasse it will be a tender green cabbage, tightly stuffed with a dressing of smoked salt pork and crumbs and garlic and olive oil (of course!), and then tied in a good cloth and boiled in ample water.

Often I have eaten a stuffed cabbage made in this fashion in the high mountains of Savoy. There we were served the broth first, just as with a *pot-au-feu* or a *poule-au-pot.* As I remember, this rich, good soup had some thin noodles boiled with it at the last, and it made a fine introduction to the fuming, delicious cannonball that next appeared on the table, to be carved for us by the head of the house, a retired mountain guide.

156

In French kitchens, potatoes are thought of as a vegetable in their own right and not as a mere adjunct to meat. Certainly they are never reduced to the near anonymity some of us have imposed on them.

Often in France they are served as a separate course, whipped into a creamy froth and then lightly gratinéed, or as a main luncheon dish demanding patience (but worth every minute of it), like *pommes de terre Anna*. In the northern provinces, especially toward the Belgian border, potatoes grow to perfection, and are usually cooked with complete simplicity, to bring out their special consistency and savor, as in *pommes de terre Dauphinoises,* scalloped with milk and cheese.

In the south the recipes combine potatoes with such local riches as cheese and eggs, or they become parts of other dishes: boiled and sliced into a *salade Niçoise* in one region, included in a *bouillabaisse* in another, even put in a *ratatouille*. In the Basque country potatoes are almost as essential to a real *garbure*, or cabbage soup, as the cabbage and goose fat. And what student would eat his "rare steak with watercress" without a generous accompaniment of "French" fries, really more a part of the dish than an added bounty?

Almost everywhere in France, small, tender steamed potatoes are served with the most delicately poached or fried fish, or peeled and browned in the juices of a roasting joint of meat, or carefully cooked in butter to be added as a delicious garnish to an entrée. Never, anywhere in that country of great culinary wisdom, are they treated as a necessary but unimportant side order to be eaten automatically or pushed aside. They are cultivated and harvested with care, chosen according to their seasons and attributes, and prepared in keeping with the wishes of the cook and the requirements of the regional cuisine. They are, when thus treated, one more proof that eating with grace can make it worthwhile to eat in order to live.

Crisp red radishes, like these in the Saint-Malo market, appear on French tables everywhere as hors d'oeuvre, to be eaten with butter and salt.

Boiling artichokes in a potful of salted water cooks them quickly and keeps their flavor fresh. But the artichokes need plenty of water—a quart each—and it has to be kept at a bubbling boil. Note that the tops and leaves have been trimmed.

BRAISING peas, lettuce and onions together blends their flavors and makes them tender.

BLANCHING beans in boiling water and refreshing them under cold water keeps them green.

GLAZING carrots in a blend of stock, butter and sugar gives them an amber coating.

Petits Pois Frais à la Française
FRESH PEAS BRAISED WITH ONIONS AND LETTUCE

Remove the wilted outer leaves of the lettuce and trim the stem. Rinse the lettuce in cold water, spreading the leaves apart gently, to remove all traces of sand. Cut the lettuce into 4 or 6 wedges, and bind each wedge with soft string to keep it in shape while cooking.

In a heavy 3-quart saucepan, bring the peas, lettuce wedges, onions, parsley, 6 tablespoons butter, water, salt and sugar to a boil over moderate heat, toss lightly to mix flavors, then cover the pan tightly and cook for 30 minutes, stirring occasionally, until the peas and onions are tender and the liquid nearly cooked away. If the liquid hasn't evaporated, cook the peas uncovered, shaking the pan constantly, for a minute or two until it does. Remove the parsley and cut the strings off the lettuce. Gently stir in 2 tablespoons of soft butter; taste and season. Transfer to a heated vegetable dish and serve in small bowls. It is traditional to eat *petits pois* with a spoon.

To serve 4 to 6

1 firm 7- to 8-inch head Boston lettuce
3 cups fresh shelled green peas (about 3 pounds)
12 peeled white onions, about ¾ inch in diameter
6 parsley sprigs, tied together
6 tablespoons butter, cut into ½-inch pieces
½ cup water
½ teaspoon salt
½ teaspoon sugar
2 tablespoons soft butter

Haricots Verts au Naturel
GREEN STRING BEANS, BLANCHED AND BUTTERED

In a large kettle or soup pot, bring the water and 3 tablespoons of salt to a bubbling boil over high heat. Drop the beans in by the handful. Return the water to a boil, reduce the heat to moderate and boil the beans uncovered for 10 to 15 minutes, or until they are just tender. Do not overcook them. Immediately drain them in a large sieve or colander. If the beans are to be served at once, melt 2 tablespoons of butter in a 2- to 3-quart saucepan and toss the beans with the butter for a minute or two, season them with salt and pepper, then transfer them to a serving dish.

If the beans are to be served later, refresh them after they have drained by quickly plunging the sieve or colander into a large pot of cold water and letting it remain there for 2 or 3 minutes. Drain the beans thoroughly, place them in a bowl, cover and set aside—in the refrigerator if they are to wait for long. If you plan to serve them hot, reheat them in 2 tablespoons of hot butter, season them and let them warm through over moderate heat.

To serve 6 to 8

6 quarts water
3 tablespoons salt
3 pounds green string beans, trimmed
2 tablespoons butter
Salt
Freshly ground black pepper

Carottes Glacées
GLAZED CARROTS

In a heavy 8- to 10-inch skillet, bring the carrots, stock, butter, sugar, salt and a few grindings of pepper to a boil over moderate heat. Then cover and simmer over low heat, shaking the skillet occasionally to roll the carrots about in the liquid. Check to see that the liquid is not cooking away too fast; if it is, add more stock. In 20 to 30 minutes the carrots should be tender when pierced with the tip of a sharp knife, and the braising liquid should be a brown, syrupy glaze. If the stock has not reduced enough, remove the carrots to a plate and boil the liquid down over high heat. Before serving, roll the carrots around in the pan to coat them with the glaze. Transfer the carrots to a heated serving dish, and sprinkle with fresh parsley.

NOTE: This technique may also be used for parsnips and turnips.

To serve 4 to 6

10 to 12 medium carrots, peeled and cut in 2-inch cylinders or olive shapes
1½ cups beef or chicken stock, fresh or canned
4 tablespoons butter
2 tablespoons sugar
½ teaspoon salt
Freshly ground black pepper
2 tablespoons finely chopped, fresh parsley

To serve 6

3 pounds fresh asparagus
6 quarts water
3 tablespoons salt

A trimmed artichoke and peeled asparagus spears show the care that French housewives lavish on vegetables. Both are at their tastiest *au naturel*—boiled until just tender, drained at once, and served hot with hollandaise sauce, as shown, or melted butter. They may also be chilled and served with a mayonnaise or vinaigrette sauce.

Asperges au Naturel
BOILED ASPARAGUS

Line up the asparagus tips evenly and cut off the butt ends to make all the spears the same length. With a small, sharp knife, *not* a vegetable peeler, peel each asparagus of its skin and tough, outer flesh. At the butt end, the peeling may be as thick as 1/16 inch, but it should gradually become paper thin as the knife cuts and slides toward the tip. Wash the peeled spears in cold water. Divide the asparagus into five or six equal bundles, and tie the bundles together with soft string at both the tip and butt ends.

In an enameled or stainless steel kettle or oval casserole large enough to hold the asparagus horizontally, bring the water and salt to a bubbling boil. Drop in the asparagus bundles and bring the water back to a boil. Reduce the heat to moderate and boil uncovered for 8 to 10 minutes, or until the butt ends are tender but still slightly resistant when pierced with the tip of a sharp knife. Do not overcook the asparagus. Using two kitchen forks, lift the bundles out of the water by their strings. Lay them on towels to drain, then cut off the strings. Serve the asparagus hot with melted butter or hollandaise sauce *(page 74)*. Or chill the asparagus and serve cold with vinaigrette sauce or mayonnaise *(page 74)*.

Artichauts au Naturel
BOILED ARTICHOKES

Trim the bases of the artichokes flush and flat. Bend and snap off the small bottom leaves and any bruised outer leaves. Lay each artichoke on its side, grip it firmly, and slice about 1 inch off the top. With scissors, trim ¼ inch off the points of the rest of the leaves. Rub all the cut edges with lemon to prevent discoloring. To remove the chokes before cooking, spread the top leaves apart and pull out the inner core of thistlelike yellow leaves. With a long-handled spoon, scrape out the hairy choke inside. Squeeze in a little lemon juice and press the artichoke back into shape.

In a large enameled kettle or soup pot, bring 6 quarts of water and 3 tablespoons of salt to a bubbling boil. Drop in the artichokes and return the water to a boil. Reduce the heat and boil briskly uncovered, turning the artichokes occasionally. It will take about 15 minutes to cook artichokes without their chokes, about 30 minutes with the chokes still in. They are done when their bases are tender when pierced with the tip of a sharp knife. Remove them from the kettle with tongs and drain them upside down in a colander. Serve the artichokes hot with melted butter, hollandaise or béarnaise sauce *(page 74)*. Or chill the artichokes and serve cold with vinaigrette or mayonnaise *(page 74)*.

To serve 6

6 twelve- to fourteen-ounce artichokes
1 lemon, cut
6 quarts water
3 tablespoons salt

To trim an artichoke before cooking, use a sharp knife to cut an inch or so off the top cone of leaves.

Then, using kitchen scissors, clip the sharp point off each of the artichoke's large outer leaves.

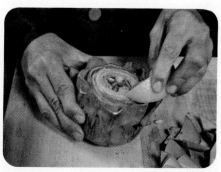

As you trim, rub all the cut edges of the leaves with lemon juice to prevent them from discoloring.

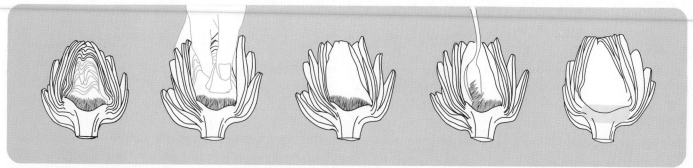

The heart of the artichoke, its most delicious part, can be reached only by removing the prickly leaves, and the hairy choke, shown in red (1).

Spread the top of the artichoke apart and pull the inside leaves out with your fingers (2), revealing the hairy choke beneath them (3).

The choke may be scraped out with a spoon (4), exposing the heart, shown in green (5). Dechoking may be done before or after cooking.

161

To serve 6

MUSHROOMS WITH CRAB MEAT STUFFING

1½ cups lump crab meat, fresh, frozen
    or canned
2 tablespoons butter
4 tablespoons finely chopped shallots
    or scallions
1 cup *béchamel* sauce *(recipe below)*
¼ to ½ teaspoon lemon juice
Salt
White pepper
18 to 24 two-inch mushroom caps

MUSHROOMS WITH SPINACH STUFFING

½ cup finely chopped shallots or
    scallions
3 tablespoons butter
¾ cup finely chopped, squeezed and
    firmly packed cooked fresh spinach
    (about ¾ pound) or 1 ten-ounce
    package frozen, chopped spinach,
    defrosted and squeezed dry
¾ cup finely chopped boiled ham
1 cup *béchamel* sauce *(recipe below)*
Salt
Freshly ground black pepper
18 to 24 two-inch mushroom caps
2 tablespoons butter, cut in tiny
    pieces

MUSHROOMS WITH MINCED
   MUSHROOM STUFFING

¾ pound fresh mushrooms, finely
    chopped
4 tablespoons finely chopped shallots
    or scallions
2 tablespoons butter
1 cup *béchamel* sauce *(recipe below)*
1 teaspoon finely chopped fresh
    parsley
Salt
Freshly ground black pepper
18 to 24 two-inch mushroom caps
2 tablespoons fine dry bread crumbs
1 tablespoon grated, imported Swiss
    cheese
2 tablespoons butter, cut in tiny pieces

BÉCHAMEL SAUCE (Makes about 1 cup)

2 tablespoons butter
3 tablespoons flour
1 cup hot milk
Salt
White pepper

Champignons Farcis
BAKED STUFFED MUSHROOM CAPS

CHAMPIGNONS FARCIS AU CRABE (mushrooms with crab meat stuffing):
Preheat the oven to 350°. Carefully inspect the crab meat and remove any
bits of cartilage, then shred the lumps with a fork. In a heavy 8- to 10-inch
skillet, melt 2 tablespoons of butter over moderate heat and in it cook the
shallots, stirring constantly, for 2 minutes, or until they are soft. Stir in the
crab meat and toss it with the shallots for 10 seconds or so. With a rubber
spatula, transfer the mixture to a large bowl.

Stir in the 1 cup *béchamel* sauce, then season to taste with lemon juice,
salt and white pepper. Lightly butter a shallow baking dish or roasting
pan large enough to hold the mushroom caps in one layer. Sprinkle the
inside of the caps with salt, spoon in the crab filling and arrange the caps in
the pan. Bake in the upper third of the oven for 10 to 15 minutes, or until
the mushrooms are tender when pierced with the tip of a sharp knife and the
filling is bubbly. Serve on a large heated platter.

CHAMPIGNONS FARCIS AUX ÉPINARDS (mushrooms with spinach and ham
stuffing): Preheat the oven to 350°. In a heavy 8- to 10-inch skillet, cook
the shallots in 3 tablespoons of butter over moderate heat, stirring constantly, for 2 minutes, or until soft. Add the spinach and toss it in the skillet for
3 to 4 minutes. With a rubber spatula, transfer the mixture to a large bowl.
Stir in the ham and 1 cup *béchamel* sauce, and season with salt and pepper.
Butter a large, shallow baking dish or roasting pan; sprinkle the caps with
salt and spoon the filling into them. Arrange the caps in the pan and dot
them with butter. Bake in the upper third of the oven for 10 to 15 minutes,
or until the mushrooms are tender and the filling is lightly browned. Serve
on a heated platter.

CHAMPIGNONS FARCIS DUXELLES (mushrooms with minced mushroom
stuffing): A handful at a time, squeeze the chopped mushrooms in the corner of a towel to extract as much juice as possible. Preheat the oven to 350°.
In a heavy 8- to 10-inch skillet, cook the shallots in 2 tablespoons of butter
over moderate heat, stirring constantly, for 2 minutes, or until they are soft.
Add the chopped mushrooms and cook, stirring occasionally, for 8 to 10
minutes, or until all the moisture has evaporated and they are beginning to
brown lightly. With a rubber spatula, transfer the mixture to a large bowl;
stir in the 1 cup *béchamel* sauce and parsley, and season to taste with salt
and pepper. Butter a large, shallow baking dish or roasting pan; salt the
mushroom caps and spoon the filling into them. Mix the bread crumbs and
grated cheese, then sprinkle them over the filling. Arrange the caps in the
pan and dot them with butter. Bake in the upper third of the oven for 10 to
15 minutes, or until the mushrooms are tender and the filling is lightly
browned. Serve hot or cold.

BÉCHAMEL SAUCE: In a heavy 2- to 3-quart saucepan, melt 2 tablespoons of
butter over moderate heat, and stir in the flour. Cook, stirring constantly,
for 2 minutes. Do not let this *roux* brown. Remove the pan from the heat
and blend in the hot milk. Then return to high heat and cook, stirring constantly, until the sauce comes to a boil. Reduce the heat and simmer, still
stirring, for 2 or 3 minutes, or until the sauce is thick enough to coat a
spoon heavily. Remove the pan from the heat, taste and season with salt
and white pepper.

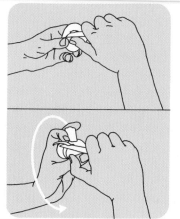

In France plump mushrooms, like those on the cutting board and in the antique French scoop, not only flavor other dishes, but are featured by themselves. On the far side of the platter are mushrooms *à la grecque*. In front of them are *(from left)* mushrooms filled with crabmeat; ham and spinach; and *duxelles (page 162)*. In the foreground are grilled mushrooms on toast rounds.

To flute a mushroom, hold it in your left hand, thumb on the cap, stem away from you *(left, above)*. Using a small sharp knife with a rounded cutting edge, rotate left hand toward you *(arrow)* so the blade cuts from center to edge of mushroom cap *(left, below)*. One design you can make—with practice—is shown above.

Bold Relatives of the Lily: The Onion Family

All seven members of the onion family sketched above and shown in color on the opposite page have important roles in a French kitchen. They are:
1. Yellow globe onions
2. Leeks
3. Garlic
4. Scallions
5. Shallots
6. White onions
7. A pot of chives

Onions, the "lilies of the kitchen," are as French as the stock pot, and just as indispensable. Except for desserts, almost all French provincial dishes contain at least a trace of some member of the onion family. For sauces, there are shallots or scallions; for soups, leeks or garlic; for *navarins* and *blanquettes*, white onions; for garnishes and herb omelets, chives. The ordinary yellow globe onion is the most versatile of all and turns up everywhere—whole, sliced, diced or chopped.

Leeks, which look like fat scallions but have a blander taste, are invariably part of hearty vegetable soups, from *potage Parmentier* to *garbure*. In France, where leeks are so plentiful they are called "the asparagus of the poor," they are often cooked and served as a vegetable.

Of all the onion family, shallots are the most typically French. They look like reddish-brown garlic, but taste like mild onions—which is why scallions can take their place in almost any dish.

The white onions that Americans call "boiling onions" get subtler treatment in French *ragoûts* and *navarins*, or are glacéed to garnish roasts. The fat yellow globe onion is at its finest thinly sliced in *soupe à l'oignon*. Big ones may be stuffed and baked like Provençal tomatoes, but their usual role is as a seasoning for stocks, stews and stuffings.

The "weeds" of the onion family are chives, which flourish in French backyards and window boxes, ready to be snipped to dress up everyday omelets, soups and salads. Green onions (which are young globe onions) and scallions (which are clusters of shoots of the white onion family) come to the French table raw as appetizers or as salad ingredients, or are chopped up and used in sauces when shallots are out of season.

Garlic, also in the onion family, is used so lavishly along the Mediterranean that it is sometimes referred to as *la vanille de Marseille*. Cooks there have found that crushing garlic makes its pungency more gentle. (Boiling garlic also tames it; the Provençals make soup with a couple of dozen garlic cloves, water, and not much else.)

Luckily, most members of the onion family are as available in the United States as they are in France. Shallots and leeks, however, tend to be winter and early spring vegetables and are not always easy to find in the markets.

Oignons Glacés à Blanc

GLAZED WHITE ONIONS

To serve 4 to 6

⅔ cup chicken stock, fresh or canned
2 tablespoons butter
Salt
Freshly ground black pepper
16 to 24 peeled white onions, about 1 inch in diameter

In a heavy 8- to 10-inch skillet, bring the chicken stock, butter, and salt and pepper to taste to a boil. Drop in the onions, reduce the heat, cover and simmer very slowly for 20 to 30 minutes, or until the onions are tender, turning the onions occasionally with a spoon. The braising liquid should have reduced to a syrupy glaze; if it hasn't, remove the onions and boil the liquid down alone. Roll the onions around gently in the pan to moisten them with glaze before serving them in a heated vegetable dish.

XI

Salads: To Refresh the Palate

A bowl of fresh, tender leaves from any of half a hundred kinds of salad greens, unadorned except by the simplest possible mixture of oil, vinegar and seasoning, is a joy to the palate—even if it is dismissed by much of the American population (and some other populations as well) as rabbit food. Many want it disguised—by coddled eggs, highly flavored croutons, dressings heady with sharp, fruity cheeses like Roquefort, slices of cooked vegetables and tomatoes, and so on.

We eat such concoctions during a dinner based on rare steak and a baked potato often doused in another rich, cold dressing, this time of sour cream with chives, though this is perhaps more a restaurant pattern than one followed in American homes.

Something good for the palate

Romans used to wear wreaths of tiny lettuces and parsley on their heads to stay refreshed during their long banquets. Frenchmen have found a more sensible use for these greens: they follow almost any entrée or main dish of a meal by putting the lettuces and sometimes the parsley into a bowl, tossing them with the simplest form of vinaigrette sauce and eating them. In this way they refresh their palates, which as true disciples of good eating they keep in excellent condition for whatever may next be tasted to the full. Such a plain salad acts as an excellent digestive, lightening and stimulating the gastric processes of all but the most reluctant human bodies.

Salad greens, freshly washed in cold water, are placed in a special basket to be shaken dry. A vigorous swinging in the air does this best. Careful drying of the leaves makes them crisper and allows the dressing to cling to the surface of each leaf.

In all French homes and restaurants, from the most modest to the greatest, this almost ritualistic part of a meal is prepared in much the same way, with the same rules:

The greens are fresh, clean and dry.

They may come from kitchen gardens, hothouses, markets, or even wild meadows or springtime ditches, but they will be mild and sweet—unless a gamy or spicy dish is served first; in that case the strong flavor may be made to linger agreeably on the tongue with the judicious help of young spinach leaves or a handful of tender sorrel or sharp watercress (with the promise of an equally forceful cheese to follow, rather than a delicate dessert).

The dressing will be made of oil, vinegar, salt and pepper. The oil will depend upon the province and also upon the flavors of the meal: a delicate nut oil, a pungent one made from olives, a mild vegetable oil. The vinegar too will depend, in provincial households, upon whether one lives in Burgundy, for instance, or in the northern cider country. Sometimes a little mustard is blended with the dressing; usually it comes from Dijon and tastes subtly of tarragon. (The most mustard I have ever tasted in a French salad was made once for an outdoor dinner in the early summer near Aix-en-Provence: inch-long slices of Belgian endive, thoroughly coated just before serving with an almost-thick vinaigrette of nothing much but olive oil and *moutarde de Dijon*. We ate it after lamb that had been roasted on a spit and wrapped with supple twigs of wild thyme we gathered while the fire was prepared.)

The salad will be made the minute it is time for it, not before; and more often than not, at family dinners, it will be made at the table, by the one designated as having the best "hand" with it.

It will never be served in small bowls or plates set above or to one side (in America, most awkwardly, to the left) of the main plate. It will be put on clean plates or, rarely, on the ones used for the entrée if the flavors are congenial. Even in the last case, it is considered a course in itself, not an accompaniment to anything.

Obviously all these rules have many exceptions. They depend largely upon the flavor of the dish that precedes the salad. They also depend upon the toughness of the component greeneries: winter lettuces are not as tender as those that bloom in the spring, and a bowl of strong-flavored curly chicory or dandelion greens will need different treatment from a pile of butter-sweet, almost gauzy "oak-leaf" lettuce hearts.

Herb-flavored vinegars are sometimes used in French kitchens, but if an herb is to be added to a green salad, a few leaves fresh from the garden are preferred. If dried they should be rubbed fine and put in the vinegar of the dressing to soften before the oil is stirred in. Whatever is added to the otherwise strict simplicity of the salad is chosen with great care so as not to break the continuity of the meal. After an *omelette aux fines herbes,* for instance, one or several of the herbs contained in it could be used, very discreetly, on the lettuce leaves.

A chicken cooked with tarragon would indicate a hint of tarragon in the salad dressing, unless a very delicate cheese or dessert was to follow.

A Gallery of Basic Salad Greens

Chicory: curly-leaved, slightly bitter

Endive: a tight cluster, a tangy taste

Dandelion greens: wild and bitter

Boston lettuce: delicate, subtle flavor

Watercress: spicy green for accent

Bibb lettuce: tender and nutlike

Romaine: stiff leaves, vigorous taste

Escarole: like chicory, but with broader leaves and a stronger flavor

These are the simple ingredients of the traditional vinaigrette dressing: oil (in flasks), plus vinegar (in cruets and the stoppered bottle, with tarragon) or lemon juice. How to combine them—with or without such variations as a touch of mustard —is the supreme test of the taste and skill of the salad maker.

Garlic? That would depend upon the regions from which the other dishes had come, and upon how sturdy the flavor of the after-dinner cheese might be. In any case, the garlic would come not from a salt or a vinegar that had been preflavored to save the cook a little work, but from a fresh clove rubbed in the bowl or tossed with the dressing and then removed, or occasionally rubbed upon a crust of bread and mixed with the salad.

Herbs are a staple of any French kitchen, increasingly encountered as one moves south. They are amusing and pretty to grow—outdoors when possible, or indoors in pots. They have their seasons like all the rest of us, and in France they are served fresh when at their prime, and then used unashamedly in dried form, to be crushed in a mortar or rubbed in the palm of one's hand with delightfully odorous results, as the recipes dictate. Often they are allowed to freshen themselves in a little wine or broth before being added to the dish that needs them. As with all things regional, they will grow sparsely or richly according to the soil and climate, and be used accordingly by cooks. Thanks to excellent modern cultivation, we can buy in dried form every herb acceptable to man (and a few that are still dubious) by going to a good market or store for them.

There are almost as many charts for the uses of herbs as there are recipes that call for them. But it is nearly impossible to find recommendations for their use in the classical green salad in French cookbooks, because it is assumed that any cook knows better than to interfere with the salad's basic function: to refresh the palate and rest the digestive processes. A salad delicately flavored with mint might follow a roast leg of lamb but it would *never* come after a steak. Why? Because, a Frenchman would answer with irrefutable logic, it would be simply unthinkable, that is why. A salad with a hint of garlic in it *might*, on the other hand, follow *tomates à la provençale* or a *ratatouille*. Nevertheless, on both counts most Frenchmen would rath-

170

er eat their salads innocent of everything but salad greens and leave the herbs to work their magic in the dishes that go before.

Most salads are literally "tossed," after being pushed lightly through the dressing at the bottom of the bowl. There are some few travelers of the late '90s left who remember the pretty salad waitresses in the Duval restaurants in Paris, wheeling a cart about the rooms and making salads from it with their bare hands, their arms elbow-deep in the big bowls. A few salads are turned so thoroughly in the dressing that they are called "tired," but this depends upon the toughness of the leaves, and on the tastes of the salad maker, the star of the performance, and his captive audience.

One such star was my friend Madame Rigoulot, under whose gastronomical spell I lived for many months. She was Alsatian, and perhaps inclined to add extra richness to many things a Normande or a Bordelaise would have left alone. One of her tricks, which I admit I have copied, was to add a few teaspoonfuls of the juice from a roasted chicken or a joint of lamb, beef or pork to the salad bowl just before the platter was removed and the salad was mixed. It carried the flavor from one course to the next in a delicious if unclassical fashion.

One of the best shows I ever saw over a salad bowl was in Marseilles, when a visiting-fireman friend of mine asked that a salad be made at the table, but absolutely without any trace of garlic. The waiter blandly went about his performance, during which he managed to crush at least three ripe, juicy cloves of the forbidden fruit in his bowl. The salt on them held down their fragrance, and then ample mustard was included, and finally a little vinegar and the oil added drop by drop and beaten in as if for a mayonnaise.

The result was a smooth, thick blend, sharp, opaquely yellow, and miraculously innocent of the dreaded smelly bulb. The lettuces were thinly coated with this dressing, and the fireman pronounced it one of the best he had ever tasted. I agreed. The waiter thanked us impassively, with one small sideways look of triumph at my own impassive face. Perhaps it was treacherous of us both, but there was local pride to be protected: who in his right senses would ask a Marseillais to leave garlic out of anything?

Perhaps the slowest and simplest salad-bowl performances I ever witnessed —and often, thank heavens, but not often enough—were daily rituals at my old friend Georges' table. After the table had been cleared of all but the bread and wine (which would be needed to assist in the consumption of the modest but excellent array of cheeses to follow), two bowls of equally generous size were placed before him, one empty and one filled with fresh greens. The wine vinegar and oil were put in position, with salt, pepper and occasionally a small pot of mustard. Georges made the dressing in the empty bowl, ignoring the one filled with crisp leaves until a sip told him he had created the right mixture, once more, of all the ingredients.

He then lifted a small handful of the salad onto the dressing, tossed it lightly through the puddle and then pushed it aside, added another handful and tossed it, and so on, with great care, until every leaf was delicately coated but neither bruised nor limp. An interesting spectacle. And given the right greens, the right dressing, the right deft, finicky touch (and perhaps the right man), it is a process anyone can duplicate—and a fine way indeed to revive oneself for whatever will follow.

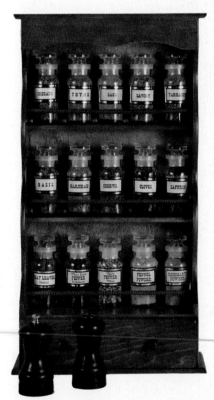

The herbs and spices that supplement salt and freshly ground pepper in French cooking are most conveniently stored in a rack. Since they lose flavor if they are kept too long, buy small amounts and store them in tightly sealed jars in a cool, dry place.

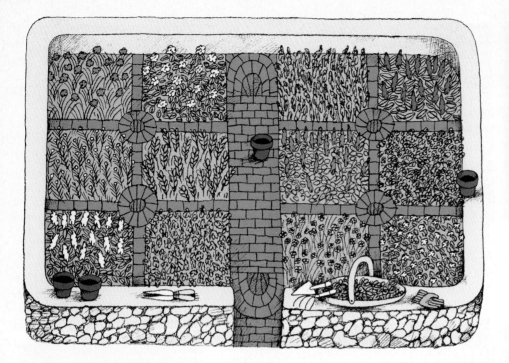

CHIVES—a delicate relative of the onion. Their long, thin stalks, which should be cut frequently, go well in salads or as a garnish for bland dishes.

SAVORY—a warm, piquant flavor. A member of the mint family, savory is a traditional seasoning for vegetables like string beans or peas.

BASIL—a refreshing member of the mint family. It is used with tomatoes in any form—the vegetable, juice or sauce—and also with eggs and seafood.

A Grow-It-Yourself Herb Garden

Herbs—flavorful, aromatic plants—are not at all difficult to grow. They have a much better flavor fresh than dried, and the best way to ensure a ready supply is to have your own herb garden.

The garden sketched above is planted with 12 of the herbs most frequently used in French cooking; the photographs correspond with the herbs' locations in the garden. Conveniently placed near the kitchen door, the garden need not be elaborate or take up much space. All it needs is plenty of sun, regular watering and good drainage.

If you don't have enough land for a garden, herbs can be grown in pots on terraces or even in sunny windows. While most flavorful when used fresh, they may also be dried and stored for later use. For drying, select herbs at their peak, pick them in the early morning, and sun-dry for several hours during the hottest part of the day (to help prevent mold). Then tie them in bunches and hang them upside down—or spread them thinly on a piece of window screening that is supported above the floor—in a dark room where the air can circulate freely around the herbs.

Many herbs are hardy perennials; some are annuals, and a few are biennials, producing seeds every other year. In this garden are *(top row, left to right)* chives, oregano, rosemary, sage. The second row contains savory, tarragon and thyme, all perennials, and parsley, a biennial. In the bottom row are the annuals: basil, chervil, fennel and marjoram.

OREGANO—strong, aromatic, slightly bitter. Its flavor is particularly suitable to robust Mediterranean dishes that use tomatoes or eggplant.

ROSEMARY—a fresh, sweet flavor. It is primarily used to flavor meats—sparingly, because when heated it releases a strong, acrid oil.

SAGE—strongly fragrant and slightly bitter. Commonly used in poultry stuffing, it can also be used to complement pork and sausage dishes.

TARRAGON—faintly licorice-like in flavor. It is best known as a flavoring for vinegar. It is also widely used for fish and for chicken.

THYME—aromatic and pungent. This must be used judiciously, because of its strong taste. It helps flavor almost all French soups and stews.

PARSLEY—slightly peppery flavor. Popular as a garnish, both to enhance the looks of food and to enrich the taste of soups, salads, stews, sauces.

CHERVIL—a cousin of parsley. Its fresh leaves are good in salads; its dried leaves go well with eggs and on cream soups or broiled fish.

FENNEL—licorice-like in flavor. Its root and stalks are eaten raw or cooked; its leaves and seeds flavor fish, soups, salads and sauces.

MARJORAM—a member of the mint family, aromatic and rather bitter. A versatile herb for poultry, lamb and vegetables that need zest.

XII

Cheese, Fruit, Wine: Purest Pleasures

A velvety cheese in its soft prime (in this case Coulommiers), a chunk of crusty bread, a basket of fine fruits and a glass of wine are for many Frenchmen the ideal ending of a meal—better than any prepared sweet.

In a country as enormous and as new as America, the regional specialties must depend more upon imported tastes than upon what has evolved over centuries of human occupation. Our good wines, especially on the West Coast, usually come from vines brought originally from Europe, just as some of our best cheeses have been developed in a relatively few years from European cultures. There are excellent wines made from native grapes in the older Eastern states, and there are completely native cheeses, like the Vermont sage cheese, and the Western Teleme Jack. But in the main we depend upon importations.

In France, our source for many of the best imports, there are seasons for cheeses, just as there are for strawberries or lamb or green peas. The cheeses used to be limited to their native regions, but thanks to improved transportation and storage (Camembert cheese now is even exported in cans, to be kept at its peak) they can be found almost in any season, and almost everywhere. Every region in the country which supports an adequate population of milk-giving animals also produces some form of fresh or ripened cheese. It will come from cows, sheep or goats; it will be mixed or plain; creamy or dry. It will be firm, soft, tough, moist, marble-hard.

From Normandy comes the king of all cheeses in the world, I think, the Camembert, as well as Pont-l'Évêque, and the gentle creamy ones called Petit-Suisse and Neufchâtel. (America has very reputable copies of them, made in the dairy country of the Middle West and on the West Coast.) From Rouergue comes one great cheese, Roquefort, and from Auvergne comes another, Cantal, the first made of ewe's milk and stored in the mysterious caves where cold wet air is laden with a powerful penicillin. Other "blue" cheeses are made, mostly from cow's milk, both in France and in America, but the true Roquefort must come from Rouergue. Cantal is a completely different type, a firmly pressed cheese, golden and mild, and good with bread and beer as well as simple wines, whereas a Camembert or Roquefort will demand, and be worthy of, the finest and fullest-bodied of the red Bordeaux and Burgundies. Another cheese well-known in America is Brie, delicately salty and pale yellow, from the Île-de-France.

The many uses of a cheese

Cheese in many cooked or heated forms can be used in any part of a well-planned meal, to add flavor, consistency and interest. It can be found in omelets, soufflés and tarts, to start a dinner or to be the main course of a lighter lunch or supper. It can form an essential part of many sauces and dishes, or it can be used to add color and flavor to dishes passed at the last stage of their preparation under a grill or into a very hot oven.

But to serve cheese as such is unthinkable to a Frenchman until the meal has passed its climax. Then is the time to finish the last few bites of bread. Usually if there is nothing to follow but some fruit, the housewife will put more bread into the low basket that has been on the table since the meal began. It is a near-truth that cheese as such is never eaten without bread in France, but there are exceptions. Probably the best example is a *coeur à la crème*, when a heart-shaped mold of creamed white cheese is served with little fresh strawberries, *fraises des bois* if possible, and often crisp dry cookies. This is a kind of compromise, combining in one dish the two (and even three) final courses of a main meal in France: cheese, fruit and sometimes dessert. Another dish that I ate many times in Alsace was called a *vacherin*. There is an elaborate dessert of whipped frozen cream, ice cream, chocolate sauce, and so on, that is called the same thing in upper-class restaurants, but the one served to me, both in Strasbourg and in the mountains, was a suave mixture of soft white cheese and sweetened cream, left outside the window sill to freeze in the winter cold for a few hours, and then served with plenty of jam and little dry cookies.

Another compromise with the cheese-dessert question is the way many Frenchmen eat Petits-Suisses, the little rolls of firm cream cheese that are flown from Paris to America, at a certain price of course, and now and then are made by our own adventuresome dairymen. They are considered less rich than most cheeses, and therefore are somewhat in the child-invalid-geriatric category in some provincial kitchens, but they can be delicious instead of a dessert, especially as I first learned to eat them (in a form I would spurn enthusiastically today as much too sweet): peeled of their little wet wrapper, piled with sugar, and then mashed thoroughly but tidily with some extra cream into an unctuous smear for one's last bites of bread. After this somewhat childish table behavior, any kind of dessert would be excessive . . . except perhaps a few crisp, cool grapes. As I remember the procedure from my initiation, which lasted some three years in Dijon, the little round white cheeses were usually served in the winter, and I ate a few dried raisins or dates or figs after them, and then drank a small cup of strong black coffee, and went off to four or more hours of classes, fresh as a buttercup.

There is a dream in many American hearts, almost as romantic as the one about the French soup kettle brewing away at the back of the old kitchen range, but much less lethal and more attainable. It conjures up a little restaurant on the Left Bank, or on a balcony overlooking St. Tropez, and it centers around some crusty bread, a piece or two of cheese, some fresh fruit in a basket, and a bottle or pitcher or carafe of wine.

It is a fine dream. Unfortunately most of us prefer to keep it sacrosanct, safely over there in Paris or the south of France. Yet we *can* have some good crusty bread if we want it badly enough to seek it out. There *is* wonderful cheese available in every part of our country, some made right there in the locality, some brought in, as honest as any Camembert that ever came from Normandy.

There *is* fine fruit the year around, thanks to ever-improving methods for shipping and storing products. In the old days, it was the millionaires who ate grapes for Christmas. Now they are not only available but delicious, then and most of the year, in every part of this vast country, except perhaps on a mountainside in Montana or in a snowbound Vermont village. And there are other seasonal floods of fruits across this vast country: cherries and strawberries ripe for the table, cool but not too cold; then the peaches and apricots and plums of summer, so rich and beautiful in a basket; grapes of course, of every color and from every part of America, tart or heavy with sweetness to savor at the end of a meal. Afterwards will come, as in every other land, the ripe apples of autumn and winter, small and crisp from a state like Vermont, or large and bland and pungent from Washington. They are, no matter how shaped or flavored, superb with cheeses at the end of any kind of meal, especially a simple one. And their rival, in America as in France, is the pear, which comes to its perfection at the year's end and which can be, when it is in that state, perfection indeed.

A good cheese preserver, designed to prevent hardening, is a glass or plastic jar with a tight-fitting lid and ridges on the bottom. A mild solution of vinegar and water is poured into the bottom to impart moisture; the ridges keep the liquid from touching the cheeses.

The good wines of America

And as for the wine, we have it. It can be found, and it can be good. It will not be the same as the wines in Paris or St. Tropez, of course, and it may have suffered not only by comparison but by different treatment in traveling, storing, even serving. But it can be good. (Sometimes red wines do not like altitude—but to compensate, whites come to life in an astounding way, and a California Riesling served by a stream in the High Sierras will have the zing and sparkle of a Zizerser in Switzerland.)

There is good red port being made in America now, and the English custom of serving a glass of it with a sharp or fruity cheese is pleasant, especially if there is time to sit and talk, over the last bites of a meal, no matter how simple it may have been. This is a custom especially well suited to our habit of dining at night, instead of at noon, since port itself seems meant for nighttime enjoyment, a rich, reassuring thing to go to bed on.

Of course fruits are basic to French provincial cooking, fresh or dried or preserved. They are basic as well to any good meal when they are in season and at their most delectable in their simplest state, fresh from their own trees and vines and bushes. They are made into wonderful tarts and puddings, from Alsace to Périgord, and in the apple regions like Normandy they are cooked with everything, fish, meat, puddings. In Touraine, the country of beautiful prunes, it is the same. Everywhere, the *clafoutis* (consisting simply of a good light sweetened batter baked over fruits) are made when cherries are ripe, and down in the eastern part of the Bordeaux region, where beautiful greengage plums grow better than anywhere yet discovered, a *clafoutis* is made with them and raisins. Farther west, in the Basque country, it is made with fresh sweet grapes like muscats, and apples. The best I ever ate was in Franche-Comté, of stoned cherries which, instead of lying at the bottom of the dish, rose up through the pale yellow batter, making pockets in it of rich purple. Perhaps they had been soaked a while in kirsch? Near the Belgian and German borders, pickled cherries are often served with meat, and of course apples cooked with meat or in sauces are common in Normandy and Brittany.

Rural, genteel, delicious, but dynamite

Several times I have been offered, in the country, a taste of the family cherry liqueur, and whether in Provence or the Île-de-France it has been a glass of good brandy, perhaps sweetened, with a big cherry in it, usually still on its stem—the prize fruit from the tree. The trick, I soon found, is to sip the liqueur, which after a couple of years of intimacy with the fruit has completely changed its original taste, and then to pop the rather ugly, mottled, swollen fruit in one's mouth, where it becomes even larger, and seems to hold in its delicious flesh all the fire of the alcohol it has lain in. It is an interesting experience, and to my knowledge limited to rural areas. I feel quite sure that if I lived in any one of them, and had a cherry tree and a good jug, I would compound the same genteel dynamite for my guests.

Almost always, the wine which has gone along with the meal, or at least the entrée, is finished with the cheese, and this of course is an indication of what cheese to serve. It would be foolish, if a light, dry white wine had been drunk with an omelet and then with *sole meunière*, to serve a very strong, full-flavored cheese like a Roquefort or a Munster: the quarrel—not only with the wine but with the flavors left from the eggs and fish upon the diners' palates—would be ruinous. Instead, a mild, nutty Gruyère, a Port-du-Salut or a completely benign Petit-Suisse would be better, in and for every sense. When a good Camembert can be found, or a moldy Roquefort, or any strong or sharp cheese which is ready for the table but not tired and stinking of ammonia or plain ugly decay, then a firm-bodied red wine, one of the best from Burgundy, will be in its right place—preferably after it has performed an equally honorable role with something like a *boeuf bourguignon* or a grilled sirloin steak. Obviously nothing could be more restful after this delicious onslaught of both taste buds and gastric juices than a piece of fresh, cool fruit, unless the meal could last a long time and not be followed by anything but a contemplative amble or a little nap.

Desserts are fun, or can be once we escape the pattern of pies and puddings. But the dream most of us carry of that little restaurant with the cheese and bread and fruit, and the last of the bottle of Sancerre, is one that risks no disillusionment by being made real. Surely our habit of dining at night lends itself to the idea of a few moments of leisure over the last nibble of cheese and good bread, the final sip of wine, and the lingering freshness of a ripe muscat.

Twenty-one of the World's Most Savory Cheeses

Cheese comes in a wider variety of tastes, shapes and textures in France than anywhere else in the world. But French leadership in cheese is more than numerical: the quality is of international repute. Twenty-one of France's finest cheeses, shown in the color photograph overleaf, are identified in the key diagram at right. What follows is a description of the essential characteristics that have won each cheese its popularity.

Camembert, one of the most popular, is in its prime a pretty cheese; its rind is a light yellow-orange with a white, powdery crust. On the inside it should be a light, pale yellow with a softness that is short of being runny. Brie is next to Camembert in popularity. It also has a soft texture and a delicate but definite taste; it should be satinlike inside, with the same consistency as Camembert. Another good cheese of the Brie family is Coulommiers, which is sold younger and less mellow than Brie itself and tastes somewhat like Camembert.

Roquefort is a salty, tangy cheese with a grayish crust and an inside that is moist and mottled with green-blue flecks. Another blue-veined cheese is Bleu de Bresse. Cantal, France's one major cheddar-type cheese, is semihard and smooth with a light lemon color inside. Saint-Paulin, a cheese similar to Port-Salut, which was originally produced by Trappist monks, is a semihard cheese, with a mild, fresh flavor and a very smooth and butterlike texture. Reblochon, with an orange-yellow crust, is a soft, pale, creamy-colored, buttery cheese whose consistency is reminiscent of that of Camembert but without Camembert's tendency to run. Because of its mildness it makes a good starting point for the timid taster whose palate has been exposed mostly to bland processed cheeses. Beaumont and Le Dauphinois resemble Reblochon in taste. Tomme de Savoie is a mild-flavored, semisoft cheese, gentle to the inexperienced palate. Pont-l'Évêque is a square cheese with a soft and pale-yellow interior. Its flavor is rich, hearty and aromatic. Fromage au Marc de Raisin, also called "La Grappe," is a pale, sweet, pasty cheese that is rolled in a crust of grape pulp, or "marc." Comté is a French version of Swiss Gruyère cheese, complete with holes. Its rind is stippled a yellowish-brown color and is slightly roughened; the inside is ivory-yellow.

Sainte-Maure, Valençay and Saint-Marcellin are all goat cheeses, generally creamy, eaten when relatively fresh, and not found in quantity outside France. Mimolette resembles the Dutch Edam but has a tangier flavor. Munster is semisoft, strong-flavored and pungent. Boursin Triple-crème and Belletoile Triple-crème are rich, fresh cheeses and are frequently eaten by themselves with a fork or spoon, with a little powdered sugar sprinkled over them to sweeten their flavor.

All cheeses are best served at room temperature, removed from the refrigerator one to three hours before serving. They complement fruit as a light dessert and they are most frequently used in this manner, but they are equally well suited to hors d'oeuvre and midday snacks.

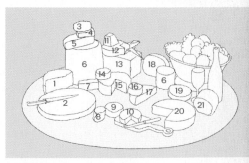

The cheeses shown on the next two pages are listed below:

1. Roquefort
2. Brie de Meaux
3. Camembert
4. Pont-l'Évêque
5. Saint-Paulin
6. Cantal and small Cantal
7. Sainte-Maure
8. Belletoile Triple-crème
9. Le Dauphinois
10. Coulommiers
11. Valençay
12. Saint-Marcellin
13. Comté
14. Reblochon
15. Fromage au Marc de Raisin
16. Boursin Triple-crème
17. Beaumont
18. Mimolette
19. Munster
20. Tomme de Savoie
21. Bleu de Bresse

Médaille d'Or, Paris 19

XIII

Desserts: The Finishing Touch

At a typical inn like the Auberge des Essarts-le-Roi near Paris, cheeses and strawberry tarts are freshly prepared for the table. The tarts are filled with berries at the last possible moment before serving so that their pastry shells will remain crisp.

Pastry shops—at least those that bake and sell nothing but pastries— are becoming rare in America. In small towns they do not exist, unless there is a deep ethnic pocket of people from other countries who consider pastry essential to life. They are gradually disappearing from large towns and cities, driven under by packaged mixes and frozen goods.

Occasionally, in a neighborhood predominantly French, Austrian, Italian or Scandinavian, an honest pastry shop will survive, and often successfully, as long as it does stay honest. In general, though, it will have to wage a losing battle with families who accept instant gelatins, "boughten" ice creams and defrosted pies as necessary endings to their meals.

It is a different story in France. Most French girls, of whatever level in the social structure, know a few basic recipes for making the end of a meal light and reviving, or for creating a rich, exciting finale. For an unexpected guest, they count on the nearest honest pastry-maker, who will provide not only the little hot cheese tarts, *pissaladières* (a type of pizza) and *pâtés en brioche* for an occasional hors d'oeuvre, but also a variety of desserts. Most good pastrymen have their own specialties, and pride themselves on their meringues in every shape and size, or their *pâtes brisées,* pastry doughs that they can provide on command in any form imaginable. Often the pastry-shop window will have a sign announcing that onion tarts are ready every Wednesday, or that *biscuits au chocolat* can be ordered Saturday and picked up after Mass on Sunday.

Much of the time, though, the modern French housewife trusts to her own training. More often than not, cheese and fruit will finish the main meal of her day. But she may want to give the family a smooth caramel custard, and then she knows just where Grandmother's mold is hanging, and just how long it will take to bake it before she must meet the school bus, and just how the pudding will taste, once it is turned out. If she has some good pears or apples, she will bake them in red wine or cider, and perhaps put a spoonful of currant jelly in each apple to give a luxurious color and taste. In the summer she will make a quick compote of whatever fruits there are, brought to a fast boil in a mixture that is half water and half sugar, drained, and then chilled in the syrup, which has been reduced a little. In the winter she will serve a compote of dried fruits.

The basis of countless confections

And of course there are two kinds of basic pastry that can be used in countless ways: the *pâte brisée* which is the same dough used in all the *quiches* and tarts that are eaten as hors d'oeuvre and main dishes, but sweetened for desserts—and the *pâte à choux,* which is much like the puffier popover recipe.

Cakes in France are different from ours. Frosted cakes are usually little squares or rounds, often filled first, and then decorated in ways traditional to the pastry art or to the regions in which they are made. When they are large enough to serve six or eight diners, they are not high and in layers, but are usually not more than two inches deep, split horizontally and rather elaborately filled and decorated.

When a cake is made at home, it is usually a very simple *biscuit,* which is not what it sounds like in English, a dry crisp cracker or a soft soda-bread, but rather an extremely light spongecake. This is baked either as vanilla- or chocolate-flavored, not more than an inch and a half thick. It may be eaten plain, or dusted with powdered sugar, or split and filled with a *crème anglaise* (and then iced or not) or cut into *petits fours* and played with at will. A *biscuit* is a refreshing thing, and easy to make once the cook understands that it does not contain any baking powder and depends upon the mixing of beaten egg whites into the batter, and that it is therefore much like a soufflé.

A *crème anglaise* is standard in any French housewife's repertory, even in these days of shortcuts. Almost any honest modern cook will confess that a fairly commendable thin custard can be tricked from packages, by using a mixture of common sense and liqueurs and knavery, but there is nothing as bland and kindly as a real "English cream," made as it was for several hundred years before it was called that. It can be thin, to pour over fresh or poached fruits. Somewhat thicker, it can half-fill a tart crust. Flavored according to the kind of cake it fills, and made thicker still, it can be spread between the layers or spooned into a ring mold.

Naturally a soufflé for dessert is as basic as one for an hors d'oeuvre or a light entrée, to the average French housewife. Once the technique has been learned, it is intrinsic to kitchen thinking. Most soufflés served as a dessert, and naturally geared to what preceded them, are kept simple and are variations on the vanilla theme. Often they are served with a sauce flavored with fruits or liqueurs, or the liqueur is baked into them, aided by whatever will help to bring out its flavor, as grated orange rind does with Grand Marnier. Occasionally, finely chopped candied fruits marinated in brandy are put into the mixture before it is baked, and then a plain vanilla sauce is served with it.

One of the most delicious desserts I ever ate was a combination of lemon soufflé and *crêpes*. The little pancakes were thin indeed, and only lightly golden. The soufflé, heavily flavored with lemon, was piled on one half of each *crêpe*, which was then folded over it lightly. The whole amazingly delicate thing was baked on a big metal platter, two soufflés to a guest, until they were done and no more. Then they were sprinkled with sugar and rushed—tantalizing and delicious—to the table.

Considering how many dessert tricks French cooks seem to have up their sleeves, it is surprising that their meals so seldom feature desserts. Instead they tend to be used as a foil for other flavors—those that have come in the two or three courses served earlier. When a really grand dessert is to be presented (as was occasionally the case when I lived with a family whose grandfather, called Papazi in his local dialect, was the dean of all pastry-cooks of Alsace-Lorraine), the whole meal leads up to it, exactly as does a meal in Bordeaux when important wines are to be tasted. Papazi's chef-d'oeuvre was a *diplomate au kirsch*, partly frozen, partly chilled, partly baked. It was indeed a production, and his daughter planned a meal to precede it which would not interfere in any way with its skillful conglomeration of textures and flavors.

When a pudding ceases to be shy

Technically a *diplomate* is a rather elaborate pudding, light but highly seasoned with candied fruits and a liqueur, and served with a *crème anglaise*. In Papazi's hands it became a structure, an edifice. It had layers of pale, delicate *biscuit*, artfully soaked with kirsch. It had hand-chosen preserved cherries, also soaked in the liqueur named for them. The custard, the whipped cream, and even the fancy mold itself, were laced with kirsch. It is a wonder the final layers of pudding ever froze, so alcoholized were they. But when the *diplomate* was ready to be slid from its heavy metal shell onto the platter waiting for it (as we were waiting too, after at least two days of preparations), it was so subtly perfumed, so lightly reminiscent of the cherry orchards in Lorraine, that only a master pastry cook like Papazi would be able to guess how many cupsful of *kirschwasser* had been swallowed up by it. The *crème anglaise*, deliberately kept free of anything but a hint of vanilla, masked the whole structure, which stood perhaps a foot tall.

The best dessert plates sat before us at a table meticulously cleared of every crumb. Papazi carved, like a famous surgeon before a group of fourth-year medical students. His daughter passed a sauceboat of extra custard around the table. The reverent hush broke in a hum of proud approval, and then the old master sat down, cracked a little joke, and we were off to a long noisy Sunday afternoon, helped along by more of the same kirsch that had disappeared into the pudding. It was a reckless and wonderful change from the very simple custards and compotes we usually ate in that good household . . . and how fine to be able to say, in any family, that we have known a master pastry chef!

Compote de Fruits
FRUIT POACHED IN VANILLA SYRUP

To serve 4

3 cups water
1 cup sugar
1 two-inch piece of vanilla bean or
   1½ tablespoons vanilla extract
4 ripe but firm pears or peaches or 8
   apricots, peeled, halved and cored
   or stoned

In a 12-inch enameled saucepan, bring the water, sugar and vanilla to a boil over moderate heat, stirring until the sugar dissolves. Add the fruit, reduce the heat, and cook uncovered at a very slow simmer for 15 to 20 minutes, or until the fruit is soft but not mushy when pierced with the tip of a sharp knife. Let the fruit cool in the syrup for 30 minutes. With a slotted spoon, transfer the fruit to a serving bowl or baking dish. Boil the syrup briskly over high heat until it thickens slightly, and pour it over the fruit. Refrigerate the fruit, and serve it chilled in dessert dishes, small bowls or champagne glasses with a spoonful of syrup to moisten each of the portions.

Poires Pochées au Vin Rouge
PEARS POACHED IN RED WINE

To serve 6

2 cups dry red wine
2 tablespoons lemon juice
1 cup sugar
1 two-inch stick of cinnamon or ½
   teaspoon ground cinnamon
6 small or 3 large ripe but firm pears,
   peeled, cored and halved

In a 12-inch enameled saucepan, bring the wine, lemon juice, sugar and cinnamon to a boil over moderate heat, stirring until the sugar dissolves. Add the pear halves, partially cover the pan and reduce the heat to low. Cook the pears at a very slow simmer for 15 to 20 minutes, or until they are soft but not mushy when pierced with the tip of a sharp knife. Cool the pears in the syrup until they are lukewarm. If you would like to serve the pear halves warm, discard the cinnamon stick and use a slotted spoon to transfer the pears to dessert dishes, small bowls or champagne glasses. Spoon a bit of the syrup over them. To serve the pears cold, refrigerate them in the syrup in a large bowl or baking dish until they are thoroughly chilled.

Pêches Cardinal
POACHED PEACHES WITH RASPBERRY PURÉE

To serve 8

6 cups water
2 cups sugar
8 large ripe but firm peaches, peeled,
   halved and stoned
1 four-inch piece of vanilla bean or
   3 tablespoons vanilla extract

SAUCE CARDINAL
2 ten-ounce packages frozen raspberries,
   defrosted and thoroughly drained
2 tablespoons superfine sugar
1 tablespoon kirsch

CRÈME CHANTILLY
¾ cup heavy cream, thoroughly
   chilled
2 tablespoons superfine sugar
1 tablespoon vanilla extract

GARNISH
Whole fresh raspberries or defrosted
   frozen raspberries (optional)

In a heavy 3- to 4-quart saucepan, bring the water and sugar to a boil over high heat, stirring until the sugar dissolves. Boil this syrup briskly for 3 minutes, then reduce the heat as low as possible. Add the peeled peach halves and vanilla and poach them uncovered at a very low simmer for 10 to 20 minutes, or until they are barely tender when pierced with the tip of a sharp knife. Refrigerate the peaches in the syrup until they are cold.

SAUCE CARDINAL: With the back of a large spoon, purée the raspberries through a fine sieve into a small mixing bowl. Stir 2 tablespoons of superfine sugar and the kirsch into the raspberry purée. Refrigerate, tightly covered.

CRÈME CHANTILLY: With a wire whisk, rotary or electric beater, whip the cream in a chilled mixing bowl until it begins to thicken. Sprinkle in 2 table-spoons of superfine sugar and the vanilla; continue beating until the cream is firm enough to hold soft peaks on the beater when it is raised out of the bowl.

To serve, transfer the chilled peach halves with a slotted spoon to indi-vidual dessert dishes or arrange them attractively on a large platter. If you wish, you can place the halves on top of one another to resemble whole peaches. (Discard the syrup or save it to use for poaching fruit again.) Mask each of the peaches thoroughly with the *sauce cardinal*. Decorate the peaches with the *crème chantilly*. Garnish with whole raspberries if desired.

Pêches cardinal: peach halves smothered in raspberry sauce and *crème chantilly* are served in a broad champagne glass.

To serve 4 to 6

1½ cups milk
4 eggs
½ cup all-purpose flour
¼ cup sugar
2 teaspoons vanilla extract
2 to 3 cups fresh black sweet cherries,
   pitted; or drained, canned, pitted
   Bing cherries; or frozen sweet
   cherries, thawed and drained
Confectioners' (powdered) sugar

Clafoutis aux Cerises
CHERRY CAKE

Preheat the oven to 350°. To make the batter in a blender, combine the milk, eggs, flour, sugar and vanilla in the blender jar, and whirl them at high speed for a few seconds. Turn the machine off and scrape down the sides of the jar with a rubber spatula, then blend again for about 40 seconds. To make the batter by hand, stir the flour and eggs together in a large mixing bowl, and slowly stir in the milk, sugar and vanilla extract. Beat with a whisk or a rotary or electric beater until the flour lumps disappear and the batter is smooth.

Pat the cherries completely dry with paper towels. Spread them evenly in a shallow, buttered baking dish or pan that holds 5 to 6 cups and is about 2 inches deep. Pour in the batter. Bake on the middle shelf of the oven for 1½ hours, or until the top is golden brown and firm to the touch. Dust lightly with confectioners' sugar, and serve the *clafoutis* while it is still warm.

To serve 6 to 8

4 egg yolks
¼ cup superfine sugar
2 tablespoons Cognac
6 ounces semisweet chocolate, cut
   in small chunks
3 tablespoons strong coffee
8 tablespoons soft unsalted butter
   (1 quarter-pound stick), cut
   in ½-inch pieces
4 egg whites
½ cup heavy cream, whipped

Mousse au Chocolat
CHOCOLATE MOUSSE

Brush the inside of a 1-quart charlotte (cylindrical) or ring mold with a film of vegetable oil. Invert the mold on paper towels to drain.

In a heatproof mixing bowl, beat the egg yolks and sugar with a whisk, rotary or electric beater for 2 or 3 minutes, or until they are pale yellow and thick enough to form a ribbon when the whisk is lifted from the bowl. Beat in the Cognac.

Set the mixing bowl over a pan of barely simmering (not boiling) water, and continue beating for 3 or 4 minutes, or until the mixture is foamy and hot. Then set the bowl over a pan of iced water and beat for 3 or 4 minutes longer, or until the mixture is cool again and as thick and creamy as mayonnaise.

In a heavy 1- to 1½-quart saucepan set over low heat, or in the top of a double boiler over simmering water, melt the chocolate with the coffee, stirring constantly. When all the chocolate has dissolved, beat in the butter, one piece at a time, to make a smooth cream. Then beat the chocolate mixture into the egg yolks and sugar. In a separate bowl, with a clean whisk or beater, beat the egg whites until they are stiff enough to form stiff peaks on the wires of the whisk. Stir about one fourth of the egg whites into the chocolate mixture to lighten it, then very gently fold in the remaining egg whites. Spoon the mousse into the oiled mold or dessert cups, and refrigerate for at least 4 hours or until it has set.

To unmold and serve the *mousse au chocolat*, run a long, sharp knife around the sides of the mold and dip the bottom of it in hot water for a few seconds. Then wipe the outside of the mold dry, place a chilled serving plate upside down over the mold and, grasping both sides firmly, quickly turn the plate and mold over. Rap the plate on a table and the mousse should slide easily out of the mold. If the mousse doesn't unmold at once, repeat the whole process.

With a wire whisk, rotary or electric beater, whip the chilled cream in a large chilled bowl until it is firm enough to hold its shape softly. Garnish the mousse with the whipped cream.

The decorative "cap" on a *soufflé au Grand Marnier (left)* is formed by making a trench around the edge *(above)* before the soufflé is baked.

Soufflé au Grand Marnier

ORANGE LIQUEUR SOUFFLÉ

To serve 4

Preheat the oven to 425°. Grease the bottom and sides of a 1½-quart soufflé dish with 2 tablespoons of soft butter. Sprinkle in 3 tablespoons of sugar, tipping and shaking the dish to spread the sugar evenly. Then turn the dish over and knock out the excess sugar. Set aside.

In the top of a double boiler, beat the egg yolks with a whisk, rotary or electric beater until they are well blended. Slowly add the sugar and continue beating until the yolks become very thick and pale yellow. Set the pan over barely simmering (not boiling) water and heat the egg yolks, stirring gently and constantly with a wooden spoon or rubber spatula, until the mixture thickens and becomes almost too hot to touch. Stir in the Grand Marnier and grated orange peel and transfer to a large bowl. Set the bowl into a pan filled with crushed ice or ice cubes and cold water, and stir the mixture until it is quite cold. Remove it from the ice.

In a large mixing bowl, preferably of unlined copper, beat the egg whites and the cream of tartar with a clean whisk or rotary beater until they form stiff, unwavering peaks. Using a rubber spatula, stir a large spoonful of beaten egg white into the egg-yolk mixture to lighten it. Gently fold the remaining egg whites into the mixture. Spoon the soufflé into the buttered, sugared dish, filling it to within 2 inches of the top. Smooth the top of the soufflé with the spatula. For a decorative effect, make a cap on the soufflé by cutting a trench about 1 inch deep 1 inch from the edge all around the top.

Bake on the middle shelf of the oven for 2 minutes, then reduce the heat to 400°. Continue baking for another 20 to 30 minutes, or until the soufflé has risen about 2 inches above the top of the mold and the top is lightly browned. Sprinkle with confectioners' sugar and serve it at once.

2 tablespoons soft butter
3 tablespoons sugar
5 egg yolks
⅓ cup sugar
¼ cup Grand Marnier (1 two-ounce bottle)
1 tablespoon freshly grated orange peel
7 egg whites
¼ teaspoon cream of tartar
Confectioners' (powdered) sugar

189

To serve 8 to 10

PÂTE À CHOUX, OR CREAM-PUFF PASTE
1 cup water
6 tablespoons butter, cut into small
   pieces
1 cup all-purpose flour, sifted after
   measuring
1 teaspoon sugar
5 eggs (U.S. graded "large")
½ teaspoon water

FILLING
1 cup heavy cream
3 tablespoons confectioners'
   (powdered) sugar
1 tablespoon vanilla extract

CHOCOLATE SAUCE
8 ounces semisweet chocolate, cut
   into small chunks
½ cup strong coffee
Confectioners' (powdered) sugar

Profiteroles
CREAM-PUFF PASTRY ROSETTES

PÂTE À CHOUX: In a heavy 2- to 3-quart saucepan, bring the 1 cup of water and the butter to a boil over moderate heat, stirring occasionally. As soon as the butter has completely melted, remove the pan from the heat and pour in the flour and sugar all at once. Beat the mixture vigorously with a wooden spoon for a few seconds until it is well blended. Then return it to moderate heat and cook, still beating vigorously, for 1 or 2 minutes, or until the mixture forms a mass that leaves the sides of the pan and moves freely with the spoon.

Immediately remove the pan from the heat and use the spoon to make a well in the center of the paste. Break an egg into the well and beat it into the paste. When the first egg has been absorbed, add 3 more eggs 1 at a time—beating well after each egg is added. The finished paste should be thick, smooth and shiny.

Preheat the oven to 425°. Lightly butter two large baking sheets. Spoon the *pâte à choux* into a pastry bag that has a ¼- or ½-inch plain tip, and press the paste out onto the sheets in mounds, about 1 inch in diameter and ½ inch high. Space the mounds approximately 2 inches apart; they will double in size as they bake. If you don't have a pastry bag, drop teaspoonfuls of the paste onto the baking sheets, allowing the same 2 inches of space between them.

Beat the remaining egg with ½ teaspoon of water in a small bowl until they are well mixed. With a pastry brush, lightly paint the top of each *profiterole* with the egg-and-water mixture. Bake in the upper and/or lower third of the oven for 6 minutes, then reduce the heat to 400° and bake for 5 minutes longer.

Reduce the heat to 325° and bake for another 15 to 20 minutes, or until the *profiteroles* have doubled in size and have turned a light golden brown. They should be firm and crusty to the touch. Turn off the oven and make a tiny incision near the bottom of each *profiterole* with the tip of a sharp knife to release the steam. Let the *profiteroles* rest in the oven for a few minutes to dry out. Then remove them from the baking sheets and set them on wire cake racks to cool.

FILLING AND CHOCOLATE SAUCE: No more than 1 hour before serving the *profiteroles*, whip the cream with a wire whisk, rotary or electric beater in a chilled mixing bowl until it begins to thicken. Sprinkle the confectioners' sugar and the vanilla over it, and continue beating until the cream is firm enough to hold unwavering peaks on the beater when the beater is raised out of the bowl.

Gently break the top off each *profiterole* or slit it in half with a small, sharp knife. Fill the bottom half with a spoonful of heavy cream, replace the top and gently press the *profiterole* together again. Dust the top lightly with confectioners' sugar. Melt the chocolate with the coffee in a small, heavy saucepan over hot water, stirring constantly until the mixture is perfectly smooth.

To serve, pour a little of the warm chocolate sauce into individual dessert dishes and float two or more of the *profiteroles* on top. Or, if you prefer, you may serve the *profiteroles* on dessert plates with the chocolate sauce poured over them.

Paris-Brest

CREAM-PUFF PASTRY RING WITH WHIPPED CREAM FILLING

Preheat the oven to 450°. Butter a baking sheet, scatter a little flour over it, and tap the edge on the table to knock off the excess flour. Then lay an 8-inch plate or pan on the sheet, pressing down hard to make a circular impression in the flour. Remove the plate or pan. Using a pastry tube with a large plain tip, make a circle or crown of *pâte à choux* 2 inches wide and 1 inch high around the pattern in the flour. If you don't have a pastry tube, drop the paste by spoonfuls, placing the mounds side by side around the ring, then, with a spatula, smooth the mounds into a continuous strand, 2 inches wide and 1 inch high. Beat the egg and water together and paint the top of the crown with the mixture. Sprinkle it with slivered almonds. Bake on the middle shelf of the oven 10 minutes, then reduce the heat to 350° and bake 10 minutes more. Reduce the heat to 325° and bake for 20 minutes, or until the crown has more than doubled in size and is golden brown, firm and crusty. Turn off the oven and make 3 or 4 tiny cuts near the bottom of the crown with the tip of a sharp knife. Let the crown rest in the oven for 5 minutes to dry out. Slice it in half horizontally with a serrated knife, and spoon out any soft dough inside the shells.

No more than 1 hour before serving, whip the cream with a wire whisk, rotary or electric beater in a large chilled mixing bowl until it begins to thicken. Add the sugar and vanilla, and continue beating until the cream holds its shape firmly. Using a pastry bag with a decorative tip, or a tablespoon, fill the bottom part of the crown with whipped cream. The cream should rise well above the rim of the pastry. Gently replace the top of the crown so that it floats on the cream. Sprinkle the top with confectioners' sugar and refrigerate the *Paris-Brest* until serving time.

To serve 6

PÂTE À CHOUX *(recipe opposite)*
1 egg
½ teaspoon water
3 tablespoons blanched, slivered almonds
2 cups heavy cream
1 tablespoon confectioners' (powdered) sugar
2 teaspoons vanilla extract

Crème Caramel

CARAMEL CUSTARD

To line a 1-quart metal or porcelain mold or six 4-ounce heatproof porcelain or glass individual molds with caramel, it is necessary to work quickly. Remember in handling the caramel that it will be over 300°, so be extremely careful with it. Place the mold (or molds) on a large strip of wax paper. Then, in a small, heavy saucepan or skillet, bring the sugar and water to a boil over high heat, stirring until the sugar dissolves. Stir in a pinch of cream of tartar and—gripping a pot holder in each hand—boil the syrup over moderate heat, gently tipping the pan back and forth almost constantly, until the syrup turns a rich, golden, tea-like brown. This may take 10 minutes or more. As soon as the syrup reaches the right color, remove the pan from the heat and carefully pour the caramel syrup in a thin stream into the mold (or the first of the individual molds). Still using the pot holders, tip and swirl the mold to coat the bottom and sides as evenly as possible. When the syrup stops moving, turn the mold upside down on the wax paper to cool somewhat and to let any excess syrup run out.

Preheat the oven to 325°. In a 1- to 1½-quart saucepan, bring the milk almost to a boil over moderate heat. Remove the pan from the stove and add the vanilla extract. With a wire whisk, rotary or electric beater, beat the sugar, eggs and extra egg yolks until they are well mixed and thickened.

To serve 6

CARAMEL
½ cup sugar
¼ cup water
Pinch of cream of tartar

CUSTARD
2 cups milk
1 teaspoon vanilla extract or 1 three-inch piece of vanilla bean
¼ cup sugar
3 eggs plus 2 extra egg yolks

Stirring gently and constantly, pour in the milk in a thin stream. Strain through a fine sieve into the caramel-lined mold and place the mold (or molds) in a large pan on the middle shelf of the oven. Pour enough boiling water into the pan to come halfway up the sides of the mold. Bake the custard—lowering the oven temperature if the water in the pan begins to simmer—for about 1 hour, or until a knife inserted in the center of the custard comes out clean. Remove the mold from the water and refrigerate the custard for at least 3 hours, or until it is thoroughly chilled.

To unmold and serve the large custard, run a sharp knife around the sides and dip the bottom of the mold briefly in hot water. Then wipe the outside of the mold dry, place a chilled serving plate upside down over the mold and, grasping both sides firmly, quickly turn the plate and mold over. Rap the plate on a table and the custard should slide easily out of the mold. Unmold the individual custards carefully, turning them out one at a time on individual serving plates. Pour any extra caramel remaining in the mold (or molds) over the custard. Serve cold.

Diplomate

MOLDED CUSTARD WITH GLACÉED FRUITS

To serve 10 to 12

½ cup kirsch
½ cup diced mixed candied fruit
2 dozen best quality (or home-made
   type) ladyfingers, split in half
1 envelope plus 1 extra teaspoon
   unflavored gelatin
⅓ cup water
1 cup milk
5 egg yolks
¼ cup sugar
1½ cups chilled heavy cream
½ cup apricot preserves

In a small bowl, combine ¼ cup of the kirsch with the diced candied fruit, and set them aside at room temperature to steep. Lay a circle of wax paper on the bottom of a 2-quart charlotte mold or any other plain, round 2-quart mold 3 or 4 inches deep. Line the mold with ladyfingers by first cutting a ½-inch circle out of a ladyfinger half and placing it, curved side down, in the center of the paper. (Save the scraps to use later.) Then cut ladyfingers into slightly tapered wedge shapes to fit and radiate around the circle—like petals in a rosette—and arrange them, curved side down, on the paper. Stand more ladyfingers side by side around the inside of the mold, trimming off any excess above the rim. Set the mold and the rest of the ladyfingers aside.

In a heatproof measuring cup or small bowl, sprinkle the gelatin over ¼ cup of water. When the gelatin has softened for 2 or 3 minutes, set the cup in a small skillet of simmering water and cook over low heat, stirring constantly, until the gelatin dissolves. Remove the skillet from the heat, but leave the cup of gelatin in the skillet to keep warm.

In a heavy 2- to 3-quart saucepan, heat the milk until bubbles begin to form around the edge of the pan; remove from the stove. With a whisk, rotary or electric beater, beat the egg yolks and sugar together in a bowl for 3 or 4 minutes, or until the yolks are pale yellow and slightly thickened. Stirring continually, pour the hot milk in a thin stream over the egg yolks. When thoroughly blended, pour into a clean saucepan. Stirring constantly, cook over low heat until the custard begins to thicken; continue cooking, stirring constantly, until the custard coats the spoon like heavy cream. Do not let the custard come near the boil or it will curdle; if it gets too hot, lift the pan off the stove to cool it.

Then remove the pan from the heat and stir in the dissolved gelatin, blending it through the custard completely. Strain the custard through a fine sieve into a large mixing bowl. With a wire whisk, rotary or electric beater, whip the cream in a large chilled mixing bowl until it forms soft peaks. Set the bowl of custard into a large pot filled with crushed ice or ice

192

cubes and water. Stir the custard for 4 or 5 minutes or until it is quite cold and begins to thicken. Beat thoroughly with a wire whisk to be sure it is perfectly smooth. Then scoop the whipped cream over the custard and use a rubber spatula to fold them together gently but thoroughly. If there are any lumps, beat gently with a whisk or rotary beater until smooth. Fold in the candied fruit and kirsch.

Force the apricot preserves through a fine sieve into a small saucepan. Stir in the remaining ¼ cup kirsch and bring to a boil over moderate heat, stirring constantly. Brush the ladyfingers lining the mold lightly with the hot apricot glaze. Ladle half of the custard into the mold, then arrange ladyfingers in a neat but informal layer on the custard. Ladle in the rest of the custard and cover the top with whatever ladyfingers are left; even the scraps will do. Chill for 4 or 5 hours, or until firm and set.

To unmold and serve the *diplomate,* run a sharp knife around the sides of the mold and dip the bottom in hot water for a few seconds. Then wipe the outside of the mold dry, place a chilled serving plate upside down over the mold and, grasping both sides firmly, turn the plate and mold over. Rap the plate on a table and the *diplomate* should slide out of the mold. If it doesn't unmold at once, repeat the whole process. Gently remove the wax paper from the top, and chill the *diplomate* again before serving.

Tartes aux Fraises
FRESH STRAWBERRY TARTS

To serve 6

Preheat the oven to 400° and bake the pastry shells (or shell) as described in the recipe for *pâte brisée*, adding another 7 to 10 minutes to the final baking to brown the shell lightly and cook it fully. Unmold the shells (or shell) and slip it onto a wire cake rack to cool.

In a heavy 2- to 3-quart saucepan—off the heat—beat the egg, the extra egg yolk and the sugar with a wire whisk, rotary or electric beater until the mixture thickens and turns a pale yellow. Add the flour and salt, and beat until well blended. Beat in the powdered gelatin and vanilla; then slowly pour in the hot milk in a thin stream, beating constantly. Cook over moderate heat, stirring with a whisk, until smooth and thick. Do not allow the custard to boil; if it seems to be getting too hot, lift the pan off the heat a few seconds to cool it. If the custard gets lumpy, beat it with a whisk or rotary beater until smooth. Pour the custard into a large mixing bowl and place in the refrigerator to cool. When the custard is cold and has begun to solidify slightly, whip the cream until it holds soft peaks. Fold it thoroughly into the custard with a rubber spatula and beat gently if there are any lumps. At once, pour or spoon the custard into the pastry shells.

CURRANT GLAZE: In a small saucepan, warm the red currant jelly and hot water over low heat, stirring occasionally, until they begin to froth and thicken. Remove the saucepan from the heat, stir in the kirsch and let the glaze cool a bit.

Meanwhile, arrange the strawberries on the custard, stem side down—and in concentric circles if the tart is a large one—until the top of each tart is completely covered with berries. Spoon the warm glaze over the berries. Refrigerate the tarts for at least 2 hours, or until the custard is firm. Sprinkle them with confectioners' sugar before serving.

6 individual 3- to 4-inch *pâte brisée* tart shells or 9- to 10-inch *pâte brisée* shell *(page 67)*
1 egg plus 1 extra egg yolk
¼ cup sugar
3 tablespoons flour
Pinch of salt
1 envelope unflavored gelatin
1 teaspoon vanilla extract
1 cup hot milk
1 cup heavy cream

CURRANT GLAZE
1 cup red currant jelly
1 tablespoon hot water
1 tablespoon kirsch
1 to 1½ quarts large ripe strawberries, cleaned and stemmed
Confectioners' (powdered) sugar

The Dessert...

. . . can be a light, refreshing finale to a series of hearty courses or can itself be the high point of the meal. Shown here are six desserts which range from the very light to the very rich *(clockwise from the top)*: *mousse au chocolat, tartes aux fraises, compote de fruits, profiterole, crèmes caramels* and *Paris-Brest. (Recipes on preceding pages.)*

A Brief Guide to French Table Wines

The guide on these pages offers a brief course in French table wines—when to drink them, what kinds to look for, how to buy, keep and serve them—preceded by a glossary of special terms used by experts to describe them.

Table wine—served at the table and accompanying food—is relatively mild-flavored and is moderate in alcoholic strength (10 to 14 per cent). The fortified wines, such as sherry, Madeira, port and vermouth, have had their alcoholic content increased by the addition of spirits. They are seldom served with food.

It should be remembered that pleasing the palate with wine or food, or both, is a subtle and subjective exercise. Whatever combinations of food and wine taste good to the taster through his own trial and error are just as acceptable as those selected according to the "rules" about which wine should be served with which food. There are, however, traditional happy marriages of food and companionable table wines that have long been approved by experts, and a number of these combinations are included here. To begin with, here is a glossary of terms:

ACIDITY: A tartness or sharpness of taste due to natural fruit acids in the wine. This is considered a desirable quality in a good wine. A marked smell of vinegar, however, means that a wine has spoiled.

ASTRINGENCY: A sharpness that causes the mouth to pucker slightly. A moderate degree of astringency is desirable in many wines.

BALANCE: A state in which the various characteristics of a well-made wine are in harmony. Thus, a balanced light-bodied wine should have a delicate taste and bouquet; a full-bodied wine should not be watery or weak.

BODY: "Weight" or substance. A full-bodied wine will impress the tongue as having more weight and more density than will a light-bodied one.

BOUQUET: The aroma of wine—not just one odor but a combination of odors, like that of a bouquet of flowers—produced by the oxidation of fruit acids and by fermentation of the wine.

CLEAN: Refreshing and agreeable to the palate and free of disagreeable taste or bouquet.

DELICATE: Applied to a wine whose bouquet and taste are light and subtle, rather than strong and coarse.

FINESSE: A high degree of distinction, applied only to fine wines.

FRUITY: Having in a strong degree the fragrance and flavor of fruit.

GENEROUS: Of full bouquet and taste.

HEADY: Strong, pungent, usually high in alcoholic content.

MELLOW: Said of a wine that is smooth, mature and ripe.

ROUGH: An excess of astringency, frequently a characteristic of young wine and often an indication of potential long life.

SOFT: Without harshness. Although good wines should have some softness, it is possible for a wine to go too far and become bland.

TART: Possessing agreeable acidity, reflecting the content of fruit acid.

VELVETY: Agreeably smooth to the taste.

SELECTING THE RIGHT WINE: In the following lists, some of the most popular French table wines exported to the U.S. are grouped under types of food they accompany especially well.

French wine names in many cases are taken from the name of the town in which the wine is produced or, as in the case of wines from Alsace, from the name of the grape from which the wine is made. Although more than one individual or firm (often called a château) may produce wine in a given town, the wines of that town will all reflect the strong family similarities that are described below. The place of origin of each wine in the famous wine-producing regions of France is noted in parentheses.

Hearty Meats, Strong Game

FULL-BODIED RED WINES—the Burgundies, Bordeaux (clarets), and those of the Côtes du Rhône—are the most robust of the French wines.

CHÂTEAUNEUF-DU-PAPE (Côtes du Rhône): A heady, strong wine of a deep crimson color, possessing a fine bouquet and strength of flavor.

CHAMBERTIN (Burgundy): This is traditionally described as having been Napoleon's favorite wine. It is produced in the township of Gevrey-Chambertin. It is a Burgundy of deep-red color, full-bodied and well balanced, with a generous and exceptional bouquet.

CORTON (Burgundy): A well-balanced wine with the delicacy, smoothness and strong bouquet characteristic of the red wines of the Côte de Beaune, the southern part of the Burgundy region. Brilliant in color, it may be rough when young, but usually ages into a robust, long-lived wine.

HERMITAGE (Côtes du Rhône): A deep-colored, strong and mellow wine that has been called the "manliest" of wines. When young it tends to be somewhat rough and bitter, but it ages well into a fine, rich wine.

NUITS-SAINT-GEORGES (Burgundy): One of the wines of the Côte-de-Nuits, the northern part of the Burgundy region, it is rich, extremely full-bodied, considered to be among the greatest Burgundies.

POMEROL (Bordeaux): Wines from the Pomerol district have a deep color, a rich bouquet, a great depth of flavor and a general velvety quality. Similar in character to the neighboring St. Émilion wines, but less known, they mature more rapidly, are slightly more delicate.

SAINT-ÉMILION (Bordeaux): Wines of this district are rich and robust in flavor. St. Émilion is quite dark in color and can live for at least 10 to 15 years without loss of quality.

VOSNE-ROMANÉE (Burgundy): This town produces some of the greatest wines in France, topped by the excellent—and expensive—Romanée-Conti. Vosne-Romanée wines are full-flavored and elegant. They age well, are long-lived (good vintages 20 years old are not uncommon) and are considered by many to be the best of the Burgundy wines.

Lighter Meats, Delicate Game

LIGHT-BODIED RED WINES—also Burgundies and Bordeaux, but less potent than their full-bodied cousins—complement the less heavily flavored meats such as lamb, veal and pork, and lighter-flavored game birds like pheasant.

BEAUJOLAIS (Burgundy): Extremely agreeable, light and fruity wines that are highly refreshing and drinkable. Delicate and brisk in taste, they are best when young, less than two or three years old.

GRAVES (Bordeaux): The wines called Graves get their names not from a town but from a geographical district in Bordeaux noted for its gravelly soil. Graves clarets have a brilliant garnet color, are well balanced and elegant wines with a distinctive bouquet and fruity taste. Most of the Graves clarets are not labeled "Graves" but are named for a château. Some of the best known include Château Haut-Brion and Château Smith-Haut-Lafitte.

MÂCON (Burgundy): Relatively inexpensive wines with a pleasant if undistinguished flavor. Like Beaujolais, they should be drunk when young.

MÉDOC (Bordeaux): The Médoc, a triangle-shaped district of more than 50 towns, north of the city of Bordeaux, is considered by many to be the most important wine district in the world. In 1855 the red wines of the whole Bordeaux region—some 4,000 of them—were officially classified in order of quality; of the top 60, all but one were products of the Médoc district. Wines called simply Médoc are very good wines, those called Haut-Médoc are much better, and those produced in five particular communes—Pauillac, Cantenac, Margaux, Saint-Julien and Saint-Estèphe—are the best of all. Médoc wines in general are light in body, smooth and mellow.

POMMARD (Burgundy): The better Pommard wines bear the names of certain vineyards, notably Les Épenots, Les Rugiens, and La Platière. The best of them are soft, smooth and velvety.

VOLNAY (Burgundy): Pleasant, delicate, smooth wines, with a pronounced bouquet. Perhaps the lightest, most delicate of all lighter red Burgundies.

Hors d'Oeuvre, Cheese, Egg Dishes

ROSÉ is a light red wine that bridges the gap between the fuller reds and the white wines. It goes well with hors d'oeuvre, particularly cold meats; with egg dishes, with cheeses that are not too pungent, and with some meats, such as veal, ham and pork, that are more delicate in flavor than beef. A Rosé d'Anjou is light and agreeable. Tavel, a rosé from the Côtes du Rhône, is widely available and popular in the United States. Rosés from the Côtes de Provence in the south of France, including Sainte Roseline, are also very popular.

Strong-Flavored Fish, Most Fowl

FULL-BODIED DRY WHITE WINES are best served with fish, like mackerel or bluefish, that have a strong flavor or with fish or shellfish that are cooked in a rich wine sauce. These wines, which want to be served quite cold, also make a fine accompaniment for most fowl.

CORTON (Burgundy): Smooth, velvety wines, golden in color, and of substantial reputation. The best of the white Corton wines bears the vineyard name Corton-Charlemagne and is one of the great white Burgundies.
GRAVES (Bordeaux): These are wines of delicacy and vigor. Clean, fruity, fresh and quite dry. They are well-balanced and generally elegant.
GEWÜRZTRAMINER (Alsace): The bouquet of this wine is flowery, and its flavor is rich and unusually fruity. Its name comes from the German word *gewürz*, meaning spicy, and its flavor reflects it.
HERMITAGE (Côtes du Rhône): Heady wines, with a full aroma and warmth, dry, but very rich. As they age, the wines take on an amber color and an attractive mellowness.
MEURSAULT (Burgundy): One of the finer white wines of France. Full-bodied, exciting and dry with a fruity bouquet, it has finesse and elegance.
MONTRACHET (Burgundy): The white wines from the communes of Puligny- and Chassagne-Montrachet are generally considered the finest white wines of France and tend to be expensive. They have a fine bouquet, are full-bodied and rich, elegant and quite mellow. Their color is pale. The best of them come from the vineyard called simply Montrachet.

Fish, Shellfish, Egg Dishes

LIGHT-BODIED DRY WHITE WINES are the best complement for light-textured fish simply cooked and served, such as sole meunière, poached trout or salmon, or broiled shellfish, and for such delicate egg dishes as soufflés.

CHABLIS (Burgundy): A very light, fresh, heady wine with a taste often characterized as "flinty." Pale gold in color, with greenish highlights, Chablis ranks among the driest and palest of white wines. The best is labeled "Chablis Grand Cru."
MUSCADET (Loire Valley): Pale, fresh and quite dry, Muscadet gets its name not from the town in which it is produced but, as is the case with most Alsatian wines, from the name of the grape from which it is made. It is a fairly inexpensive wine whose popularity is on the rise in America. It generally should be drunk quite young, less than three years old.
POUILLY-FUISSÉ (Burgundy): A crisp, dry, fruity wine with good bouquet and a sturdy and vigorous character. It is a wine of high reputation, somewhat fuller-bodied than other wines in this category. It has a delicate color with pale green tints.
POUILLY-FUMÉ (Loire Valley): A clean, pleasant, delicate wine with some softness and a fruity flavor and bouquet. It tends to be less dry than other wines in this category.
RIESLING (Alsace): Acknowledged to be the best of the Alsatian white wines. In common with most Alsatian wines, it tends to be somewhat more fruity and fragrant than other dry white wines, and has a fine bouquet.
SANCERRE (Loire Valley): Wines from this town share the clean, pleasant, soft and delicate qualities of the Pouilly-Fumé wines from across the Loire River, but lack their elegance and are somewhat lighter in bouquet. They tend to be short-lived, even among Loire Valley wines, which generally have reached their prime after five years.
SYLVANER (Alsace): A good wine and quite popular although considered to be inferior to Riesling. It tends to be lighter, softer, and more flowery than Riesling. Quite pleasant to drink.

Desserts

SWEET WHITE WINES are generally served with the dessert course, although some people prefer them in place of the drier white wines with fish or egg dishes. However, as sweet wines tend to satiate the appetite rather than stimulate it, they seem more appropriate at the end of the meal.

SAUTERNES (Bordeaux): A deep golden wine, sweet and rich-bodied with a marked bouquet. It gains its distinctive flavor from the fact that the grapes are picked when overripe. The Sauternes age extraordinarily well and some may be drunk when more than 40 years old. The great ones, such as Château d'Yquem, are considered truly noble wines.

VOUVRAY (Loire Valley): Tart and slightly sweet when young, sweet when old, with a natural tendency to sparkle, Vouvray is a versatile wine.
CHAMPAGNE (Champagne): Champagne is one French table wine that experts agree can be drunk with happy results at any point in the meal or can be served alone on festive occasions. It is also the one French table wine that you are advised to purchase by brand name rather than by vineyard or district name. Some of the better brands include Bollinger, Möet et Chandon, Mumm, Piper-Heidsieck and Taittinger. Champagnes are categorized by their relative sweetness or dryness: those marked *brut* or *nature* are the driest of all; the label *sec* (literally, "dry") means moderately sweet; *demi-sec* is sweet. Champagnes are fruity, light and sparkling.

Buying and Storing Wines

The best advice anyone can give a novice wine buyer is, "If you don't know your wine, know your wine merchant." Choose a store that stocks a wide range of wines and has the proper facilities to store them correctly.

Don't attempt to set up a wine cellar with one shopping expedition. Instead, buy for a specific occasion, choosing the most appropriate wines for the food to be served. After you have experimented, you can settle upon the wines that best suit your taste. Only then does it make sense to take advantage of bargains to build up a wine collection in your own home.

In certain years when growing conditions for grapes have been ideal, the wine produced is of especially high quality. Conversely, in an off year, the grapes—and hence the wines—will be of lesser quality. Vintage charts are available that attempt to indicate the good, bad and indifferent years for the various French wine-producing regions. Though helpful, they are often simply not detailed enough to be meaningful—for example, wines of a particular year may be excellent in one town but mediocre in the neighboring town. Again, the best source of information is a good merchant.

Some of the great, old wines may leave a sediment in the bottle. Such a wine should be purchased at least a week in advance of the time it is to be served and set upright to allow the sediment to settle slowly to the bottom of the bottle. In serving, care should be taken to handle the bottle gently so as not to disturb the sediment. Although most wines do not have any sediment, experts agree that even these seem to benefit from an overnight rest.

Nothing elaborate is needed for the storage of wine in quantity. Only a cool, dark spot with a constant temperature is required and this usually can be found in an apartment closet or under the cellar stairs of a house. The ideal temperature for storing and aging wine is about 55°. You can keep wines for several months at higher temperatures. The worst enemy of wine is sudden changes in temperature.

Bottles of table wines should be stored on their sides in order to keep the wine in contact with the cork, so that the cork will not dry out and admit air. There are many kinds of wine storage racks available, to keep the bottles on their sides and to allow easy access and removal.

Serving Wines

Like the rules about which wines go best with which foods, the rules about serving wines are the result of long experience and general common sense. But they are not inflexible and should be adapted to your tastes.

If only one wine is to be served with a meal, a tulip-shaped, 6- to 8-ounce glass is the best choice. (There are special glasses for each major type of wine, but their use is dying out in all but the most elegant formal dining.) Whatever the shape, the glass should be clear, not colored, so that the color and substance of the wine can be seen and appreciated.

Fine red wines of any age benefit by being uncorked about an hour or two before being served, which enhances the bouquet and gives them time to "breathe." White wines may be opened just before they are poured. The flavor of red wines is best appreciated when they are served at room temperature—between 64° and 68°. Dry white wines and rosés should be served chilled, between 44° and 54°. Champagne and sweet wines should be served thoroughly chilled, between 40° and 45°.

Never warm up a red wine artificially to raise it from cellar temperature; let it reach room temperature by sitting in the dining room overnight. White wines and champagnes can be chilled on the bottom shelf of the refrigerator: about two hours for white wines, three for champagnes and sweet wines. Or you can chill them in ice buckets. Never put ice in wine.

Glossary

À BLANC: a preliminary cooking in a solution of salted water, lemon juice and flour, for the purpose of blanching foods or retaining the whiteness; also, cooked in butter or by braising or poaching, without browning

À BRUN: browned before poaching or braising; also cooked until brown

AGNEAU: lamb

AIL: garlic

AÏOLI: garlic-flavored mayonnaise

À LA BOURGUIGNONNE: in the style of Burgundy; cooked in red wine

À LA GRECQUE: in the Greek style; cooked in a marinade of herbs and olive oil

À LA MODE: in the style or manner of, as, *à la mode de Caen*. When it is written without a place name (e.g., *boeuf à la mode*), it is understood to mean *à la mode de chez nous* or "in our manner"

À L'ANCIENNE: old-fashioned, or in the old style; often a simple stew or fricassee

AMANDE: almond

ANCHOIS: anchovy

ANGUILLE: eel

APÉRITIF: a beverage served as an appetizer, often a fortified wine (one to which alcohol has been added)

À POINT: cooked to medium rare, usually said of beef, especially steak

ARTICHAUT: artichoke

ASPERGE: asparagus

AUBERGINE: eggplant

AU CHOIX: of your choice; *de choix:* prime quality

AU GRATIN: sauced food topped with bread crumbs or grated cheese and butter, baked in the oven until the food is cooked and the top is browned (*gratiner* means to brown the top under a broiler)

AU JUS: served with natural, un-thickened pan juices

AU NATUREL: served in a natural state (e.g., asparagus *au naturel* is simply boiled)

BAIN-MARIE: a large pan, or "bath," in which to keep a pan of food (such as a sauce) warm or to cook it slowly on the stove. Unlike its smaller relative, the double boiler, the *bain-marie* is filled with water so that a saucepan placed inside it is surrounded by water as high as halfway up the sides. A *bain-marie* can be used on top of the stove to maintain slow, even cooking, or in the oven to prevent a crust from forming around such food as a *pâté* or a caramel custard

BANANE: banana

BAR: bass

BARDER: to bard; to cover a bird or roast with strips of fat in order to protect such delicate parts as a chicken breast, or to provide automatic basting of meat

BÉARNAISE: in the style of the Béarn region; a type of hollandaise flavored with shallots, wine, vinegar and tarragon usually served with meat, fish, and egg dishes

BÉCHAMEL: a basic white sauce of white *roux* (flour and butter) to which milk is added

BEURRE: butter

BEURRE BLANC: a warm sauce for fish, consisting of butter creamed into a mixture of vinegar, wine and shallots

BEURRE CLARIFIÉ: clarified butter, obtained by heating the butter until it liquefies, whereupon the clear liquid, which burns less easily, can be separated from the whey, or milk solids

BEURRE MANIÉ: paste of flour and uncooked butter for thickening sauces

BEURRE NOIR: a hot sauce of butter cooked until it browns

BLANCHIR: to blanch; to plunge into boiling water for the purpose of softening a food, to remove unwanted flavor, or for partial cooking or precooking

BLANQUETTE: a stew of veal, lamb or chicken in a cream sauce

BOEUF: beef

BONNE FEMME: home style; usually a dish simply cooked, accompanied or garnished by several vegetables

BOUILLIR: to boil

BOUQUET GARNI: a combination of herbs, usually parsley, thyme and bay leaf. Tied together, they are added to a dish during cooking to flavor it, and removed before serving

BRAISER: to braise; to cook in a tightly covered pan with a small amount of liquid at a low temperature

BRIOCHE: a very buttery yeast dough enriched with eggs, baked in a variety of shapes and sizes, and served as rolls for breakfast or at tea; dough also baked around sausages, meat or fish mixtures, making a decorative case

BROUILLÉ: scrambled

CANAPÉ: a small, open-faced sandwich or appetizer; a small, crustless slice of bread sautéed in butter on which foods may be served, such as asparagus, mushrooms or squabs

CANETON: duckling

CÂPRES: capers

CAROTTE: carrot

CÉLERI: celery; *céleri-rave:* celery root, or celeriac

CÈPE: the Boletus, one of the largest and best of the wild mushrooms

CERISE: cherry

CERVELLES: brains

CHAMPIGNON: mushroom

CHANTILLY: lightly whipped cream

CHARCUTERIE: a butcher shop specializing in pork and sausage

CHAUD-FROID: a cold sauce with cream and gelatin, used for coating chilled foods such as poultry or fish

CHOU: cabbage

CHOUCROUTE: sauerkraut

CHOU-FLEUR: cauliflower

CHOUX DE BRUXELLES: Brussels sprouts

COCOTTE: any heavy, covered casserole or Dutch oven that can be used both on top of the stove or in the oven

COMPOTE: fresh or dried fruits cooked and served in a flavored sugar syrup

CONCOMBRE: cucumber

CONFIT: preserved; as *confit d'oie*, pieces of goose, cooked and then preserved in their own fat; or as *fruits confits*, fruit that is cooked and preserved in sugar or alcohol; or vegetables in vinegar

COQUILLE: shell; a shell or ramekin in which food is served

COQUILLES SAINT-JACQUES: scallops, sold in their shells in France

CÔTE: rib; a chop of any meat, or part of the rib section of beef

CÔTELETTE: a chop or cutlet

COTRIADE: a fish soup, the Breton version of *bouillabaisse*

COUPE: a shallow dessert dish

COURGETTE: zucchini

COURT BOUILLON: a seasoned or flavored stock for cooking fish or vegetables

CRÉCY: after a region of France that grows exceptionally fine carrots, hence *potage Crécy* or anything cooked or served with carrots

CRÈME: cream; also any custard-based sauce or dessert

À LA CRÈME: served with cream or a cream-based sauce

CRÈME ANGLAISE: a light custard sauce of egg yolks, sugar and milk used in desserts of fruit or pastry

CRÊPE: thin pancake of egg and flour-batter. As a main dish (*crêpes salées*) or *hors d'oeuvre*, *crêpes* are rolled around a filling and often covered with a sauce. Dessert *crêpes* are called *crêpes sucrées*. *Crêpes Suzette* are dessert *crêpes* flavored with orange butter and flamed with brandy

CRESSON: watercress

CROISSANT: a light, flaky pastry made of yeast dough rolled in a special way with butter and formed into a crescent shape before baking

CROÛTE: a large piece of stale bread, toasted, or sautéed in butter or oil; *en croûte:* in crust

CROÛTON: a small *croûte*

DAUBE: any larded meat or poultry braised with vegetables and liquid in a covered casserole

DÉGLACER: to deglaze; to remove most of the fat from a cooked dish and add stock or wine to make a thin sauce of the browned bits that cling to the pan

DÉGRAISSER: to degrease

DUXELLES: a mixture of finely chopped, cooked mushrooms and shallots or onions used in sauces and fillings

EAU DE VIE: literally, "water of life"; any alcoholic spirits distilled from wine, usually brandy

ÉCHALOTE: shallot, a small variety of onion

ÉCREVISSE: fresh-water crayfish; *queues d'écrevisses:* crayfish tails

ENTRECÔTE: a boneless steak cut from the rib-roast section of beef, presumably from the first cut on the loin end, ribs 9 to 11

ÉPINARD: spinach

ESCALOPE: thinly cut slice of meat, usually veal

ESCARGOT: snail

FARCI: filled or stuffed

FERMIÈRE: literally, "farmer's wife"; braised or pot-roasted meat with vegetables

FINES HERBES: a mixture of finely chopped fresh green herbs, usually parsley, tarragon, chives and chervil

FLAMBÉ: flamed, by pouring cognac or other liqueur over food, setting it alight, and letting the alcohol burn away

FOIE: liver; *foie gras:* liver of an especially fattened goose

FONDS DE CUISINE: basic stocks for sauces and soups

FONDUE: a Swiss dish of melted cheese, white wine and kirsch; also a type of cheese croquette, *fondue bruxelloise;* also vegetables cooked very slowly in butter

FRAISAGE: the kneading of dough

FRAISE: strawberry; *fraises des bois:* small, wild strawberries

FRAMBOISE: raspberry

FRICASSÉE: pieces of poultry, sometimes meat, cooked in butter or fat and then simmered in liquid

FRITURE: fried in deep fat; generally refers to a platter of very small fish

FROMAGE: cheese

FRUITS CONFITS: glacéed or candied fruits

FRUITS DE MER: literally, "fruits of the sea"; crustaceans and shellfish served together, often raw, and as an *hors d'oeuvre*. Also called *bouquet de mer,* or "flowers of the sea"

FUMET: a concentrated broth extracted from fish, meat or vegetables by slow cooking

GALETTE: a round, flat cake

GARNI: garnished or trimmed

GÂTEAU: a cake

GELÉE: jelly; *en gelée* means food served with a gelatin coating

GLAÇAGE: a frosting or glaze

GLACE: ice cream, sherbet or flavored ice

GLACE DE VIANDE: a meat glaze extract achieved by boiling down the stock to a syrup

GOUJON: a gudgeon (a tiny freshwater fish)

GRATINÉ: served with a browned top crust, as in a sauced dish that has been put under the broiler to brown (see also *au gratin*)

GRENOUILLES, CUISSES DE: frogs' legs

HACHER: to mince or chop very fine

HARICOT: bean; a *haricot vert* is a green bean, a *haricot mange-tout* is a wax bean and a *haricot sec* is a dried bean

HOLLANDAISE: a sauce of egg yolks, butter and lemon juice

HOMARD: lobster

HORS D'OEUVRE: a first course

HUILE: oil

HUÎTRE: oyster

INCORPORER: to fold, gently blending one mixture into another without breaking or mashing

JAMBON: ham

JULIENNE: thin, matchlike strips of food

LAITUE: lettuce

LANGOUSTE: a sea crayfish or rock lobster with no lobsterlike front claw

LAPIN: rabbit

LARDON: a thin strip of pork fat, ham or bacon pushed through the interior of meats with a larding needle; also short strips of pork or bacon that cook with various stews such as *coq au vin* or *boeuf bourguignon*

LARD DE POITRINE FUMÉ: bacon

LÉGUMES: vegetables

MACÉDOINE: a mixture of raw or cooked fruits or vegetables, served hot or cold

MAÏS: corn

MAISON: literally, "house"; added to the name of a dish (*crêpe maison, terrine maison*), it means cooked according to the special recipe of the house, or restaurant

MAÎTRE D'HÔTEL: headwaiter; or served with butter flavored with lemon juice and parsley

MARINER: to marinate

MARINIÈRE: shellfish steamed in a broth of wine and other seasonings, such as mussels (*moules à la marinière*)

MARMITE: a soup kettle or stock pot

MARRON: chestnut

MATELOTE: a fresh-water fish stew

MÉLANGER: to mix; to blend food

MERINGUE: beaten egg white and sugar, usually referring to pastry

MEUNIÈRE: fish seasoned, floured and sautéed in butter, served with a sprinkling of lemon juice, parsley and foaming melted butter

MIJOTER: to simmer

MIREPOIX: finely diced carrots, onions, celery and sometimes ham, cooked slowly in butter and seasonings and used as a flavoring for sauces, fillings, stews and braises

MOULE: mussel

MOUSSE: froth; any light dessert such as a cream or custard, containing beaten egg whites or whipped cream; an aspic of puréed fish or meat

MOUTARDE: mustard

NAVARIN: mutton (or lamb) stew with onions and potatoes

NAVET: turnip

NOISETTE: hazelnut; or a small, round, nut-shaped cut of meat. Also a nut-brown butter sauce

NOUILLE: noodle

OEUF: egg

OIE: goose

OIGNON: onion

PAIN: bread

PATATE: sweet potato

PÂTE: any dough, paste or batter for bread, rolls or pastry

PÂTE BRISÉE: pie dough, short pastry

PÂTE À CHOUX: cream-puff paste

PÂTÉ: a mixture or blend of ground meats, poultry or fish, seasonings and often wine, baked in a crust and served hot or cold. When the same mixture is cooked without the crust in a dish lined with strips of fat, it is called a *terrine,* after the earthenware dish in which it is cooked. In common usage, both are called *pâtés*

PÂTÉ DE FOIE GRAS: a delicacy made with goose liver and usually truffles, baked in a *terrine* with a very finely ground pork stuffing; *foie gras* without the stuffing is called simply *foie gras* or *foie gras au naturel*

PÊCHE: peach

PERSIL: parsley

PETITS FOURS: small, fancy cakes; cookies; also fruits dipped in *fondant* (sugar frosting)

PETITE MARMITE: clear, strong bouillon garnished with meat and vegetables, topped with *croûtes* and grated cheese, and served in individual earthenware pots

POCHER: to poach

POIRE: pear

POIREAU: leek

POIS: pea; *petits pois frais,* fresh green peas; *pois cassés,* split peas

POISSON: fish

POIVRE: pepper

POMME: apple

POMME DE TERRE: potato

PORC: pork

POTAGE: soup

POTÉE: any preparation cooked in a pot, but usually a hearty soup of pork and cabbage

POULET: a young chicken, such as a broiler or fryer; *poule:* a stewing chicken

PURÉE: sieved or ground into a fine pulp

PRUNEAU: prune

QUEUE DE BOEUF: oxtail

QUICHE: an open-faced pastry shell filled with a savory custard mixture

RADIS: radish

RAFRAÎCHIR: to refresh; to plunge vegetables from boiling water into cold water to stop the cooking process; to chill anything, especially fruits, by icing or refrigeration

RAGOÛT: stew

RÉDUIRE: to reduce liquid by boiling to lessen the quantity and concentrate the flavor

RILLETTES: a variety of pork *pâté* in which shreds of fat and lean meat are simmered with seasonings, then packed into jars; used as a spread on bread or toast

RIS DE VEAU: sweetbreads

RIZ: rice

ROGNON: kidney

RÔTI: a roast; roasted

ROUILLE: a hot red-pepper sauce served with *bouillabaisse*

ROUX: a mixture of butter and flour cooked together and used as a thickener in sauces

SALADE: salad. A plain green salad is a *salade simple* or *verte*. A *salade composée* is one containing several ingredients

SAUCISSE: small sausage; *saucisson:* large sausage

SAUMON: salmon

SAUTER: to sauté, or cook, in hot fat over high heat on top of the stove

SEL: salt

SOUFFLÉ: a sweet or savory mixture containing stiffly beaten egg whites that cause the dish to puff when baked in the oven

SUCRE: sugar

TARTE: an open pie usually filled with fruit

TOMATE: tomato

TOURNEDOS: individual steaks cut from the center part of a fillet of beef

TRANCHE: slice

TRIPES: tripe

TRUFFE: truffle; a mushroomlike underground fungus much esteemed for its flavor and aroma

TRUITE: trout; *truite au bleu:* literally, blue trout; freshly killed and cleaned trout are plunged into a solution of salted, boiling water and vinegar and cooked until done. The vinegar turns the trout skin blue

VACHERIN: a cylindrically shaped cheese; a meringue case originally made to resemble the cheese, but now highly decorated and used as a container for whipped-cream desserts, fruits or ice creams

VEAU: veal

VELOUTÉ: literally, rich and velvety; a basic white sauce made from poultry, veal or fish stock, and white *roux* (flour and butter); a cream soup made in the same general way

VIANDE: meat

VIN: wine

VINAIGRE: vinegar; *vinaigrette:* a sauce of vinegar and oil

VOLAILLE: poultry

Recipe Index: English

NOTE: An "R" preceding a page listing refers to the Recipe Booklet. Size, weight and material are specified for pots and pans in the recipes because they affect cooking results. A pan should be just large enough to hold its contents comfortably. Heavy pans heat slowly and evenly and cook food at a constant rate. Aluminum and cast iron conduct heat well but may discolor foods containing egg yolks, wine, vinegar or lemon. Enamelware is a relatively poor conductor of heat, and foods cooked in it can scorch too easily. Many recipes therefore recommend stainless steel or enameled cast iron, which do not have these faults.

Recipe Index: French

General Index

Credits and Acknowledgments

The sources for the illustrations that appear in this book are shown below. Credits for the pictures from left to right are separated by commas, from top to bottom by dashes.

All photographs by Mark Kauffman except:
4—Louis Goldman from Rapho Guillumette—Lee Lockwood from Black Star. 12—Drawing by Leo and Diane Dillon. 52, 53—Richard Meek. 56—Ben Rose. 61—Charles Phillips. 64 through 98—Drawings by Matt Greene. 106, 115—bottom right—Richard Meek. 135 and 143—Drawings by Matt Greene. 158 —Top right Charles Phillips. 161 through 164—Drawings by Matt Greene. 169—Richard Meek. 171— Charles Phillips. 172—Drawing by Lionel Kalish, top right Charles Phillips. 173—Center right Charles Phillips. 177 and 179—Drawings by Matt Greene. 182—Richard Meek. 189—Richard Meek.

For their help in the production of this book the editors wish to thank the following: In New York City—Sam Aaron, President, Sherry-Lehmann, Inc., Wine and Spirits Merchants; Bazaar de la Cuisine, Inc.; Bazar Français; Michael Bertolini Antiques; The Bridge Company; Tom Durkin Antiques; Madame Fernande Garvin, President, Fernande Garvin & Co., Inc.; Dr. Howard S. Irwin, Associate Curator, The New York Botanical Garden; Georg Jensen, Inc.; Lea Kates, Director, Public Relations, Foods from France, Inc.; La Cuisinière, Inc.; Nathalie Laguerre; Herbert Lanning Antiques; Yvonne McHarg; The Mediterranean Shop, Imports; Gilbert Pelham Antiques; The Pottery Shop, Inc.; Mittledorfer Straus, Inc., Importers; Stuyvesant Square Liquors; Gregory Thomas; Eliza Gill Werner; Corning Glass Works, Corning, N.Y.; and Charlotte Lee and Helen Whitman, co-owners, Tool Shed Herb Nursery, North Salem, N.Y.

Sources consulted in the production of this book include: *French Provincial Cooking* by Elizabeth David; *Larousse Gastronomique* by Prosper Montagné; *Mastering the Art of French Cooking* by Julia Child, Simone Beck and Louisette Bertholle; and *Michael Field's Cooking School* and *Michael Field's Culinary Classics and Improvisations* by Michael Field.

Printed in U.S.A.